Helen M. Mackenzie

FOR THE LOVE OF SANG

In 1980 writer Rachel Anderson, her husband
and their three children aged 6, 11 and 13 opened
their hearts and their home to Sang. He was of
uncertain age, thought to be about nine, and of
Vietnamese origin – a war orphan. This is the
story of what happened when Sang moved in for
keeps as part of the family.

'From the start the only thing we were
absolutely sure of was that we all loved
him so much. Despite the fact that he
brought rage, self-destruction, chaos and
spiritual despair into our family, we knew
we had to hang on to him because he was
meant to be with us. But we could never
have anticipated the anguish of caring for
a child who was profoundly traumatized,
irreversibly brain-damaged, and whose
small, malnourished body frequently
disintegrated into uncontrollable violence.'

From the time when Sang arrived from the
children's home, Rachel kept diaries 'as a way of
staying sane'. In 1988 she set about turning them
into a book about all that has happened since. The
result is an inside view of what it is like to adopt
an older, disabled child of a different race.
Reading it is a most moving experience.

This book was written during my stay at the Carmargo Foundation, in France, January to June 1988.

For up-to-date information on adoption and long-term fostering, the people to contact are:

British Agencies for Adoption and Fostering
11 Southwark Street,
London SE1 1RQ
tel. 071 407 8800

Parent to Parent Information on Adoption Services (PPIAS)
Lower Boddington,
Daventry,
Northants NN11 6YB
tel. 0327 60295

FOR THE LOVE OF SANG

Rachel Anderson

A LION PAPERBACK
Oxford · Batavia · Sydney

Copyright © 1990 Rachel Anderson

Quotation from *Dust of Life* copyright © Liz Thomas 1977,
Hamish Hamilton

Published by
Lion Publishing plc
Sandy Lane West, Oxford, England
ISBN 0 7459 1914 6
Lion Publishing Corporation
1705 Hubbard Avenue, Batavia, Illinois 60510, USA
ISBN 0 7459 1914 6
Albatross Books Pty Ltd
PO Box 320, Sutherland, NSW 2232, Australia
ISBN 0 7324 0234 4

First edition 1990

British Library Cataloguing in Publication Data
Anderson, Rachel
  For the love of Sang.
  1. Mentally handicapped children. Mothers – Biographies
  I. Title
  362.30852

  ISBN 0-7459-1914-6

Library of Congress Cataloging in Publication Data
Anderson, Rachel, 1943-
    For the love of Sang / Rachel Anderson. — 1st ed.
    ISBN 0-7459-1914-6 (alk. paper) : $7.95 (U.S.)
    1. Interracial adoption   2. Handicapped children
  3. Children, Adopted — Family relationships
  4. Vietnamese   I. Title.
  HV875.7.U6A53   1990
  3627'34'0973—dc20   90-33380
                                              CIP

Printed and bound in Great Britain
by Cox & Wyman Ltd, Reading

CONTENTS

Prologue

My mother took me to the Odeon as a treat. After the main film, we stayed to watch the newsreel and heard about a football match and advances in industry. Finally the optimistic voice-over told us about some heavy fighting. Again I didn't fully understand.

'I thought the war was over, Mum?'

'Sssh. This is Korea.'

So though our war was over, here was another war. And wars, so I had been brought up to believe when my father made propaganda films for the Ministry of Information, were won or lost on the strength of the newsreel.

The screen was full of jungle. British soldiers, easily recognizable to any eight-year-old by the soup-dish shape of their tin hats, ran across the foreground and jumped on to army trucks. The eager commentary indicated that, whatever they were doing, it was a good thing. Then we saw other people, not soldiers, poorly clothed and oriental, being helped on to another truck by some soldiers.

'What are they doing?'

'Sssh. They're taking them to a safe place.'

Then suddenly the whole screen seemed to be taken up with the sight of a small child, a baby, sitting naked and alone in the middle of a dusty track as the last of the soldiers tramped past. The camera lingered on it for several moments and we could see, though not hear, that it was howling, and that it was alone, and that it was being left behind.

Who would pick it up? Where was its mother? Would it never stop crying?

The newsreel was over. The silver swagged curtains swooped down. The cock crowed. And nobody in the cinema audience protested about that poor little baby left behind unattended, unexplained, silently screaming in the middle of the screen.

Home we walked, my mother and I, through the golden afternoon; and I tried not to cry that the comfort and safety of our familiar world had been devastated.

We always had toast and dripping for tea in the kitchen with my younger sisters and brother, and with whoever was helping my mother look after them, and with some of the lodgers too. I couldn't let all that lot see me crying. So I ran to hide my shame and inadequacy in the lavatory. My elder sister called to me through the door.

'Hey, you all right? Is the door stuck? Why don't you come and have some toast?'

This tenderness and concern for my well-being only made it worse. That child, still howling, and nobody bothering.

My mother came next to talk to me through the lavatory door.

'What'll happen to him? They left him all alone. The people went past.'

'I'm sure he's all right,' she said without conviction. 'I expect one of the soldiers noticed and jumped off the truck and came back for him.'

A week later, she was preaching to a gathering of Brownies and Sunday school pupils in a church two streets away. The Sunday school children were dressed as coloured angels with paper wings in shades of the rainbow. Pink angels, mauve, indigo, lime and blue, massed and rustling in the choir stalls. The theme of her talk was the importance of caring for one another. We were all, she told us, and especially those of us enrolled into the Brownies, supposed to help other people in whatever way we could. She described the abandoned Asian baby we'd seen in the newsreel as an example of someone in

8

another part of the world in need of our help.

She looked so sincere and so pretty in her floral dress, standing on the chancel steps with pastel-coloured angels massed behind her like a herbaceous border. But on the way home I had to tell her that she was wrong.

How could we seven-, eight- and nine-year-olds, trained to make cups of lukewarm tea and to carry old ladies' shopping bags, possibly do anything for babies left beside the dusty road so far away?

'Of course we can't actually pick them up and look after them,' she said. 'But we can pray for them.'

So I said my goodnight prayers for any Asian war children left on the roadside. Soon the anguish of the Korean war passed from the news, and I didn't have to pray about them any more.

God didn't forget. Twenty-nine years later, he sent one of them to me.

1
GETTING READY

For twelve years there had always been a small child at home. Now, Michaelmas term, was our youngest child's last months at playgroup. The end of babyhood for all of us. He and I went blackberrying on sunny afternoons. On wet ones, we made Christmas cards. He learned to tie his own shoe-laces, to write his name. The slow rhythm of mothering our last pre-school child was soon to end.

Then I dreamed unexpectedly about our unknown daughter. To my surprise, she wasn't African but half Indian, aged five or six, with dark hair which was not crinkly but glossy.

We'd talked about it for years. Now we had to do something about it. It was time to start looking for her. After supper, David and I sat down and wrote six letters to six adoption agencies.

A schoolfriend of Lawrence's wandered into the room and leaned over my shoulder.

'You type quick,' he said with admiration. It is sometimes very easy to impress ten-year-olds. 'What're you doing?'

Since David and I were starting our quest for an extra child, it seemed churlish to tell this particular child to go away and mind his own business.

'Writing letters,' said David, addressing the envelopes in a businesslike way which was meant to mean, Why oh why, little boy, do you spend so much time in our house and so little in your own?

11

'Our neighbour just got a pain in her stomach,' said the boy, peering to read what I had typed.

'Oh yes.'

'It means she's going to have a baby in the summer.' And he wandered off to find Lawrence to play with.

Eventually, replies to our letters began to arrive. 'We are sorry that the pressure of work has delayed . . . ' 'At present our lists are closed for all children . . . ' 'At the moment the general situation is extremely difficult . . . ' 'Unable to take up your application because we are already committed to a great number of families and we would be unable to give you the attention and time that would be required.'

Two replies were optimistic. One invited us to a general information meeting in South London, the other to an eight-week Prospective Adoptive Parents Course to be run by the local social services. Both were later in the year. We accepted for both. Three months later an adoption officer from the social services rang to see if we were still interested in coming to her course.

'There'll be discussion, a film show, a visit to a children's home, detailed explanation of legal procedures. It lasts eight weeks. If all goes well, you should have your child placed with you in a year.'

A year! If we have room for a child, we want her now.

'You said you wanted a West Indian, didn't you?'

'Well — ,' I said cautiously. I didn't want to seem grasping. It might be a trick question. One's motives in specifying non-white were bound to be suspect. 'Or West African. It was just that we've lived in Nigeria and know a bit about Yoruba culture. We've got links with Jamaica too. We've just been there for my husband's work . . . ' I trailed off. Where we'd been and what we'd done suddenly seemed irrelevant.

At tea-time Hannah, who was twelve, said, 'If we do have to visit a children's home, I'd rather not come. I don't want to stare at other children. I don't want them to think we're shopping for one of them.'

12

During the next year, in our attempt to adopt, we made and received about two hundred telephone calls, had some twenty home visits and went to about thirty different meetings. Our first was the local authority's Prospective Adoptive Parents Course. It was held in the DHSS conference room which was brightly, too brightly, lit with fluorescent strip lights. Twenty parents and would-be parents sat stiffly in a semi-circle in silence. We were offered cups of institutional coffee. We had all come to learn about children in need of love, in a room devoid of all human feeling. Metal filing cabinets, government-issue-type chairs. Not even a dying pot-plant. Was this the sort of atmosphere in which children's lives were sorted out?

There were two social workers, a thin vicar's wife and Joy, who was short and broad with a slightly medieval air about her. She wore flowing dresses to the ground and a sweeping cloak. She carried a huge umbrella, nearly twice as big as herself.

'This first meeting will be very informal,' the thin vicar's wife began cheerfully. The silence was more profound than ever. We all shuffled uneasily on our office chairs.

The topic was, 'What effect does having children have on your life?' Later, photocopied sheets of 'available children' were handed round for us to inspect. At the end of the course, the social workers explained, we'd be choosing a child from these lists, one that suited our requirements. It seemed very like the shopping that Hannah so much dreaded. We felt disappointed, too, about the kind of children shown: many were already so old. How come they hadn't been 'available' for eight, ten, twelve years, and suddenly were? The social workers weren't able to explain. Many were handicapped. After being shown a documentary film about a spina bifida child, I knew that we could never ever adopt a handicapped child. Nor could we cope with Down's syndrome. The idealistic vision of our bonny, if disturbed, five-year-old daughter was fading.

At the next course meeting Joy, who had been designated

'our' social worker, asked David in an aside during the coffee break, 'You would be interested in a baby, wouldn't you?'

Why offer *us* a baby when there were many childless couples on the course who were desperate for a 'new' child. We'd long ago put babies out of our minds and were thinking about all those eight- and nine-year-olds. Yet a baby can be so much much more one's own. We both said yes instantly. Yet there *are* no babies on the lists. Afterwards, we both wondered what she had meant. David thought it was a red-herring question to test us. We feel on test all the time.

The next day, without prior warning, Joy appeared at our front door. The remains of the children's breakfast was still on the table which made her laugh out loud as it was nearly lunchtime. I'd been working hard at my desk and hadn't bothered to clear it. Now I wished I had and wondered if it would gain me a bad mark for being a sloppy mother.

I was amazed when Joy asked me if we might, just might, be the sort of parents willing to take on a mixed-race baby and feed it? Breast, that is.

'I've never fed someone else's baby,' I said. 'But my sister has.'

I remembered the morning in Nigeria when, with a deep sense of loss, I finally gave up feeding Donald. Not merely a loss of my own youth, but the loss of doing something infinitely intimate with and for somebody else. One can't get anywhere near that feeling just by watching someone else doing it.

'We're all concerned,' said Joy, 'about the high failure-rate of adoptions. They shouldn't be failing. The bonding that breast-feeding would bring about might be the one thing that could change all this. You'd better talk to David about it, hadn't you?'

That night, I dreamed of our child again. She was much younger now and, like small babies sometimes are, strangely androgynous. I was not feeding it, merely holding it in my arms. I knew in my dream that it wasn't Donald, Hannah or Lawrence that I cradled but a total stranger.

14

The course meetings dragged drearily on. We learned a lot of jargon, and how tangled up in the dead hand of bureaucracy was the whole adoption process while any impression of real children in need of love and nurture seemed stifled by the lifeless paperwork that supposedly described them.

We were despatched in fours, two couples per visit. The Home, on the edge of a large estate, was a red-brick modern house, indistinguishable from all the rest, superficially warm and friendly with reasonably cheerful-looking children. It was supervised by a friendly unmarried woman who worked a three-day shift. Two teenagers were making themselves scrambled eggs while half-a-dozen other children listlessly cleared out the jig-saw cupboard and the huge television, unwatched, flickered away on its high-up shelf. Two more small children hung about in the hall. The place was no gaunt, cruel orphanage, yet there seemed to be something missing.

Why, on a bright summer's evening, were none of the younger children playing outside in their garden as all the other inhabitants of the estate were doing? Answer: because the garden was as lifeless as a public park: concrete, wire-link fence, municipal swings. No vegetable plot to dig or trespass on, no flowers to pick or trample on, no football to kick.

Why was the house-aunty so exaggeratedly welcoming to us, treating us like honoured guests in her home, while ignoring her charges? It was not her home. She had another proper home elsewhere four days a week. We were led straight into a teenage girls' bedroom, without knocking, without asking permission, without even saying hello to the two girls who were in there. It seemed that the official assessment forms which we studied at the course meetings were shown more respect than these living children.

The visit confirmed our instinct that homes *must* be better for children than even the best of Homes.

As we left the Home, our co-couple, in their late forties and without children, told us that they were fed up with the adoption course.

'There's too much shilly-shallying. We aren't getting anywhere,' said the husband.

'In all the meetings, we just talk and dither about,' said his wife.

'And all the talk is always about healthy normal children. But the children on that list they keep showing us are all disabled. There's a discrepancy somewhere. Why don't we talk about the problems of the real children who are available and get on with it?'

'We just want a kid,' said his wife.

We agreed, but we all knew that, come the next meeting, none of us would dare to risk exposing ourselves as critical of the system on which we were totally dependent to find our child.

If God is indeed guiding our lives and the lives of the children who wait, is he, I wondered, sitting in on these infinitely tedious meetings?

We were learning that to want to adopt a child, even a so-called 'hard to place' child, one had to be very eager, and very, very persistent.

Joy rang unexpectedly to tell me she was leaving social services in one week.

We felt very betrayed. The course was still only halfway through.

Joy rang again to tell me she knew of a child needing a home immediately, and were we interested? Josette was eighteen months old, three-quarters West Indian, seriously disturbed, possibly a bit retarded, and with feeding problems. Already I felt I knew everything about this small sullen toddler, needing desperately to be loved and snuggled. But were we ready? Were we suitable? My piles had been awful all weekend. What an inappropriate mother I might make, as bad as the natural mother who couldn't care for her. My mind whizzed off piles and on to cots, nappies, chicken pox and mashed carrots.

David and I thought about Josette, dreamed about her, prayed about her, talked about her and waited expectantly for her social worker to come down from the Midlands to see us. He was desperate to find Josette a home, preferably our home. He was right. The summer sun was shining. The roses in the back garden looked beautiful. Our children played amicably. It did indeed look like the ideal family. He told us how Josette was small for her age, frightened of men, had been in hospital for force feeding, and at present there were attempts 'to reconcile her with her mother, or vice versa'.

What did this mean, we wondered? That the mother was told she must feed her baby? Or that the baby was told she must look her mother in the eye? Josette's mother was sixteen, mentally retarded, loved Josette but didn't know how to look after her, had another child a year older, and was now expecting twins. Ye holy gods! How can so much be crammed into one sixteen-year-old's life?

'What Josette needs ideally,' said her social worker, 'is a happy family like this for a few years until her own mother matures and gets herself together. At the end of that time, Josette can go back.'

It seemed ironic that we had proposed ourselves as lifetime adopters of a child of five upwards, yet were now being offered a baby to foster for a while.

'We wouldn't of course tell Josette's mother where she was,' said the social worker. 'There's some history of violence with Josette's father. He's a much older man. Though with your consent, visits might be made on neutral territory.'

So it wasn't just Josette that needed looking after. It was her entire extended family.

For a week the presence of Josette had been in the house. We felt we had seen her high-chair in the kitchen, watched her toddling, cheery and rosy, learning to walk by clutching at David's finger for support. Now we couldn't see her so clearly.

After our decision there was a terrible emptiness in the house. We knew that we had failed her. Yet there was also an underlying certainty that we'd made the right decision. We knew we weren't strong enough to bear extending our family for four or five years only to have one part of it taken away. It hurt too much already as we felt Josette fading. We believed that, for us, the arrival of the new child had to be final and irrevocable, so that there could never be any rejection, ever, by anybody, of anybody. We weren't tough enough to do it any other way.

The children continued to talk of this new brother or sister as though he or she were a certainty. Whenever we were all together in the car, they joked in the back and squashed up tight against each other, leaving a large amount of empty space for the invisible fourth person.

Some time after Josette, Donald said, 'We don't want a baby in this family. Babies are disgusting.'

Lawrence said, 'It'd really be best if he was about ten.' He was ten himself. I was surprised. I had still thought we were hoping for a girl, and a lot younger than ten.

While their interest remained constant, other people's was waning. At the final course meeting, the number of parents had dwindled to eight couples. By now, Joy too had left.

During the coffee break, the remaining social worker spoke to me about one of the Down's syndrome children on the list.

'Lively little lad. In need of love', read his caption.

'Yes,' I said. 'He looks very sweet. But we feel sure we couldn't ever adopt a mentally handicapped person.'

The social worker smiled her gentle smile. 'You'd be surprised what one can sometimes find the love to do.'

The meeting was nearly over when suddenly one of the husbands stood up, eyes shining, nostrils flaring and announced that he and his wife had just received a letter from social services telling them 'their' social worker, the vicar's wife, was shortly leaving the area. 'So what's it all been for?' he asked angrily. 'First the other one went. Now you're off too. That leaves nobody. What on earth are we meant to do now?'

He sat down red-faced amidst shouts of agreement from the rest of the group. He had stirred up everybody's simmering frustration and disillusion with the system.

A young woman who hadn't uttered a word before now stood up and said, 'Yes, what are we supposed to do? Go out and find a social worker? Get one in off the streets? Or find a child? How do we find a child without a social worker? Or do we give up altogether?'

'I feel,' said the vicar's wife, enigmatic and gentle as ever, making no apologies for the fact that she too was leaving, 'that you're all very determined people. You've all come this far. I doubt if any of you will give up.'

And of course we didn't. We chased off across country to visit agencies, went to any information meetings we heard about, pestered Joy at her home number and subscribed to adoption information journals which didn't locate us our child but reminded us that the need was still there.

One adoption officer rang back, deeply suspicious of our having mentioned our experience in West Africa on an enquiry form.

'You do realize that they can be very, very dark? People say they want mixed-race. They don't realize how dark some of these people can be. They think they want a light-skinned child.'

Some of our relations had got to hear of our plans. My eldest sister Marian wrote to me sharply reminding me that an extra child would cost me my 'freedom'. I secretly hoped that it was envy which made her reprove me so. She too had three children. We grew up in a family of five children.

My brother Eddy's reaction was slightly different. 'It's quite brave of you,' he said. 'I wish I could be an objective observer on the progress of this child.'

'But you will be.'

'No, already I'm involved, just by listening to you. It's odd to think he must be alive somewhere now.'

David said we ought to tell our parents.

'If we tell them right from the start,' David said, 'they won't mind. They must be involved if we don't want to upset them.' However, he hadn't yet brought himself to mention it to his own parents.

On a visit to Norfolk at half term I kept looking out for the right moment to talk to my stepfather Paul. Then my mother said out of the blue, 'Now, about all these children I hear you're adopting, I suppose they'll all be black?'

Both she and Paul raised several unexpected objections. Paul didn't think he could bear a lifetime, he said, of having to 'talk to someone boring. An adopted person, having different genes, might well be boring.'

I wondered why having different genes should presuppose boringness. I had different genes from David and found him far from boring. Most spouses have different genes, most that is, except him and my mother who were constantly at pains to point out that they were distantly related cousins. They were strong on the importance of family connections. Did they, I wondered, see the introduction of an adoptee into the extended family as running counter to the strong family tradition?

Paul spoke of 'the diversity of talents' with which he said all his stepchildren had been blessed and said it would be wrong to deny, through lack of time, these talents their outlet.

My mother raised her glass and another objection.

'Money. Do you realize what keeping extra children costs?'

Since we were raising three, and already hard up on it, I said I didn't think one more would make much difference.

'Obviously Rachel needs an outlet for being kind to children, but suppose David were to change his job?' She implied he might move to school-teaching or some other branch of education, 'Then Rachel might find more than enough outlet for all her good works.'

I felt as furious as only a daughter can be with her mother. Why did she have to call wanting a bigger family 'good works'?

I was very surprised to hear from my sister Marian that there had been a foster-family recruiting campaign in her local supermarket, and she had recently become foster-mother to a fifteen-year-old boy. Quite a change-about from her telling *me* not to 'lose my freedom'.

When David's father wrote pointing out *his* views on the disadvantages of our adopting somebody, they were different objections from those raised by *my* parents. He described our three children as very special and as highly-strung as race-horses who, because of their special nature, needed handling with great care. They might, he said, be severely disrupted by the introduction of a difficult, unruly and probably less sensitive and intelligent outsider. He pointed out that I, as mother, would bear the greatest burden of child-care and asked if I was strong enough, mentally, to cope. I wrote back trying to explain about my certainty that all children are special, not just our own.

Six months after we began the search, we were with another social worker, young, sulky, with a straggly beard, whose approach to adoption was different from Joy's enthusiastic bubble. His technique was to raise as many objections as possible.

On his first visit to the house, he said he didn't like our books.

'You're intellectuals, I suppose?'

David's occupation on the form was university lecturer.

Mervyn gave us his opinion on books, and explained that a lot of people read far too many of them.

He didn't like our brand of liberal Anglicanism and said he'd noticed that the particular church we went to was full of insincerity. He didn't like my work, given on the form as freelance journalist. 'I thought you just wrote novels and stuff?' We put up with the personal rebuffs because we could see no other way of getting assessed and approved as adoptive parents.

Mervyn proposed 'open discussion' on education, sex, religion. When Hannah and Lawrence eagerly joined in to hear what we had to say about education, sex and religion, Mervyn became angry and said he would prefer them to stay in another room.

21

Mervyn came once a fortnight for the next eight months. His visits usually lasted three hours. They left us drained and deflated. It felt like a game we had to play even though we weren't told what the rules were. We tried hard to believe it had some purpose. We learned some more jargon. Mervyn's agency had a policy against 'sandwiching', that is, placing a child whose age is between the ages of two children already in the family.

Meanwhile, we followed up an advertisement from another agency about a brother and sister, Nina and John, aged eight and nine. We were shortlisted but were relieved (so we told ourselves) when they were found a home with someone else. Then we had a phone call from our local social services asking if we still wanted to be on *their* adoption list or with Mervyn's agency. 'Because you see, Madam, you can't be on both.'

On Mervyn's eighth visit he said that as we clearly had a 'non-violent marriage' and were from 'untroubled middle-class backgrounds', he doubted if we could cope with the real problems of a West Indian child and outlined for us a hypothetical fourteen-year-old girl who was over-sexed, alcoholic, drug-taking, extremely violent, and would use the kitchen knives against us if she could ever get hold of them.

'You do know that these West Indians have a very different sex-drive from us?' said Mervyn. 'What would you do if you found out that she was on the Pill?'

'I'd be extremely relieved,' I said.

It was the wrong answer. We never found out what the right one was.

Eventually Mervyn told us that, despite his grave doubts and misgivings, he had decided to complete his assessment.

'But you do realize,' he said, 'that I have the power over you both? It's important, in a job like this where one's making big decisions, that the people who're dealing with me should know just where they stand. OK?'

On David's thirty-seventh birthday, at six o'clock, the children and I had everything ready for when he got back from work, the meal in the oven, the candles and white wine on the table, the children's presents.

At a minute past six o'clock I got the call from Mervyn letting us know that when his panel committee had met that morning, they had rejected us.

'Oh yeah, and another thing, I think I forgot to mention it before. I'm only a temporary worker. I'll be leaving in May.'

We shouldn't have been surprised to be turned down. We weren't. We were devastated.

Hannah burst into tears and ran and hid in the kitchen. Lawrence muttered to himself, outraged and indignant. Donald sat very quietly at the table clutching the flimsy birthday card he'd drawn on typing paper.

David came home for his celebration supper to learn that he was not, after all, an 'approved father'.

The next day he said, 'We must start again at the beginning.' We must, he said, write to each of the agencies who, fourteen months before, had offered even the remotest ray of hope. We must also begin our round of telephoning again.

I felt less sure. Mervyn had said we should take the committee's decision as 'an omen'. Perhaps they were right and we were unsuitable parents? David insisted it was a momentary setback and reminded me of the numerous parents we'd met at adoption meetings who'd been through the most extraordinarily divergent assessment treatments. One family had five adopted children yet in form-filling terms were always judged as thoroughly inappropriate people to parent. Both had suffered clinical depressions. She had been previously divorced. They were initially turned down because of their agnosticism. Later, when they were converted to Christianity and became members of the Pentecostal church, they were termed religious 'fanatics'.

'But once you'd adopted the first child,' I had said, 'it must be easier to adopt the next?'

'No. We've had to go to a different agency each time. After our fourth, the social worker said she'd make a note we weren't ever to have any more from anywhere. She said she didn't approve of large families.'

The intense sense of *needing* a child and of feeling it was right to follow up this need didn't go away, and soon confidence to continue began to creep up from the ashes of failure like thin smoke. I believed we were right to go on. If we'd been turned down by twenty agencies, then perhaps I might have begun to suspect that God was trying to tell us something. As it was, I thought I heard him telling us, very quietly, to carry on, though there were times when I wished he'd talk more loudly and more clearly.

However, if we truly believed that everything in our lives was under God's control and didn't keep on trying to work out answers for ourselves, then this small incident was not a year wasted but some kind of a step forward. A benefit. It wasn't necessary for us to see how.

'Perhaps the child we're meant to have,' said David, 'hasn't even become available yet?'

2
BEGINNING AGAIN

On the fourth of March the house was peaceful, the morning sunny, the children at school, David at work. A book review lay on my desk in the middle of being written. At ten o'clock God began muttering again.

With a curious conviction that I had to telephone Joy, I left the review and looked for her telephone number. When I didn't get through, I felt compelled to keep trying.

I didn't then know that Joy was one of the practical believers who trusted in the power of prayer to accomplish even the most mundane task. She was that morning praying for a solution as she hung her washing on the line.

I didn't pray. I merely followed instinctively the urgent sense that I had to speak to her. I wasn't even sure what I might say if I did get through.

'I'm sorry to bother you . . . ' I began. 'I don't know if you'll remember . . . ?'

She didn't. I told her we were one of the couples on the course. Suddenly she placed us. 'Oh, you were the ones with the breakfast still on the table when I came round? I did like that!'

It seemed an odd thing to be remembered for.

'Aren't you fixed up yet? You wanted a baby, didn't you?'

'Our youngest says babies are disgusting.'

'But you wanted a girl?'

'Well, I thought we did. We put that down on the form at first. We didn't realize what the children felt. It turns out our

25

elder son says, a boy. And our daughter too, she'd rather stay the only girl.'

'Would nine be too old for you?'

I explained that we no longer felt dogmatic about age, race or type of child. So many theories and counter-theories had been thrown up in the past year and a half, though we had learned that there was a far greater need to find homes for older children, and boys especially. I told her how, after a prolonged assessment, we'd recently been rejected as adopters by Mervyn's agency. Joy didn't seem too bothered. Her main commitment was to take as many children as she could out of institutional homes and into families.

'D'you think you might be interested then,' she asked, 'in a boy of nine?'

So this was a *real* child she was talking about? I began to tremble. My hand shook so much I could hardly hold the phone.

'He must be with other children so a childless couple won't do. And he's got to be in your town to be near his best friend. And you say you don't mind about colour? I know it's awful to ask, but some people really do mind. There's rather a lot to explain about him. If you are interested, I'll come round as soon as I've been on to my boss. And you better have a word with your husband.'

The conception of the fourth child happened that morning on the telephone.

'He's Vietnamese by the way,' Joy added.

'Don't get too carried away by anything, darling,' David warned me on the phone. 'Just in case. We haven't even met him yet.'

But he then became carried away himself, cut short his afternoon seminar and hurried home on his bike.

When Joy in her flowing skirts and billowing cloak sailed round, her earlier excitement was somewhat dimmed. Since a home had to be found for this little boy as quickly as possible and since he was said to be nominally a Catholic, it had already been arranged that a poster showing his photograph

26

and a telephone number was to be pinned up at the back of the Catholic church in town. 'Will you be my Mum and Dad?' read the caption. Joy had the poster in her briefcase and her boss had just told her that, even though we had now appeared, the original plan must go ahead as arranged. She was due to meet the priest right away.

She billowed off again. I went back to the book review. David settled down to work at the kitchen table. Two hours later, Joy returned, bemused but more elated than even before. She couldn't understand why but the priest had unexpectedly changed his mind, deciding that permission could not be given for advertising children in the church after all.

Was this some kind of divine indication that we were the chosen parents? Joy seemed to think it was. She peeled the photograph of the little boy off the poster and, like a midwife handing over a newly delivered infant, presented it to us.

'He's all yours,' she said.

We pinned him up in the middle of the wall. The photograph showed an Asian child with light brown skin, pink cheeks, and thick long black hair. He would have been a very pretty child grinning out into the room had it not been for the huge mis-shapen mouth with a swollen upper lip and a mouthful of extraordinary teeth — crooked, missing, discoloured — attached to raw red gums.

'Looks like a dentist's nightmare,' said Lawrence when he and Donald came in from school.

'He's very fond of animals,' said Joy. 'They say he ought to be out in the country. But I think finding the right family is more important.'

We had a tiny backyard, no room for a farmyard. Upstairs Lawrence had two cages full of constantly breeding gerbils and a tankful of snails and river aquatica.

'We could get a cat?' I suggested.

'And a dog,' said Lawrence. 'Mum always said we'd have a dog as soon as we adopted someone.'

'He's very lively,' said Joy, trying to recall the child for us. 'He talks with his hands all the time.'

'You mean he's deaf and dumb?'

'No, but he waves them about a lot, like a Frenchman stereotype.'

Joy suddenly remembered that she'd never done an inspection of the house. 'Just for the official record,' she said. It was a tall thin terraced house with two rooms on each floor. At the top, in the attic bedrooms with sloping ceilings, Lawrence and Donald shared one little room, and Hannah, who was now just thirteen, had the other.

'Where would he sleep?' Joy asked.

'On the bunk bed under me,' said Lawrence.

Donald still slept in a small nursery-sized bed, and the lower bunk was kept for visitors — or the fourth child.

'He's not sharing a room with me!' said Donald. 'I'm not sharing with a baby.'

'He's not a baby. He's a big boy.'

Hannah asked if Donald would like to come into her room. 'Mine's the best room in the house,' she said. 'And then you and I can share secrets.'

The little boy's name, Joy told us, was Sang. 'Pronounced Shang.'

He had lived in the same Children's Home, some ninety miles away, for the past five years. His very best friend there, Nguyen, was to be adopted by a family in our town who'd known both boys for several years. As they already had five children of their own they didn't feel able to take on two more. Since the two boys were so close, everybody involved — the agency, Joy, the housemother, Nguyen's family-to-be — felt that their friendship should, somehow, be enabled to continue.

This other family, Joy explained, were now just waiting till Sang too had been found an adoptive family before Nguyen moved in with them. The adoption of both boys would be extremely straightforward since there were no contesting natural parents involved.

Joy made phone calls from our house to arrange for us to visit the Children's Home at the weekend and to visit Nguyen's adoptive family that very evening. It all seemed to be happening so fast. In only ten hours we'd moved from dismay at our failure to this wonderful excitement and involvement with a whole new future.

A London agency telephoned to say we were shortlisted as parents for two West Indian half-sisters, Louise and Maggie. First, not enough prospective children. Now too many.

The housemother's two-page report told us how Sang was an imaginative child, good at sports and games, that his co-ordination was developing well. He had achieved continency a year before, could look after himself and loved helping with household chores. He couldn't yet read but loved books and spent hours with them. Because he had been environmentally retarded with no chance of development till the age of three he went to a special school where he was catching up on everything, and 'by the time he is a teenager will be like his peers.

'He has a very generous nature and since we have discussed family life for him he has shared the pictures and work he brings home from school — including cooking!! between me and the "mum and dad". He is going to help "the dad" with gardening, collecting and cutting the wood, doing the rubbish, and "mending the house", and "the mum" is to be helped with the washing up, table-laying and the mess in the house. He talks about "the mum and dad" every day. He is very demonstrative in his affection and, without realizing it, is aching for family life.'

As to those terrible teeth, the report said that it had been decided to delay starting orthodontic treatment until he had a family. Clearly we would be letting ourselves in for hours in hospital waiting rooms.

But the rest of it seemed almost too good to be true. Unlike many children who'd passed through half-a-dozen homes or fosterings, here was a straightforward child who'd remained five years in one place. He didn't throw kitchen knives, take drugs and was not reported as having emotional troubles.

However, the possibility that we would be offered the victim not of social or marital disaster but of war had never occurred to us. Did we really want a Vietnamese? I couldn't even think where Vietnam was. At the time when so many orphaned babies were being airlifted out of Vietnam, we'd been living in Nigeria, where the country's own political instability and military coups got press coverage to the exclusion of anything happening elsewhere in the world.

I thought we knew nothing about Vietnam. Suddenly, to my astonishment, I realized that Hannah and I knew about the very place where this child had spent his infancy.

Joy told us how, before coming to Britain, he had been in an orphanage called the Hoi Duc Anh. The name sounded familiar, and I remembered reading about it in a paperback I'd found the previous summer when visiting a parish church in the West Country. I'd been lingering over the bookstall at the back trying to find among the display of solemn and worthy books a good holiday read. *Dust of Life* was the autobiography of a single-minded English girl determined to help the people of Vietnam. First she worked in an orphanage, later she set up a community for girl prostitutes and ex-prisoners. Since the young author was, at twenty-one, nearer to Hannah's age of twelve than to my own, I offered her the book to read, and she had been so stirred by Liz Thomas' life of self-sacrifice and enthusiasm for getting things done by by-passing bureaucracy that she had declared she was, similarly, going to give away all her possessions and devote her life to the service of others. She did indeed strip her room of its knick-knacks and spent the Christmas school holiday helping Meals on Wheels. Now I rushed round the house looking along all the bookshelves till I found that copy of *Dust of Life* and checked the place names. Here it was, the orphanage where Liz Thomas had started her work, the Hoi Duc Anh which meant, she wrote, 'Association for the Protection of Children'.

She described the dirt, the damp, the enormous rats breeding in the rubbish dump by the kitchen and frightening the children as they ate their food.

She described the babies' room where the child Sang would have been.

'There were three rows of cots, with ten cots in each row. Like the handicapped children in Room Four, the babies were left on their backs twenty-four hours a day. The only time they were washed was when they had their diapers changed and that was a quick wash under the cold tap . . . The babies were fed four times a day, with about eight ounces of warm diluted tinned milk. They were never taken out of their cots to be fed. Instead, the women would settle each baby on its back, put the bottle in its mouth, and put a pillow under the bottle to keep it in an upright position. After a couple of minutes, the women would come round and collect up the bottles again, regardless of whether the baby had finished or not. Some of the babies were slow feeders. Others dropped their bottles and so would lose their feed. When the women had collected the bottles together they would drink the left-over milk themselves, or give it to their own children from the same bottles. Most of the babies were very underweight and thin.'

If this little boy was meant to come to us, how odd of God to begin his preparation so long ago at a Wiltshire parish church bookstall.

Waiting for the weekend when we would meet him, doubts began to grow, worries to gnaw. Donald grew more vociferous. Two boys, he said, was the best number to have in a family. Three would be too many.

David said we must just keep praying for him and the right thing, whatever that was, would happen. Donald said it was more important to pray for the other boy, Nguyen, whose legs didn't work properly. Perhaps it was easier for a six-year-old to accept the needs of a physically handicapped child whose problems he can see before him.

Joy rang mid-week with bad news. 'We've all got to pray

31

a lot about this one,' she said. As both boys were officially stateless, with no papers to prove their identity, the legal aspect of their adoptions would not be as straightforward as her agency had anticipated.

I went to sleep thinking about this small dim stranger. I woke up thinking about him. David kept dreaming of him.

Just like an ordinary pregnancy, I began to suffer from continual nausea and queasiness. My best friend Pat said, 'Don't be silly. You're imagining it.' That's what they said about morning sickness too.

On Sunday morning, Donald was running a temperature. We didn't dare take it to see how high. Could a child run a psychologically induced fever? We arranged for him to spend the day with friend Pat, but no, he insisted he must come too.

After an hour's journey, he looked a lot worse and his eyes were glassy and sunken. We stopped to buy a bottle of Lucozade and some junior disprin from a newsagent's shop. Half an hour later, Lawrence too turned green and was sick, though somehow remained optimistic. Despite these setbacks, despite the grim grey day, it felt uncannily as though we were being borne along the motorways on a wave of support and the goodwill of our friends.

The Children's Home, a vast Edwardian-style mansion set in suburbia and surrounded by rhododendrons, seemed at first to be deserted. Nobody answered when we rang at the front. We walked all round the outside and found a way in through some french windows to a sitting room where an astonishingly beautiful Asian child of about eight was sitting on a full potty mewing. She stared blankly at us and began to crow unhappily.

The housemother was plump and elderly, more of a house-grandmother. Sang and Nguyen were out. We chatted nervously about everything under the sun except parentless waifs and adoptions.

At last we heard noises in the hall. Nguyen hobbled in on sticks with calipers. Then Sang, more shyly, was standing in the doorway just behind, peering round his friend.

Nguyen said, 'Hello.'

Sang said nothing, just grinned. He was so small, so frail, while Nguyen, despite the sticks, seemed so sturdy, muscular and robust.

We stayed for lunch. Some of the other inmates were severely handicapped, writhing, gurgling, wailing. The lovely little girl from the potty was helped stiffly to her chair and coaxed to feed herself. Mostly she dribbled and crowed. Donald was appalled. He wouldn't stay in the noisy dining-room but stood in a dark corridor outside. Was it fever or fright?

Lawrence tried to help the little girl beside him with her plastic beaker and was rewarded with screams of terror.

We helped wash up, played with Nguyen and Sang, walked on a nearby golf course and were shouted at by a golfer. Nguyen got stuck trying to climb through a fence with his rigid polio legs and had to be carried.

Sang seemed to be gentle and shambling. His legs, with untied shoe-laces, flopped about. His hands and arms waved about, just as Joy had said, in loose uncoordinated movements. Nguyen spoke in a high sing-song voice. Sang's was slurred and bumbling. We couldn't understand much that either of the boys said.

So now we'd met them. But what next? We stayed for tea and still nobody mentioned the purpose of the visit. Did these boys not know what plans were in store for them?

Nguyen must have realized for, at tea-time, he told us in his sing-song way that he was to be adopted one day soon. He asked if we knew the people. We were able to say that we did.

Sang said, 'One lay *I* gonna hay mumdad own.' What did he mean? One day I'm going to have a mum dad of my own.

'Sang,' I dared ask. 'Would you let us be your friends?' I dared not say 'parents' in case the housemother didn't want us to mention it. 'Special friends? And would you like to come and stay with us in our house for a visit?'

'I'd like to come,' said Nguyen.

33

'Yeah,' said Sang. 'And Nguyen coming too.'

'And would you like a picture of us so you'll remember what we look like?'

'Yes,' said Nguyen. 'I'd like a picture.'

We let each boy choose a photograph from the selection we'd brought for this purpose, then Lawrence went and helped stick the pictures on pinboards above their beds. Then goodbye, and we'll see you again soon, and the long, long drive home through the dark.

'Well?' we all asked each other. 'What do you think? Could we adopt him?'

Lawrence said, 'He's very sweet.'

Hannah said, 'Yes.'

David said, 'But how could you have a relationship with a child if you can't communicate with him? All relationships are based on communication, on mutual understanding. If he can't talk, how does one communicate?'

'Babies don't talk,' I said. 'Yet one still communicates. Maybe it's because he missed out on all the nursery rhymes and bedtime stories and word games that ordinary children get?'

'But plenty of children don't have mummies who read to them. Yet they still learn to talk.'

'Nguyen can't talk normally because he's deaf in one ear,' said Lawrence. 'The housemother told me. He's had operations.'

Was Sang deaf too? He seemed able to hear, though not always to understand. He seemed able to think he was speaking.

The visit had been a great strain. Hannah wept and had to be consoled.

Donald, still feverish and clammy to the touch, said, 'I don't expect we will adopt him, will we?'

'If God wants it to happen, I suppose it will. If not, then it won't.'

To while away the long journey, we each tried to think of what we'd liked best about the Children's Home. Donald

34

without hesitation said, 'The plastic PlayPeople! I wish I had lots like that.'

'Sang would miss them if he came to our house,' I said. 'D'you think we should get some?'

'You mean buy some?' Donald was astonished at the suggestion. Bought toyshop toys came very rarely into our house. 'New ones? For him?'

'Well no, for everybody. For our family. For you and for him and for anybody who wants to play.'

Donald perked up. 'Will we go and buy them when he comes to stay?' Then he fell asleep across Hannah and Lawrence discussing with himself the advantages of cowboy and Indian PlayPeople over knights in armour.

3
SANG COMES VISITING

'I'm convinced,' said Joy, 'that this is one of the easy ones. Sometimes cases are fraught with problems. They drag on for years. But you're all committed. Of course, you do realize that you won't be paid?'

Paid! Did discussion of filthy lucre have to enter into this infinitely delicate transaction of moving a child into our family?

Anyway, yes we did realize that normally, the local authority or agency in whose care the child is, pays out a fostering allowance during the pre-adoption 'trial period'.

'An unsatisfactory arrangement,' Joy told us. 'If people are going to adopt, I don't believe they ought to be paid. Or, if they are, it ought to carry on after, like in the States.'

This Vietnamese boy was a rare species. There was no care order on him. He was an abandoned person who entered the country as an infant refugee, by courtesy of the Home Office on a 'block-booking' entry visa.

Donald, whenever he heard the word 'adoption' mentioned, was vociferous in his disapproval, then began to vacillate. One day he said angrily that he didn't want to hear any more about it ever again. Shortly after, he began to sob because he'd begun counting off the days till Sang's visit and suddenly realized he'd been counting wrong and Sang wasn't due for another week.

Friday March 21 and the house was cleaned and tidied in

readiness. Spring-cleaning for a nine-year-old? Waiting for his arrival I found myself trembling and close to tears. There should have been somebody with me to hold my hand. Yet he mustn't be confused by too many people around. I wanted him bonded, like a duckling, to ME. We so want it to work. We so wanted him to love us, just as we thought we were beginning to love him.

Nguyen's family fetched both boys from the Home. Sang was as sweet and endearing as we'd remembered. He burbled happily, though I couldn't understand what he was saying, while I took him on a tour of the house, showing him the bunk bed he was to share with Lawrence, and the gerbils' cages, and the view of the ancient rooftops and distant plane trees. I explained to him where the toy cupboard was and the brick box. I showed him the back garden, pointing out the thirty-six daffodils newly bursting into flower. He grinned at all I said and held my hand.

'Where you flee?' he asked upstairs.

'In the bed I showed you,' I said.

'Where he flee?'

'Who? Donald? My youngest boy?'

'No. Dee other. Big man.'

'Oh David! Yes, he sleeps here.'

'Where?'

'Here, in our bed. It's a double bed, room for two.'

'Where he flee?'

'Here too.'

'You jokey,' he laughed. 'Where he dat man really flee? Not same bed!'

As soon as the others were back from school, Donald, Sang and I set out on the PlayPeople buying expedition.

The centre of town was crowded with shoppers.

'Lotta pee!' Sang said. 'Where you get pee fra? All dey pee where you ger 'em?'

He asked again and again. At last I discovered what the query was all about. *Where do you get the people from?* He wasn't asking about toy people. He meant the real ones crowding about on the pavements.

'They get born,' I said. 'People are born.'

'Yeah, but where you ger em? What shar (shop) you buy 'em?'

Surely he knew where you 'get' people? I thought it was a trick question, like some of Lawrence's schoolfriends sometimes asked, to see if I'd dare say, how babies were born.

'We don't buy real people in a shop. They're born as babies.'

'Babies born, yeah. Know dat! Big, big one. Big one people, where you ger big one?'

So Sang knew that babies were born but not where the big people came from?

He held my hand tightly. Donald resented this so much that he refused to take the other hand but walked apart from us as though unconnected. However, once home with the new cowboys and Indians set and busily setting out the little figures of men and horses, dogs and fences, beside Sang on the floor, Donald said he'd changed his mind and he did like Sang staying.

'I ha bar now,' Sang announced.

It took several tries before we understood. It was time for a bath. I took him up. Despite what the two-page report on him had claimed, he could neither bath nor undress himself. He didn't know how to undo buttons before taking off his shirt, nor how to remove his shoes before trying to pull off his trousers, so he was soon entangled in a tight mass of half-removed clothes. Why did nobody teach him how to undress himself yet claim that he could?

I had expected that Donald, along with not sharing a mother's hand with this new person, would prefer not to share a bath. But he trotted up behind us, undressed calmly, and climbed into the bath as happily as though sharing with Lawrence.

The Home may not have instructed Sang in the art of undressing, but they obviously did a lot of washing. As though desperate for approval, Sang rubbed and scrubbed at his face and chest with a bar of soap. Bathing two little boys, one blond and pink, the other dark and soapy, was a quiet, beautiful pleasure.

But the rest of the weekend deteriorated into a nightmare of fatigue. Sang wanted me in sight all the time. When I went to the lavatory he stood outside banging on the door and shouting.

'I gonna star count! Twen, twenone, twentwo, twenthree, twen, twenone, twenfour, twen!'

When I emerged constipated from the lavatory, he gave me a succession of large wet affectionate kisses. I could hardly say he was bonded. But clearly he wanted *somebody* to belong to. Indeed, he wanted, wanted, wanted all day long. The other children, without realizing, also wanted. At the front of my mind and David's was the knowledge that all four children had to go on feeling loved. Nobody must be rejected just because Sang needed so very much more. But with all these extra people in and out, out and in, we seemed to be stretched till we were thin and transparent.

There were far far too many people in and out of the house that weekend. The college chaplain wanted to meet our social worker and it transpired that they had known each other from some previous place. Joy's two sons came along too. While chaplain and Joy discussed old times, the sons played machine-gunning with Sang up and down the stairs. Nguyen's entire adoptive family came to lunch. Too much come-and-go. Too much noise and talk. So tired I could hardly think. I burned the whole of the meal: four litres of chicken risotto, black and sticky and foul in the bottom of the casserole.

Sang was so inept, had so little understanding of how the world worked. He certainly seemed to have no idea why he'd been sent to stay with us.

'You know my Nguyen?' he asked.

'Yes, of course. We saw him yesterday. He came here for lunch, didn't he?'

39

'Nguyen he gonna lib new mumdad.' Did he not realize that the people Nguyen was now staying with were his prospective family? 'One lay (I) gonna get mumdad.'

Had he really no idea that we were to be that new mumdad? Had the housemother not reminded him that this was the reason he was visiting?

Lawrence asked outright, 'What Mum means is, would you like to come and live here and be part of this family? Have my mum as your mum?'

Sang didn't seem to think his housemother would allow him to. 'What she gon say? She not let.'

'Of course she will. She wants you to have a family of your own.'

Sang shook his head. 'No she don't.'

'But your friend Nguyen's going to his family,' Lawrence persisted.

Lawrence and Hannah tried to encourage him, though they said that naturally he was free to *choose* what he wanted. Such young idealists who believed in democracy and freedom of choice. Had he understood any of what they were saying?

As Nguyen's family had fetched the boys from the Home, I made the return journey. On the train I felt very self-conscious of these two loudly chattering Eastern boys in my care. The trip along the corridor to get Nguyen to the lavatory was very arduous. Sang didn't want to be left behind, yet wasn't strong enough to hold open the doors.

At Waterloo, the train hardly stopped long enough for me to get the boys off. Sang became paralysed with fright and wouldn't step down on to the platform. I coaxed him to the door and then lifted him down. Then I lifted Nguyen out, while Sang clung to my legs behind me, and set him down on the platform but, until both crutches had been got out of the carriage and fixed to his arms, he could not stand unaided. Two German tourists rushed towards us.

'Oh thank you so much,' I said. I thought they'd come to

help. Far from it. They'd decided that ours was the one compartment they wished to enter. As I turned to grab Nguyen's sticks and both boys' luggage from the train while both boys clutched me from behind, the tourists pushed past with their own large cases.

'Mind that child!' I snapped as Nguyen wavered and lurched sideways, losing his grip on my skirt. But either they didn't understand, or we weren't as conspicuously desperate as it felt.

When I handed the boys over to their housemother, she didn't ask either boy about his weekend and was unwilling to arrange with me about the next visit.

'We'll have to see,' she said vaguely. 'There's a lot of calls to be made.'

With Joy we arranged an approximate timetable. Sang would come for some more weekends, make a ten-day stay during the Easter holidays, then, provided we had arranged suitable schooling, was to move in permanently for the start of the summer term.

There was to be a procession around the cathedral. We assembled in the draughty cloisters and were each given our palm crosses to hold while the clergy and choir had huge six-foot high palms cut from trees in the Holy Land. Lawrence began to explain the significance of Palm Sunday to the two younger boys. Sang was thrilled by this notion of imminent death.

'Who deh?' he cried with delight. 'Who de deh?'

He spoke a lot about death. He'd already told us that his housemother would soon be dead. He asked when I would die, and if my friend Pat, who was in her early thirties, was old and would soon be dead.

'No, Jesus won't be dead *this* Sunday,' Lawrence explained patiently. 'That's Good Friday. And anyway, it's not when it really happened.'

'We see him deh? Where he deh? He be dere chur deh? Inside?'

Since a church, for Sang, seemed to symbolize death, a

41

mighty cathedral was an even more spectacular death. Will we, Sang asked, once inside the cathedral, see the dead one 'In bohr?' He meant in a box.

'No. Now Sssh.'

The service began out of doors with the priests' tall palm leaves flapping in the wind, their robes billowing out like spinnakers, their singing voices rising and falling and carried away over the gothic buttresses. Sang rushed forward until he was almost on top of the canon conducting the service.

'Want see! Want see! Who deh?' Sang cried and when nobody took any notice, shouted out, 'Aw rubbish!' and began repeatedly clapping his hands over his head and grinning back at the congregation.

Please God, if you can see us and hear us, forgive our new boy his unusual behaviour. And please God don't let the people stare so much.

Sang woke with a squark of joy like a parrot, then ran to the bedroom window, leaned far out and crowed to the quiet world a dawn greeting.

Usually on the first of April we each try to out-trick one another. Last year, Lawrence filled the sugar basin with salt, Hannah brought me a cup of tea in bed, but made it with Marmite, the breakfast was laid by David with empty cereal packets, and I re-laced the boys' shoes from top down to bottom. But this year, no jokes. Sang wouldn't understand them. He'd be even more confused. Explaining normal life was hard enough. Trying to explain practical jokes would be impossible.

Sang liked to wear his 'boo' (boots) all day, usually on the wrong feet. He liked to clump about town clinging to my arm, talking incoherently, loudly and unstoppably. How pretty he was, with his dear little nose, his glossy hair, his pink cheeks. Gradually we had ceased to see the alarming mouthful of yellow and black crooked teeth. But we did notice there seemed to be something misshapen about

42

his feet. One dragged slightly when he walked. Joy, surprised that we hadn't realized the cause, explained it was the effect of rickets, as was his bony, irregular rib-cage. Slopping about in rubber boots certainly wasn't going to help his feet grow straight. So as a means of luring him out of them, we bought him sturdy new lace-ups, even though the ones he already had still fitted and even though we felt it might seem presumptuously parental. Nobody from the Home said anything, so we assumed it was all right to begin taking responsibility for his welfare.

Sang wanted to go on a picnic. But at dawn, he clomped down to our room in his new shoes, laces trailing, to tell us, 'Sfaining!'

On Sunday morning, he clomped down again, jumped on us in bed and said, 'All right! Sun here! I make de sun!' He tugged at our curtains trying to open them to show me. 'Look, look, I made a him!'

Lawrence later explained how he'd listened to Sang on the bunk bed below 'make the sun' by talking to it. 'Like a general addressing his troops.' He was ordering it to stay out. Then he sang to the sun. The sun obeyed and shone until we'd had our picnic. When it rained again, we made cardboard spaceships out of toothpaste boxes. That is to say, Donald was made one and Sang, who didn't appear to know how to handle scissors, sellotape, or cardboard, had one made for him.

The visits were very wearing. By the end of each one we were all of us shattered. Yet we missed him dreadfully when he went away. His presence, despite the demands he made, brought a marvellous new feeling of elation and optimism into the family. A feeling that we were very united and were all going in the same direction, towards loving Sang.

David set about arranging schooling. It was suggested that Sang would probably catch up enough to be able to move into ordinary schooling by the time he was eleven. Two of the teachers at Lawrence and Donald's primary school, on meeting him with us at a school concert, said that they'd be happy to have him, backward or not, in either of their classes. So why, since it would surely be better for him to be at the same school as his two new brothers, didn't we send him there straight away? But David, trying to proceed as correctly as possible, felt that if Sang had been in a special school before, he should continue in one.

The staff at the special school were easy-going and co-operative. (The system of 'statementing' a child for special education hadn't yet been introduced.) They had room for Sang and agreed to take him as our son, with our surname, even though he was not yet adopted. The headmaster was calmly optimistic.

'Nine years old? That's not too late. A lot of our children here, I'm afraid, are living in care. These institutional children need a lot of looking after to help them. No, nine isn't too late. But he's a very insecure child, isn't he?'

I was rather annoyed at this suggestion of 'insecurity'. He'd got us, hadn't he?

When David took the four children plus some friends to the cinema to see a children's space adventure, we had a first experience of this other darker, stranger and more insecure aspect which the headmaster had noticed. Perhaps we, in our enthusiasm, didn't want to see it. Perhaps in our naivety, we didn't recognize it, just as we couldn't recognize rickets.

Once seated in the darkness of the cinema, Sang began to rock quietly from side to side, then more vigorously, then so violently that he shook the whole row of seats, banging hard into those sitting on either side of him. He gurgled wildly and roared and grimaced throughout the film.

'I was so frightened,' said David. 'I tried to restrain him, I tried to put my arm round him. He became so violent I thought he was going to have a fit. He was completely out of control, had no idea what he was doing, what his body was doing. It was very frightening.'

When they arrived home, Sang was still high as a kite, almost as though drugged. He talked rapidly and incoherently and jumped jerkily about waving his arms, and couldn't sit still for tea. Was this normal behaviour for an institutionalized child, we wondered. Why did no one mention it before? Would we dare take him to a cinema again?

'He needs a psychiatrist, I suppose,' David said half joking.

'Or a good stable family?' I said.

The arrangement for Sang to move in for the start of the summer term floundered and came to nothing. The weekend visits, too, were becoming erratic and elusive and the house-mother remained uncommunicative about agreeing to firm dates and any fixed plan. Sometimes when we were expecting him to come, there would be a vague, last-minute reason why he couldn't.

Twice David reorganized his teaching timetable, drove to the Home and spent the night there as a way of staking a claim. Only then was he able to bring Sang back for the weekend as planned. Once, a visit was cancelled because Sang needed 'to spend more time at home with the other children'.

Although nobody said so, we had an uneasy feeling that, having originally made the decision to find an adoptive family, there was now a change of heart about it.

But it was too late. *We* had not changed our minds. He was ours, or as much ours as a child who didn't know who he was or where he belonged could be.

He must come. The more we got to know him, the more David and I felt that we, and only we, could offer him all that he was not getting — stimulus, security, a rich, full and purposeful life. Maybe he was already being loved, but in an impersonal way with different and constantly changing adults to take care of him. They were often short-staffed, and we knew that he wasn't getting the consistent individual attention that he so urgently needed both for learning how to make spaceships out of toothpaste cartons and for straightforward physical care. Each visit, he arrived with his thick hair matted at the back of his head like a blackbird's nest and I had to painstakingly comb through, hair by hair, to remove the knots and tangles. My other children would probably have squealed or resisted such a tedious process but Sang never complained and even seemed to relish the time it took. His scalp, beneath the matted hair, was covered in scars and coin-sized bald patches. I recalled in Liz Thomas' book her description of how the babies' heads were frequently covered in enormous boils and festering sores which she and another volunteer had to lance with a razor blade.

'Why I not hab Easter egg?' Sang asked.

'But you did have an Easter egg,' said Lawrence. 'In fact, you had more than we had. You had the same ones like we all had here and you got that monster chocolate one at your Children's Home.'

'Why I not got car own?'

'You have. It's everybody's car.'

'Why I not Cub? Lawrence Cub. You say I be Cub.'

Sang had visited Lawrence's Cub Scout campsite one weekend and been awed into temporary silence by the wonder of so many boys in green jerseys running about with sticks making a fire.

'Of course you shall be a Cub. Just as soon as you live here permanently, we'll get you enrolled.'

'Why I not lib here all de days? Why not fair. Why?'

Patiently and calmly, I had already explained a dozen times, always with a firm quiet voice, that he would come and live with us as soon as we had heard that he was allowed to. But now, finally, I agreed with him, equally emphatically, that it was indeed not fair.

'I absolutely concur,' I said. 'Your rotten dental hygiene, your homelessness, your lack of family or status. I agree. It's all utterly unfair. And the vagueness of the arrangement whereby you come to stay here is unjust too. It's appalling, and I wish I could do something about it. For your sake and for mine.'

The long speech quietened him for a few minutes. But soon he began again at the beginning.

'Why I can't stay ebber? You say I stay ebber.'

But though he asked repeatedly why he couldn't stay with us forever, much about our family began to displease him. It was unfair, he said, that Lawrence had gerbils and Donald had stick insects while he had no animal. So we got him a glass tank of stick insects, all of his own. He looked after them for half an hour, then said he hoped they'd die and he didn't want them.

'Want big nominal. Not fmor. Want hor!' He meant a horse.

'You couldn't keep a horse here!' said Lawrence, ever practical concerning the needs of animals. 'There's no room.'

We diverted Sang's repeated cry for a horse by talking about the rabbits they used to keep at the Home. Sang was disgusted by the mention of rabbits.

'Want hor! Can't ride rabbit!'

His concentration span was short. We strove to keep him occupied, the others loved. If only he could read, or look at books, or listen to stories for even a few minutes. We persevered in reading to him but he didn't appear to like it. So much for loving books! His chief occupation was asking questions, the answers to which he did not remember.

'Wha we ha supp? Wha tine? Wha we ha puddn? How old her? How old him? How old I nine? Yeah, I nine. Nine bigger si. How old you, big man? Why you not get me Star War toy? Just liggle one? Why not? I not stay here no more. I go get goo(d) mumdad get me toy.'

It was no doubt hard on the other children to be sharing their parents every minute of every hour. Sometimes when Sang was sitting on my lap chattering incomprehensibly, Donald reverted to babytalk too as though he were about three, but rather than draw nearer to reclaim his share of attention, would edge further away. Yet when it was time for Sang to leave, he said with apparent sincerity, 'I wish you hadn't got to go.' Lawrence too said, 'I do wish he'd move in sooner.'

Five weeks into the start of the new term and we were still

47

plodding on with the unsatisfactory and spasmodic weekend visits involving the one hundred and eighty mile round-trip to fetch him, and the same again to take him back, often with him chanting all the way, 'It not fair!'

A colleague of David's had a daughter whom she adopted at eight years old. After only three weekend visits in quick succession, her daughter moved in. My friend Pat, too, who is a social worker, agreed that this visiting period had been dragging on too long.

We began to wonder if, after all, he would ever be allowed to move in permanently. Instead of merely a vague, 'Let's wait and see how it goes, shall we?' we began to be told, 'Maybe after the summer holidays? That's a better time to change schools, when everybody's changing.'

Only much later did we discover that one of the reasons for the constant stalling had been that not everybody involved in the decision about Sang had been in favour of placing him in a family. Some felt that he should remain in the Home with the companions he had always known. The housemother, though she had initially approved of an adoption, also began to have second thoughts about it.

At the time, all we knew was that something strange was going on and we weren't being told about it. Joy was only able to say that there were problems with finding Nguyen an appropriate school in our area for boys with his particular handicap.

David became angry. 'We're not trying to adopt Nguyen. We're trying to adopt Sang.'

The extreme possessiveness we began to develop for Sang was perhaps the beginning of the bonding. It was certainly what enabled us later to feel that, however difficult things were becoming, it was up to us to resolve them for him.

Joy came to the house to discuss with us, between us, how we could sort out the hold-up. Sang seemed to realize, though only hazily, that her visit was in some way connected with him. As soon as she'd left, he went into a frenzy of over-excitement. He ran upstairs and down again

48

machine-gunning at top volume. He brandished sticks, he flung himself at me and sucked my arm as I stirred the gravy for Sunday lunch. He grinned, jumped, laughed, and repeatedly clapped his hands over his head.

'Gonna get new mumdad!' he yelled.

'All right, but let's have lunch first, shall we?'

'Not stay here! Get new mumdad!'

'That's all right, but I can't help you find a new mum and dad and make the food at the same time.'

Then, the hysteria turned to anger and he began to fling himself about on the floor, to writhe and twist as he roared for new mumdad.

We knew the screaming must be ignored. But he would not be ignored. Hannah nudged me as I stood at the stove cooking. 'He's really very upset,' she said reproachfully. 'He can't cope. I think it's the social worker coming. What are you going to do?' She obviously didn't approve of us leaving him there in distress.

David too recognized the need to do something. We couldn't just leave him under the table and have lunch over him. He opened a bottle of wine, handed me a full glass and took over the gravy.

'You see to him. I'll take the lunch outside and take care of the others.'

I sank down to floor level and tried to hug Sang but he wouldn't be hugged. He resisted and struggled, yet he seemed also to be trying to stay close.

'Gonna get new!'

I went on trying to hug. Reserves of spare love had to be found from somewhere. I crooned into his ear a story which he'd never heard before. How could he? I'd only just invented it, thinking it up as I went along, a mouthful of wine for every paragraph, half true, half embellished truth.

'D'you know this story, Sang, I wonder?'

'Gonna get new!'

'About a dear little boy, about nine?'

'Can't care.'

'Who wanted a new mum and dad?'

'Rubbish.'

'Well, one day, there was a mum and dad, a very nice mum and dad, who wanted a little boy all of their very own.'

'Rubbish.'

'To have and to hold. To live with them in their house always. They didn't want a girl of nine, or a girl of eight, or a boy of eight. They really wanted a boy of nine. Maybe a little toddler would be nice? About two years old? Oh no! They didn't want a toddler. What about some dear little twins of nine?'

Sang began writhing again on my lap, anxious.

'Can't care!'

'No, they didn't want twins of nine.'

Relief. He stopped writhing and waited, the angry, stone-like, face turned expectantly up.

'They wanted a boy of nine. Now, one day, they met a woman who said to them, "I know of just the dear little boy for you. He's exactly nine, and he's got a dear little face, and he smiles a lot. He's got nice black hair, and he likes football, and he's very brave and strong."'

A flicker of interest.

'So the nice mum and dad asked, "What's his name?" "Ah," said the woman, "I'm not sure. I can't remember. It's something that begins with S. Stephen? No. Sean? No. Simon? Ah, here we are. Yes, he's called Sang, pronounced Shang."'

'Dat me.'

'Yes.' Gulp of wine. 'That was you!'

'Dat me story.'

He smiled and stood up.

'I not sad now. I happy. We go ha din.'

Hand in hand we went and joined the rest of the family round the garden table. So simple, deceptively simple, telling a story. But do we have the reserves of love, of energy, of wine to see us through? Is it right to *reward* a crisis with a story when all the books say ignore tantrums or you only make them worse?

Sang was due to return to the Home in the morning. If this uncertain to-ing and fro-ing was upsetting for us, what must it have been like for him?

It was a short night. At six o'clock, heavy footsteps across the ceiling of our room. Sang was on the prowl. I got up. He was fully dressed in daytime clothes, soaking wet with wee, sitting on the floor beside his and Lawrence's bunk bed. I brought him down, washed him, changed him into dry pyjamas, back to bed. Six-fifteen, more heavy footsteps. Sang now prowling from bed to bed upstairs, shaking the children and telling them to wake up. Firm but kind, I put him back to his bed. At 6.45 he got up and went into Hannah's bed and, as she put it, 'Clung on tight. He just clung on like a little monkey, tight, tight, his arms round my neck, his legs round mine. He wouldn't let me go, so I just had to stay there and cuddle him. He was so wet! And his breath was awful!' she added cheerfully.

What guardian angels could give a fastidious thirteen-year-old girl the generosity to embrace in her bed a nine-year-old stranger smelly with halitosis and urine?

At leaving time, Sang refused to get into the car but clung to the front door screaming.

'I not go! Why I go back now? Why you bry (drive) me? Why not Big Man? Why Donna not come? Why you gonna do when I no here? After I no here?' I closed the front door so that the people passing along the street wouldn't hear.

'Dopt! I not like dopt! No dopt! Stay here.'

He was finally lured into the car with a piece of chocolate and grumbled and grizzled for the next two hours.

As we drew up in front of the Home he began a new kind of noise, like a wild wolf howling in a forest with a broken leg. I had a strong urge to turn the car round and drive him straight back to our house. But by acting impetuously we might lose him forever. We lived in fear of the great 'They', the committees of decision-makers who ruled our lives. We had to play out the games of negotiations correctly.

The housemother had gone out. Sang refused to be consoled by any of the other staff. So I led him into the gardens, lay down in the grass with him, and held him in my arms and sang to him and told him stories. When he was finally quietened, I had to hand him over into the care of a new helper whom Sang appeared not to know.

As I drove home through rush-hour London, I could hardly see out of the windscreen for tears. So I stopped in Trafalgar Square and rang a friend, chaplain of the London Hospital, and asked him to help us, somehow, anyhow.

'You must have a direct line to the Almighty,' I demanded.

A week later, Joy rang us, gasping and sobbing with emotion. Something awful had obviously happened for she could hardly speak. Had Sang been hurt in an accident? Had it been decided Sang could never come to us again?

But no, Joy was sobbing with relief and delight as she told me that 'the way was clear'. Then she dictated to me what to write in a letter we had to send to the director of social services to inform them that Sang was, in fourteen days time, moving into our house 'to be fostered with a view to adoption'. I didn't cry. I'd done enough of that last week. But I rang David in college, and Pat, and one of my sisters. I had to tell everybody.

At half term, he's coming!

Donald said, 'I think it's jolly unfair that I'm always the youngest. And even though Sang is coming, I'll still be the youngest.'

I said, 'Well, we could get you a baby, or a person younger than you, later on, if you like?'

What hubris. Waves of apprehension swept over me.

4

ARRIVING

A Saturday in May, the last Sang-free day of our lives. From tomorrow, he'll be here forever. Can we take it? Yes, yes!! The suspense has gone on too long.

David went alone to fetch Sang, staying overnight to ease the transition. It was half term. Lawrence was at Scout camp and Donald had been invited to spend the night with his best friend. So Hannah and I savoured the pleasure of twenty-four hours together in a quiet house with three floors and six rooms of personal space. In the evening, after a day's work at the typewriter, and with all Hannah's homework done, we went to see a film about a tug-of-war child in a marital breakup. I hoped it would have a message for us. But the problems of Dustin Hoffman and Meryl Streep's screen child seemed too clear-cut and simple while the cute kid himself behaved too quietly to seem real.

Donald's overnight stay away was bad timing. He had been very homesick and, so his friend's parents said, anxious all the time that Sang would arrive before he himself was home. Lawrence rang from a telephone box near his camp. Camp was a miserable failure. He wanted to be home.

Sang too was unhappy. David's appearance at the Children's Home had been, for him, totally unexpected. It seemed that nobody had told him what was happening.

Lawrence returned from Scout camp. Profound misery descended on the household. After supper, trying to be like any ordinary happy family, we settled down around the television. They began showing the film of *Oliver*, the tale of the abandoned orphan boy who dared to ask for more. Why couldn't they have shown any other film? Donald went waxy pale as though about to start having a convulsion. He'd had them on and off for a year or so. Lately, they seemed to have become more frequent. What caused them? If they didn't stop soon, he'd have to go for tests.

Donald's eyes became dark and sunken, his skin clammy. He sat ominously still, then whispered quietly, 'Mum, I've got that funny feeling again.'

I carried him up to his bed where he asked me to stay with him, holding his hand, until he fell asleep. Most unusual for us both. I sat there for an hour in the twilight wondering, have we got enough love to go round? They all seem to need so very much more. We must have enough.

When he was asleep, I went to unpack Sang's things. I had wondered before: when a child comes to live with you, does he bring his own clothes with him, or does he share his brothers'? This wasn't a query covered by the Prospective Adoptive Parents Course. Yet caring for one's child's covering, the dressing of him, the easing each arm into its sleeve, the teaching him to select what to wear, the changing of his underclothes when dirty is such an intimate and important part of mothering.

Before, Sang always came provided with a neat little case, presumably packed by an adult, containing a change of shirt, pants and socks, and for each visit a large, brand-new wrapped bar of soap and a huge new tube of toothpaste.

This time, his luggage was a miscellaneous bundle in two plastic bags as though somebody had thrown together whatever was to hand regardless of its usefulness or current owner. Twelve pairs of cotton shorts, four pairs of trousers, eleven T-shirts mostly with other people's names written in, yet only two pairs of underpants marked 'age six' and one-and-a-half pairs of pyjamas. Most of the T-shirts were so tiny they couldn't have been Sang's own for many years. And where was his red towelling dressing-gown which had accompanied him before? And his green birthday tracksuit of which he had frequently said, 'Dat my fabrit'?

As I folded away one tiny T-shirt after another I wept with anger into the drawer. There were no toys, no teddies, no books or personal possessions, nor any of the cars and football stickers which Donald and Lawrence had been buying and giving to him. Anger strengthened my belief that, however badly we might cope, it was nonetheless better for a child to receive the personal care that comes within a family than the impersonal care of an institution.

On Tuesday, child benefit day, while a spaghetti sauce for lunch was simmering on the stove, I left Hannah 'on guard' over her three brothers and cycled speedily along to the post office, cashed the benefit orders, and pedalled frantically on into town to the toy department of the biggest store. As fast as I could, I chose from a glass case a koala bear for Hannah, a small fierce lion with a shaggy mane like Rastafarian dreadlocks for Lawrence, a traditional, grown-up looking teddy for Sang, a baby bear for Donald. The bill, of just over twenty pounds, used up the entire child benefit. I pedalled rapidly home with the toys in my bike basket, put on the spaghetti to boil while I made four notices — 'I want Donald', 'I want Hannah', 'I want Lawrence', and 'I want Sang' — and pinned them to the appropriate animal. I hid koala, shaggy lion, baby bear and brown bear in the back garden among the leaves of the rosemary, the sage, the red tulips and the ivy. Were eleven and thirteen-year-olds too big for teddy games? If they were, they didn't show it and hunted among the leaves as enthusiastically as Donald. Sang was mystified by the toy which was waiting for him. When each toy was united with its new owner, we laid four extra places round the garden table so that the animals could join us for lunch.

Joy dropped round to check up on us. She seemed shocked that I had just spent two weeks' child benefit on soft baby toys for the children. I had rather shocked myself.

When we first met, Sang mostly called me, 'Plee Mi'

(Please Miss) and David was 'Michael' or 'He Big Man'. I explained after a while that Michael wasn't David's name and that 'Please Miss' wasn't mine, indeed wasn't anybody's name.

'You can call me that if you like,' I said. 'The other things people sometimes call me are Rachel, darling, Mum, Aunty Rachel, madam, and Mummy.'

'In France they call her *"madame,"* don't they?' said Donald.

'I thinka I call you Merm,' said Sang. 'I thinka call he Dad.'

Sometimes during the half-term week, when he threw himself about like a weird dog, shouting and yelling at the air, I felt he hadn't a hope of catching up and learning how to behave like a more normal child.

Joy rang to check how we are. Surely, I suggested to her, he'd have been better placed with an older, childless couple who had more patience, time, experience?

'Nonsense,' she said cheerfully. 'A childless couple? They wouldn't have lasted more than one week.'

But we hadn't lasted a week either. He'd been here for five days, and the low times were so many. Then I talked out loud to myself. 'Rachel, you are wonderful! Look how well you're managing!' I shouted aloud so that I could hear myself. So God could hear too. Can you hear me God? Can you see us down here? Can you help us handle these children? Can you help all of them adjust to what we've done?

'You always said,' said Lawrence reproachfully, 'that when we adopted somebody, we'd have a cat or a dog.'

So a kitten was located, a descendant of one that I had had as a child. I arranged to meet its owner, Jill, and her daughter Martha, for the handing over halfway between our homes, at Sissinghurst Castle.

We picnicked together in spring sunshine, lying about on fresh green National Trust grass. All Sang's favourite food was there: zizzy gring, chiklin and crip (fizzy drink, cold chicken, and crisps). The black fluffy kitten was handed

56

from lap to lap to be fondled and petted. Only Sang wouldn't touch it and withdrew whenever it came too near. So much for his being very fond of animals.

Hannah was invited, on the spur of the moment, to go back to stay with Jill and Martha. It seemed important that, despite our newly structured family, the children should still be able to keep former friendships. So off Hannah went and I was left with my three boys and a new kitten.

The grounds of Sissinghurst are just the right size for children to explore on their own, the cottage garden, the herbs, the lake. Lawrence raced about, up the twisting steps of the tower where Vita Sackville-West used to write, then down again and off to find the orchard, back to the car to check up on the kitten now sleeping on a jersey on the back seat.

But for Sang, the moment we stepped through the red brick archway into that enchanted place, it was the beginning of a dark downward spiral. Was it sparked off by Hannah unexpectedly going to stay with a teenage friend? Was it jealousy of the cat for getting all the attention? Was it directed at me for talking to another adult during the picnic? Or was it, simply, that there was too much beauty here for him to bear?

Like an approaching storm, he began by grumbling. He kicked his feet along the gravel. He fell over. He pulled my arm. The storm grew closer. He kicked me in the leg. He shouted. He roared. He yelled. People turned to look, then carefully ignored us. Donald hurried ahead to walk sedately on his own so as not to be seen with us. Six is so young. He looked so small as he disappeared round the corner of a clipped yew. I was sure he was lost to us forever.

Sang wasn't going to get lost. He followed me into the White Garden. Tumbling roses with golden hearts, little paths bordered by sweet-smelling box hedge. When we had lived in a top-floor tenement in Glasgow, I used to dream of this garden, of how one day I might have a plot of my own and make it like this.

'I not come!' Sang screamed after me, coming all the same. How carefully I took no notice.

'I can't care! don't like flower. Schupit, schupit flower. What you doin'? I can't care! Why you not wait me?'

Lawrence came back to find us. Sang screamed deep in his throat.

'Please please let's go,' Lawrence begged. He was right. All the gardens had begun to look horrid, stupid, black. What had we taken on, ruining this perfect spot, making it seem so hideous to us all?

A neat and tidy little family passed us on the narrow path, all in matching blue anoraks. Two parents, two teenage girls. One of the girls was Anglo-Saxon blond, the other Asian, but you could tell they were sisters.

I ran after them and for some reason put out my hand and touched the father's arm. So was there hope? Did other couples receive impossible children and discover, uncover, their Eastern inner calm?

'Is she your adopted daughter?' I was asking the obvious and the impertinent.

He looked at me coolly. Sissinghurst isn't the place to accost people about their children. You murmur quietly here about plants and shrubs and Virginia Woolf.

'Yes,' said the man. 'Our Serena's been with us since she was a baby.'

Sang cast vicious and threatening looks all around. Why hadn't we had one like theirs? Tall serene Serena. Why had we been sent by God this monster?

We trailed back to the kitten in the car and I felt ashamed. I'd wanted that perfect family to break the terrible isolation of being an adoptive parent. Now I wished I hadn't tried to speak to them. It wasn't their fault they'd made me feel worse by their calm success.

On the drive home, Lawrence and Donald played a game of choosing a name for the new kitten, working through wildly ridiculous alternatives.

Sang growled, locked in his own angry world. Then for no reason, he suddenly cheered up. The relief of being released from the grinding whining was too much to bear.

Only a mile from home, also for no apparent reason, I found myself swerving off the main road up a side lane, bumping the car along the ditch to come to rest, bonnet in hedge. I laid my head on the steering wheel and wailed.

'Mummy, what's the matter?' said Lawrence wrapping his arms round my neck.

'Mummy,' said Donald, stroking my hair.

'I don't know,' I said. 'I'm so sorry. It's just everything.'

To cry in front of my sons, my three sons. I am crying for your new brother. I hate him. He is so pathetic. But it wasn't that. It wasn't his awfulness. It is my own inadequacy, faced with this extraordinary child. I don't know how to cope. I don't think either of us do. He's so unlike any child I've come across.

Each new outing was like another hurdle to be negotiated, and the next one looming ahead was going to church together as a family.

The university chaplain once advised Lawrence, when he complained about church being boring, that 'too much church-going is bad for you'. We heeded this advice and limited regular church-going to the monthly parish communion when there were cakes and biscuits with local chat in the vestry afterwards.

We kept putting off going with Sang. Partly this was to protect him from the stress that any outing, even merely out on to the pavement in front of the house, seemed to be causing him. It was also to protect ourselves. We feared that the presence in our midst of this infant stranger with bizarre behaviour would mark us out as items of curiosity. There is much social judgment within a parish congregation. One is known, and yet strangely not known. In my grandfather's parish, I often felt myself to be an outsider, a clearly visible impostor, only there because of whose grand-daughter I was, not because I had any understanding of the spirit. Others who busied round with the brass or the flowers seemed to be closer to the meaning of the service.

We couldn't put it off any longer. We had to maintain

usual life for the sake of the other children as much as for ourselves.

The way to church was a pleasant stroll along the river. Sang had a small tantrum as he left home, but then skipped happily along clutching my arm. Despite his anxiety, he'd obviously been into churches enough times to have learned to cross himself efficiently on entry, not unlike the thorough, all-over way he used a bar of soap in the bath, and to mumble some authentic-sounding prayerlike noises. But once the service began, he lost any semblance of churchlike behaviour, either Roman or Anglican. He rocked violently, clambered along the length of the pew, waved both arms in the air, clapped his hands, and crowed. All the usual sound effects.

Our lives have been changed, yet the order of the litany goes on unchanged. Lord have mercy upon us, miserable offenders. Just because our tiny world had been broken did not mean that the sequence of the words had changed. The clarity was still there despite our confusion. Let us pray. I believe in one God. Come unto me all that travail and are heavy laden. Yes, we come, heavy heavy laden. But we have failed. Rock, rock, rock, suck. Are we forgiven for failing? God loved the world so much that he gave his only son to the end that we all believe in him. If he gave his one and only son, can't we give a little part of our lives? Rock, rock, crow, suck.

But it is not a little part of our lives that we were giving. It is our whole lives, daily, twenty-four hours round the clock, and our children's lives, and each other's lives.

As we prayed the same words as last year, as five years ago, or ten, I realize that I didn't have to pray. Others were doing it for us. We could be swept along on their praying. All I had to do was sit, or kneel, or stare. Only after the order of the service was over am I flung back into the process of maintaining an air of normality when all seems so far from normal. Be matter-of-fact and chatty about this loud, uncouth, and very, very foreign child disturbing everybody's peace. May the peace of the Lord be always with you. And also with you.

'Isn't it interesting,' said David as we walked home, 'how sometimes, in a new situation, different parts of the service take on a new meaning?'

While my way of coping was to let the service wash over me, his way was to search constantly for new levels of understanding.

'For instance, "The breaking of the bread, is it not a sharing of the Body of Christ". Christ's body was broken. Now we feel we're being broken. And through being broken, we can become more like Christ. Renewed. Better than before.'

It sounded close to sacrilege to me. Did we have to see this child as the Christ-child in our lives? There is only one Christ-child. But I agreed with him that hearing words, participating in acts which reflected our own sense of breakage, gave hope that we were not alone, that others had been along here before us.

5

OUR NEW BOY

When David had to go to Glasgow for three days to supervise degree exams, it felt as though he was going to be away for ever. While he packed, we bickered rattily about the bus ride which, from now on, Sang would have to make each day. He said it was too long. I said it couldn't be helped.

Children who attend special schools, we'd learned, had to be provided by the local education authority with some form of transport. Because we lived near the depot Sang was always going to be first to be picked up. We were to stand on the doorstep and, soon after eight o'clock, the white Bedford van would come lumbering down the street to collect him before going out to the distant villages, finally reaching school, a mere two miles away, at 9.15 a.m. At 3.15 p.m. the whole thing would be repeated in reverse order and Sang would be deposited back on our doorstep at twenty to five. Thus, in order to be educated at a special school, he would have to spend three hours a day, every day, travelling.

David knew precisely how jolting and dreary that journey was for, on Sang's first morning, he travelled on it too while I walked Donald, as usual, along to his school, then leaped on my bike and pedalled across town to be at the special school gates as the bus drew in. Sang's request was that both Merm and Dad would see him in.

'Yes, yes, yes!' I shouted at David. 'Three hours a day *is* a long time for a little boy to spend on a bus. But if that's the system in operation, we should be grateful it's there, instead of complaining.'

Besides, we'd need the extra time after Sang was picked up in the morning to settle Donald into his normal school routine. Without the bus, how else would we get Sang to school?

'And anyway, if you're going off to Scotland, I can hardly deliver two small children in opposite directions simultaneously, can I now? I'm not superwoman for goodness sake!'

The headmaster, whom we'd consulted, saw the long bus rides which most of his pupils endured as positively beneficial, providing them with a neutral buffer-zone between the different demands of home and school.

David departed for Glasgow. The topic was dropped.

Sang came home after his second day aggressive yet buoyant. David wasn't there to witness the buoyant side which was, I concluded, proof of the benefits of the buffer-zone theory. I was there to endure the aggression which was doubtless another by-product of that long journey.

By early evening, I was so tired from being recipient of both buoyancy and aggression that I had to keep clutching at the kitchen wall to steady myself as everything seemed to be continually spinning round.

I started supper an hour earlier than usual so that I wouldn't collapse in tears or nausea before the children were in bed. I wanted to leave time for a long bath for the two little boys. Gentle play in warm water is supposed to have a calming effect.

Donald, who'd been playing contentedly on the living-room floor with the little plastic PlayPeople, decided to bring them all upstairs to put in the bath. Sang co-operated and carried some of the plastic horses.

There's no doubt, I reassured myself, that Sang is a wonderful bonus for Donald. A constant elder brother and playmate, lessening Donald's need to continually strive to catch up with the big ones. He and Sang can play silly games together without the onus of looking babyish.

As I was running the bath, David rang from Glasgow. Both

small boys, watching me talk on the phone, pulled down the cuffs of their jersey sleeves and began to burble into them, in imitation of me nattering excitably on the phone. I laughed out loud.

'Yes darling,' I told David. 'I'm tired out, but everything's fine.'

In the bath, with toy knights, cowboys, horses and a plastic dog, the noise and excitement sounded like twenty boys rather than two. There seemed little of that supposed soporific effect.

Then, suddenly, in place of cries of joy, was a piercing shriek followed by roars like lions. I turned round to see the bath filled not only with floating coloured mannikins, but with a quantity of brown excreta. Sang stood immobile, soiled all over, screaming as though in pain. Donald, slightly soiled, clambered rapidly out and began to dry himself. Toys and poo bobbed about on the surface.

I lifted Sang out. He ran naked, wet, and streaked in poo along the passage to my bed where he crouched in a huddle roaring at the ceiling. Meanwhile, Donald leaned into the bath trying to 'save' the toys. I added some disinfectant to the water but he became hysterical that I had ruined the toys forever with the disgusting smell of pine. The bath plug-hole was blocked and the water wouldn't run away. Sang continued to roar. The volume of a nine-year-old's roaring was astonishing considering how small he was.

On the top floor, quietly doing homework in their rooms, were the big ones. I called to them for help.

It took us half an hour to shower down, calm down, and dress in pyjamas the two boys, to clear the bath, clean the toys and floor, put all the dirty towels in a bag for the launderette. Donald quickly recovered and the big ones read him a story. Sang, now clean but still wet and naked, refusing to be dried, crouched like a smouldering volcano in the middle of my bed. I coaxed him on to my knee and tried to talk to him. He was so distant from himself, so unaware, that I found myself talking to him in the third person.

'Poor little Sang is so unhappy. He's had nine years without a mummy or a daddy. He needs nine years of cuddling to catch up. He's had no mummy to cuddle and care for him.' On and on I crooned, always repeating the same things. 'But now he's all right. And here he is, and he's going to sit on my lap and have a cuddle.'

Gradually, he curled up with his long rickety knobbly knees on my scratchy, plastic-coated *Good Housekeeping* apron, head down in fetal position, and sucked. He would suck anything, thumbs, my own or his, plastic apron, jersey, door knob, or new mother's cheek.

At last, many hours later than I'd planned, all were bedded down, stories read, prayers said, kisses given, doors at the right angle. But this latest outburst, both the emotional and the new physical display, alarmed me. Had he done it on purpose or was he without control over his bodily functions which we were just going to have to learn to cope with? I hadn't coped very well. I didn't think I could cope again. What if Hannah and Lawrence weren't around next time?

I rang Joy for advice. The automatic answering machine told me she was out. I rang Pat. A babysitter told me she'd be back late. I rang David's number in Glasgow. No reply. I already knew he was out at a dinner.

Somewhere, we had the number of an agency which gives support to any adopters facing any problem. I found the scrap of paper. The service, I read, operated only on certain days a week, between certain hours. Not today, tonight. I wished we had neighbours next door like we used to, instead of a constantly changing series of renting tenants. I wished Nguyen's adoption had already happened so that I could talk to his new mother.

I rang the Samaritans. They have such odd numbers, all naughts.

'Hello? Yes, listen, I mean look, I'm not actually a suicide case, and I don't want to block the line if a real crisis needs you, but you see, it's like this, it's just that . . . well I'm not an emergency, but I do need — .' What did I need?

The male voice said would I like to re-call him on a different number which would leave the emergency one, with all the naughts, free? I did so. I nearly didn't. My hand was trembling. Perhaps I was an emergency?

On hearing his voice a second time, I felt convinced I knew it. Ours is a small town. Most people knew most people vaguely by sight. And what about by sound? A calm, confident, yet not overbearing voice, thirtyish, bearded. It was so familiar. It was surely one of the humanitarian teacher-friends we had? I didn't know what I wanted from him. So I disguised myself, changed my reason for ringing. Instead of explaining that I felt there were too many people in my life, I reversed the problem and pretended I was unhappy because there weren't enough. My husband was abroad on business, I said. It seemed sort of true.

I knew I wouldn't ring the Samaritans again, not because of their failure to say the right thing, but because of my own to be honest. To have said, 'My new son has just shitted in the bath all over my youngest son and the new toys and it's taken me three hours to clean up and unblock the waste pipe, and I feel distraught and disgusted and inadequate,' sounded lame. I bumbled and murmured and finally told the compassionate listener what I should like him to say to me.

'I think, if you could kindly tell me to go and make a nice cup of coffee, then watch 'The News at Ten' for half an hour, and then go to bed, I think I'd do it.'

He told me, and I did it.

The June days were exceptional, each new morning bright and clean and clear. By 8.30 in the morning it was already so hot they were using water sprinklers on the roses in the park. By 8.40 a.m. I was there too, sitting on a bench waiting for the washing to finish at the launderette. It was easy to count our blessings instead of sinking.

As I hauled home the wash-bag, I met the bus escort lady. She'd just got back from delivering the children to school.

'Sang's settling in so well with the other children!' she

told me. 'He's really doing wonderfully! I'm so pleased with him!'

Her pride made me proud. With abundant cheer, I hung the festoons of washing in the hot sun to dry. But we were like yo-yos, up for a bit, then down again.

Joy rang up. She'd got my call recorded on her answering machine. The one-and-a-half hours she now spoke to me offering professional advice did not, to me, seem to make up for those vital minutes when there had been nobody.

Her advice wasn't very encouraging either.

'Normally,' she said, after I'd explained the poo episode, 'in a child of his age we'd have to refer immediately to the Child Guidance Clinic. But in this case, I really think we'd do better to just wait and see, and keep quiet about it, don't you?'

I had absolutely no idea.

'By the way, d'you feel any *embarrassment* about his speech? Are the other children embarrassed about him? D'you feel you could back out now?'

What a ridiculous question when he's only been here for less than two weeks. But I supposed she had to ask it.

The real worries I confided to a notebook.

a. Continuing and perpetual exhaustion.

b. The tiny stresses which arise between the other children, not openly about Sang but indirectly caused by his arrival. As Lawrence, describing himself, put it, 'I feel more tension with Donald since Sang came, than I do with Sang.'

c. The laundry bag and Donald's dismay at being walked to school beside it! The increased mountain of washing was, indeed, a by-product of our new life. Donald begged me, please please would I take him to school first, without the laundry? So, in future, even though the launderette is only two doors down from school, I have to make separate trips.

d. The neighbours when Sang screams and screams without stopping.

The children have usually welcomed the special occasions

when their own home is turned into a chapel. When the telephone table becomes an altar, the milk jug a chalice, and the bread board is blessed by the university chaplain, it's much less boring than real church. Afterwards, the gathering generates into a student party with more wine and more Holy Spirit and carryout curries and singing and talking, and the children don't have to go to bed till late.

But at the first knock, as I hurried to the front door, Donald went quite suddenly into a babyish emotional collapse. As seventeen students and the chaplain bundled out of their cars and into the house, Donald clung to my skirt behind me. He wanted me, only me, all of me, no sharing. He didn't want to stay and sing with the students. He wanted to sit on my knee upstairs with the door shut, to have a bath alone with me there. Not Dad, not Hannah.

Together in the steamy bathroom we listened to the sound of the singing and praying downstairs come wafting up through the old floorboards. I felt almost glad that Donald was showing these signs of stress. It had been almost unnatural that, for so much of the time, he remained so calm, dignified and accepting of the disruption to his life. We had supposed he might occasionally say, 'Hate the new boy. I don't want him here any more.' But instead of making a rejection of Sang, he made this repossession of me.

As I dried him, his arms limp as though he were incapable of drying himself, he whispered that he didn't want to have to go to tea with his best pal after school ever again. Was he afraid that if he didn't come straight home after school, he may lose his place here?

At the weekend, a period without the structure of school, the raging sessions were more frequent, though we still couldn't always figure out what would provoke one. The mood of violence descended out of nowhere to grip hold of him like some kind of seizure over which he had no control. It was alarming to see our sunny, smiling child change so suddenly and so radically. My God, I wondered, was he schizophrenic or psychopathic?

One Saturday morning, Sang roared and rocked, moaned and yelled for an hour and a half. For the first time, he attacked physically if David or I went near. He bent back fingers, pinched, and tore with his fingernails. He kicked so savagely with his feet that we were forced to take off his heavy shoes as we were afraid he might hurt himself more than anybody else. Tears sprouted from his eyes and ran down his face, yet he didn't appear to be weeping in what one might call an 'ordinary' way.

During these attacks, he seemed to lose all self-awareness, so to ignore him as one would an angry toddler in a tantrum seemed inappropriate.

In our tiny house, there was no escape from the fury. Donald looked down at Sang as he thrashed on the floor and said, 'I think Sang's angry. I think you ought to cuddle him more.'

It was a reproach. But for goodness sake, we were *trying* to cuddle, to hug, to reassure. We had heard about 'hug therapy' as practised in the States. The theory seemed to be that by holding tight to the child, one provided the physical contact he sought when he bit or punched, and the adult's body absorbed some of the violence that the child felt, while defusing their own natural urge to stop the roaring by hitting the child. Body contact was the aim, not with a blow but a hug.

In fact, as we discovered, it required enormous confidence and skill to hold a violent child who bites, kicks and pulls back your fingers when you get near. David, being stronger, was better able to hold on, and gradually to turn the rage towards physical bear-games of loving and rock-a-bye-babying.

Then, unexpected relief. On the evening of that long ninety-minute attack, Sang slept right through the night for the first time ever. Was our newborn baby growing up, just a little?

David and I planned to go to the end-of-year department dinner in college, our first evening out together since Sang's arrival. But since he was so volatile in his moods, we didn't know who we could safely get to babysit. Sometimes, even the tiniest change in routine seemed to throw him. Then, through the housemother, we were put in touch with a student who, when a schoolgirl, used to look after Sang and some of the others at the Children's Home as a volunteer worker.

At five o'clock, two hours before we were due to leave, Sang, watching me ironing my dress, began his descent into the dark places of his mind. He wrenched at my hand. He groaned, he howled, he thumped.

'Isn't it nice for me and Dad to be able to go out together?' I reminded him brightly as I did my hair with Sang jostling and punching. 'Sometimes children have nice treats, don't they? Like picnics and ice-cream. And sometimes, grown-ups do.'

Sang snarled, half fascinated, half horrified, as he watched me make up my face.

Though unable to express it in words, his mounting anger seemed to be directed at us for daring to *want* to go out. Or was it anxiety because he thought we were never coming back? Or perhaps it was uncertainty because the others were so unperturbed? Or perhaps, despite my explanations, he just didn't understand any of it?

With this angry companion hindering my preparations, it was hard to keep up any enthusiasm for wanting to go out, let alone for feeling relaxed and glamorous.

'Dad and I like each other so much,' I persisted chattily, 'that quite often we want to be together having a nice time. That's what parents *often* do when they like each other. Dad and I like each other a lot. We chose each other, to be married and live together always.'

As we left the house, he was standing glowering and growling on the doorstep wrapped in the cheery embrace of Hannah, flanked by Lawrence, Donald and a somewhat unenthusiastic babysitter.

At the dinner I was placed next to one of David's more

elegant and languid colleagues who chatted so charmingly about Italian opera it mostly took my mind off the domestic trials at home.

Sang's retribution began next morning long before anybody else was awake. At dawn, he stormed down to our room, wet and steaming, and an inch from my face, shouted, 'Why you not get up? I hit you in safe (face). Yes I do. Schupit. Schupit. Shud up. I break you finger. You schupit babe. I hit you Waa! List that! Waaaaaaaaaa! Ha! I make noy (noise) you in safe (face)!'

Abuse so early makes one wonder whether the previous evening's dainty chat about Rossini was worth the price. This, however, was a different and more self-aware kind of anger from the uncontrolled writhing-on-the-floor. David got up, led Sang into the privacy of the bathroom, closed the door and tried to explain firmly and quietly what being rude to your mother is all about.

Every day now there's a period when the stress is so great, whether or not Sang is having a roar, that I wonder why we are doing this? We'll surely all break soon? One of David's colleagues, a professor from the University of London with whom he's been invigilating exams, tells David that he's had seven children, of whom one was adopted. When the boy was thirteen, the professor was still having to get up in the middle of the night to attend to the boy's night needs. This now-elderly man offered only one piece of advice to David. He told him that we must remember 'to take care of each other too' and 'try never to get too tired'.

After the children had all grown up, this man's marriage broke up and his wife committed suicide. Save a child. Kill a marriage.

Yet still he didn't resent adopting the child?

'I feel it's the best and the most useful thing I ever did in my life,' he told David.

We have to remember to keep a sense of proportion, not allow child interests to obsess our lives or come between us. But the calm empty times, the occasional silence in the

71

house, have gone forever. There is tension for two hours each morning before he leaves for school. There is tension in the afternoon as I await his return. I fetch Donald from school, play with him and chat about his day, help him make his tea-time snack. Then it's Hannah and Lawrence's turn for attention. They unwind from their day, tell me about life and classroom gossip before settling to homework, music or television.

At 4.30 I find I am beginning to tense, to brace myself for WHAM! BAM! the full blast of our last child's return. I sit down quietly and compose my thoughts into a mood of relaxation. The bus hoots in the road outside and we hear the slow grinding of the diesel engine ticking over. I must hurry to be on the doorstep to receive. Like a lucky dip, what will I pick off the bus today? A deeply affectionate toddler who clings, hugs, whimpers, holds on with repeated stutters of 'Merm, Merm, I love you, I wanna you'? Or a wild thug who pushes past, refuses all contact, yet simultaneously demands it, who rages, clings and pinches? Whichever child it is, I have to take notice of him yet ignore his behaviour. I have to give him his tea which has to be prepared always in the approved way: a syrup sandwich, and a mug of weak Nescafé with one spoon of brown sugar which has not been stirred, for he likes to lick the unmelted sugar out of the mug afterwards. If, absent-mindedly, I leave the teaspoon in the mug, he will hurl abuse as punishment for my neglect.

Please God, make it easier. One day I find myself pouring out a large slug of Vermouth at 4.30 just before the bus is due in.

And always, always, everywhere, throughout the house is the lingering smell of cooked sausages.

'Sausage my fabrit,' Sang has told us many times.

He cries if anybody had more on their plate than he does. David cooks sausages for breakfast. Four fat sausages and Sang is happy. It has become a ritual. Sausages *every* morning. If there are no sausages, Sang cries and won't eat anything else. David makes sure that there always are sausages, checking the evening before when he comes in from work and going to a late-night shop in town if the fridge is bare.

'It's my war-work,' he says. 'If sausages make him happy, it's an easy enough thing to arrange. And maybe it's making up on the protein he missed as a baby?'

'Is there protein in sausages?' I wonder.

'All right, making up on the bread he won't eat,' says David.

I have bought some tinned chipolatas and hidden them in the food cupboard, just in case we run short.

Filling the house with the pervading smell of sausage seems a peculiar way of showing one's love. There is nothing about coping with the feeding habits of adoptive children on the preparation course. In fact, I recall nothing from the course that bears any relation to what living with Sang is actually like. With a new baby, you can buy a book which tells you how to manage each step of the way. There is no such book telling us how to manage a fully grown boy about whom we know so little. Yet people seem to expect us to know. They seem to think we know what we are doing. People enquire curiously, 'And how do the other children take to him? How do they feel about him?'

What do these enquirers expect to hear? Maybe that the other children are totally put out by him? That they find him a grinding bore? That they kick him whenever they see him? If Sang were a newborn brother, would people ask such questions? Surely, they would know that we all love and welcome the newcomer and want him to be happy?

Joy rings to ask if she might bring a trainee social worker round to show the woman how well we are all coping, and in particular how well we all 'relate to one another within the family context.' Is basic survival with a child who bites now termed 'relating well'?

Joy and her apprentice sit side by side on the sofa with coffee and view me relating to my children as each returns from school. Sang occasionally lies on the floor and writhes around the table legs. I feel like a mother bear on view in a zoo.

After supper, when Joy has gone, there is a big scene. Is it because Sang realizes we have all of us been inspected? Is it because Donald has decided that he will, after all, resume going to tea with his long-standing schoolpal? Or is it because, in 'relating well' to Sang, I told him I was fed up with him hitting me?

Whatever the cause, he screams and roars. Later, he sulks.

'I not lib here more! I get mumdad. I get good one. You not my fren.'

'No, I am not your friend,' I agree firmly. 'I am your mummy.'

Surely he has to learn to distinguish between mother and friend, to learn that, however angry you are at your mummy, unlike a friend, she does not go away.

At least, not this mummy. Or not yet anyway.

6
SETTLING

Cousin Bertie's christening was to be a big family event in Norfolk with an even greater than usual gathering of cousins, second cousins, uncles, sisters, great aunts and extended friends.

Like any parents of a new child, we were proud of Sang and we wanted the rest of the world to see him, know him, admire him too. I was apprehensive only about the initial meeting with my mother since, along with a number of others of her generation, she had all along been so vociferously against our plans to adopt. She was, nonetheless, supposed to love all children so much. So would she now?

A hot midsummer weekend, the trees shimmering in the sun. All the grandchildren rushed at their granny for hugs. Sang was prodded forward. He took her hand, asked if he could call her 'Granny', and held on tight. He giggled, and made incomprehensible but clearly well-meaning jokes. She seemed so entranced that, though dressed up in her silky church-going best, she grabbed a pair of wellies from the porch and suggested that everybody go for a quick ramble in the woods and a trip on the lake.

'Oh, but he's such a *character*!' she said, as though perhaps she'd been expecting him not to have had any character. 'Are you going to put the adoption in *The Times*? People *do*, you know.'

In the mass of people at the party after baby Beatrice's christening, Sang seemed to have been always with us. This radical change in routine, this demanding and sociable party, far from upsetting him or sending him into one of his uncontrollable outbursts, seemed to cause him only to need to cling on very very tightly to either David's or my hand all the time, as was perfectly natural for a child suddenly meeting many strangers. Otherwise, he behaved impeccably and it was so easy to be proud of him, to want to show him off. I introduced him formally to each person I chatted to, friend, relation, the rector, the sidesman, my sister-in-law's father. This extended family is enormous, with numerous children, so an extra one here or there seems to make little difference. The introductions were more to help cement Sang's sense of identity, to help him through the confusion of this mass of new people, so familiar to the other children, yet total strangers to him. We had to offer him the sense of his arrival at some definite point within some definite family community. It seemed important, too, to declare publicly that this newcomer, with brown skin, black thick hair, and slanting eyes, was to be received and accepted from now on as part of the family.

'Aunt Gladys,' I said. 'This is Sang, our new son.'

'Jill, have you met Sang, our son?'

'This is my son, Mrs Raymond, Sang, who came to live with us last month.'

Sang responded quite well to this game of being introduced and each time held out his hand, a random choice of left or right, to be shaken. Indeed, he responded so enthusiastically that at one point when I'd said hello to the doctor's wife without having first made any explanation to her of the child clutching my arm, Sang whispered, 'She not know me. Why you not tell her?'

Introduction accomplished, Sang clung quietly, grinning all around him.

Nineteenth June. Our wedding anniversary. Fifteen years. We never imagined it would be like this, surrounded by six young children. Lawrence's French *correspondant*, a morose know-all, was staying for two weeks and Hannah invited a schoolfriend. But what a large happy family we felt. I packed a celebration picnic supper into the back of the car — cold chicken, white wine, and a meringue cake which somehow managed to get dropped upside down so had bits of grass in it. We ate it lying under the willow trees in the college gardens, before going to a musical comedy staged by the college staff which was unbelievably bad and we didn't mind a bit.

Next day, Joy dropped in unexpectedly to check up on us. This time Sang was the model child, almost normal, and settled to some drawing. But Donald seemed fraught, overwrought, somehow unhappy. Joy said it was because of his 'sense of displacement'. I found it hard to accept that this bogie, 'displacement', should always be attributed as the cause of infant unhappiness. Surely, in the process of growing up, much that is profoundly unsettling happens to *all* children, whether or not they suddenly acquire a demanding new elder brother to contend with. Children frequently pass through good patches and bad. Moreover, Donald, as the youngest, was accustomed from the moment of his birth to being in the bustle of a home already full of other people bigger than him coming and going.

We still seemed to have to spend as much nervous energy appeasing the peripheral workers involved on the case as we did caring for our children. Joy also announced that the housemother of Sang's Children's Home expected him to go back and 'stay the weekend to see all his old friends'. It seemed that after one month, it was too early for such a return visit. Sang would find his loyalties divided between his new home and his old Home. If only Sang were my own child, No, no! I could say. Not yet, not yet. Too soon!

But Joy endorsed the idea of the visit. So David and I resolved that, since this visit seemed unavoidable, it should last only one night, and that David, Hannah and Lawrence as visible tangible reminders of the new life should go too.

We solved the problem of squeezing four children with assorted needs into two attic rooms by partitioning the larger room into two tiny ones, one each for Donald and Hannah.

Lawrence and Sang were to stay in the other room, one above the other on the bunk bed.

'Rabbit hutches!' Lawrence said disparagingly of the new tiny bedrooms, hiding his own anguish at not being in one, though he had uttered no outward protest about having to go on sharing. He didn't point out that it would be more logical for Sang and Donald, whose lives and habits were closer, to be together. Nor did he moan about any injustice of the youngest member of the family getting a room to himself. He didn't protest about having to move all his clothes, books, toys, snail tanks and gerbils into half as much space as before to make room for Sang. He didn't even refer to the subject.

When I'd thanked him for being so generously open-spirited and not making a fuss, he merely shrugged and appeared nonchalant.

'Dunn't matter,' he said. 'I still pretend it's my room all on my own. Anyway, Sang's not up here much, is he? He's downstairs with you most of the time.'

While Donald pottered and chattered beside me, organizing his books into sizes and straight rows, I painted his attic rabbit-hutch with leftovers from other re-paintings about the house. We had a quarter tin of dark red for one wall, some white and half a tin of yellow for the rest. Painting someone's walls can be an act of love. One thinks all the time about the person who's going to be in the room. It seemed such a short time ago that I was painting these same walls and moving beds about in readiness for Donald's arrival into the world. We'd wondered then how we'd cope with space. Now the children were larger, and there was one more of them, and we were still wondering.

After his books, he sorted his private possessions. These seemed mostly to be obscure scraps of paper, saved twigs and beach stones.

He too, even in his immature way, seemed to be aware that this brief interlude together was to be valued for it might never happen again. He was an easy-going companion and didn't allow himself a single cross word or childish paddy. It felt so different from some of those long days of his earlier childhood that we survived together, when he was clearly tetchy and bored to have to be in his mother's company.

Perhaps in some ways Joy was right. Donald *had* been changed by Sang's arrival, but only for the better. Not 'unsettled irreversibly by displacement', merely transformed from spoilt youngest brat to courteous youngest child. Sang's arrival had *not* displaced him from his position as youngest, for he still held it. Nor had Hannah to relinquish her position of privilege as eldest. So, if the theory of displacement had any truth, it was Lawrence, neither youngest nor eldest nor, in these days of sexual democracy even shown the special favours for being firstborn male, who was likely to feel displaced. Yet he too continued to be generous and caring about his new brother without making any big deal about it. We had such very high expectations of him. And he seemed to live up to them.

By Sunday afternoon Donald, already beginning to miss the company of the others, cooked a welcome cake: chocolate sponge, thin as a floppy biscuit, sagging slightly in the centre.

They arrived home for high tea.

Sang's first words, addressed to nobody in particular as he got out of the car and on to the front doorstep, were, 'I hate you. I hit you safe.'

Maybe displacement theories did have some truth?

He strode into the house seething.

Donald's welcome cake was out on the table with WELCOME HOME in wobbly blue icing on top.

'I not want dat schupit cake. No good cake.'

'It's not just to welcome only you darling,' I said. 'It's to you all. We've missed all of you.'

Hannah and Lawrence, usually ebullient on returning from an outing, were so self-effacing as to be almost not there. I wondered what had happened during the visit. David told me how Sang had been very very quiet, almost repressed. Now his rage was unleashed. After tea, when he refused the welcome cake, came screams of 'Why you no leab me cay? (cake) You liar, you. Liar!'

Liar was a term of abuse having nothing to do with truth or untruth, used indiscriminately to cover anybody's misdeeds.

In bed he refused to accept a goodnight kiss, instead turning his face to the wall. Donald, too, dismayed by the scene about the welcome cake, wouldn't bring himself to say goodnight.

As I trudged downstairs I felt curious despair, not over two angry little boys tucked up in their beds but about the bundles of second-hand clothing which I had to pass on my way.

We had become reception centre for a depressing quantity of cast-offs. The house was awash with them. Like jetsam and flotsam at high and low tides, small piles of them flopped on every stair right to the upper landing. Downstairs in the tool cupboard, black plastic bin-liners overflowed. In the bathroom yet another newly arrived boxful waited to be unpacked. Clothing with zips broken, seams unsewn, in vile colours and of unspeakable man-made fibres, all waiting to be washed or sorted, mended or stitched. Dozens more mis-shapen, well-used garments were crammed into drawers waiting for children to grow into.

One acquaintance, on hearing we had a new adopted son, drove twenty miles to donate a boxful of her prep.school son's outgrown, outworn, underwear, which included six pairs of threadbare Y-fronts.

'I don't suppose your children would wear them,' she said, cheerfully unloading her car boot. 'But they'll do for Sang.'

Since she'd never met him, how did she know they'd 'do' for him? And why should he be a second-class citizen who'd wear up other people's greying underpants?

Picking through at a jumble sale, one is at liberty to select or reject. It was a very different process to be personally presented with pass-ons by their previous wearer who usually likes to relate the history of each shrunken jersey. One had to turn a blind and grateful eye to the thin knees of the pyjamas which one knew will rip on the first wearing. Or the blue anorak, size 10, which would fit nobody in the house, yet which the donor insisted 'still has a little bit of wear left in it'.

Why should one have to seem grateful when, by receiving these offerings, one was providing their donors with an acceptable alternative to the pain of throwing long-loved treasures into the bin? I recognized this kind of old-clothes patronage, having done it myself when passing on some baby dress without seeing its faded, dribbled-on appearance, thinking only of when my baby first wore it, realizing how long ago that was and hoping that, by granting the baby dress an extension of useful life on someone else's child, I would extend my own.

Till now, we'd happily relied on pass-ons and jumble for ourselves and our children. But now, how I wished I didn't ever again have to accept any of these horrible, festering old clothes. How I wished there could be all new clothes for each of the children including our all-new boy.

He is in the wrong family. Surely, he should have had the chance to be the youngest and to blossom? Behaving as a toddler of three or four years old, he can be funny and cute and petted and spoiled. Behaving as a nine-year-old, he shows only the worst aspects of being nine. His new speciality is going up to people and shouting 'Pig!' in their face with a great deal of spittle. He wanders away in the middle of meals shouting, 'Eeeergh! yuk! yuk!' He creeps up behind adults and older children and whacks hard with any long object to hand, cricket bat, yard-broom, ruler, for no apparent reason.

Maintaining a basic code of domestic civility hurts when our inclination is to give in to all his impossible demands, to give him all he wants and has missed out on. But we would have to be firm, for this constant rudeness was catching.

After a day out in the woods, Donald, in a rage, emptied the picnic rubbish out of his rucksack on to the carpet because he said his rucksack was 'too sticky'.

David asked him quite kindly not to leave his rubbish on

the carpet but to pick it up and put it in the bin. Donald refused. 'Why should I?' he said.

David whacked him on the bottom.

Donald retired to bed crying.

Sang, good as gold and grinning with delight, asked, 'What the matter Donna? He cryer. You smacking!'

Sang himself seemed to have been smacked a good deal for we noticed how sometimes, when one put out an arm to hug him, he quickly ducked his head, or put up his hands as though to protect his head in expectation of a hit rather than a hug. One of the young volunteer helpers admitted that they did sometimes hit the children if they were very naughty. The housemother confirmed this. 'Well sometimes you just have to, don't you?' For bedwetting, Sang had been smacked on the bottom with a hair-brush.

Soon after the rubbish-on-the-floor incident, a disgruntled Donald asked, 'Why does Dad have to smack *me*? It's not fair. He never smacks Hannah and Lawrence. And Sang doesn't get told off *at all*.'

Hannah and Lawrence instantly took up his cause and accused us of being unjust parents. Sang did far 'worse' things than Donald, they said, but Sang was always a special case, excused, made allowances for, while Donald was not. It was anyway extremely unfair, they said, that Donald should ever be smacked considering we said we didn't approve of smacking.

David and I felt chastened and humiliated. While we had been acutely conscious that we must never strike Sang, not ever ever, we hadn't noticed our double standard regarding Donald. We made a parental resolution never to smack Donald ever again, and told him so.

Hugs all round. But if double standards couldn't be operated, that would have to mean that there must be fewer allowances made for Sang.

One evening, he came off the school bus happier than usual for he was clutching a tube of Opal fruits. Wretched people,

82

well intentioned no doubt, insist on giving the poor unfortunates on the special bus, sticky sugary treaties. Sang had saved his tube and now in the kitchen began to eat them, cramming two and three at a time into his mouth in front of the others, turning his oozing mouth towards them so they should see.

'Sang darling, in this family, if somebody's given some sweets, they share them with the others.'

'No!' Two more were unwrapped and stuffed into a viscous sickly lime-green and citric-pink open, chewing mouth.

'Because you see, it's rather greedy and not very kind to eat sweets in front of other people without offering the packet round.'

'Can't care!' Sang sidled close up to me as I stood cooking at the stove and hugged me. 'I like you,' he said, changing the subject. Chew, dribble, chew, another sweet.

I didn't say, Well I don't much like you when you've got that greedy look in your eye. I said, 'When a person eats all his sweets by himself, he sometimes gets a horrid mean feeling. When he shares them round, he doesn't have so many sweets all to himself, but he feels nice both inside and outside because he can see all the other people are feeling nice too.'

'No.'

'And sometimes, other people might have sweets or chocolate given to them and they may not want to share them with you if you aren't sharing now.'

Grind, grind, grinding mother. Is it really worth such an effort and such a boring dreary lecture to try and help a child be morally responsible for his own actions? In the Children's Home there were quite simply large notices pinned up everywhere, in the hallway, on the staff noticeboard, even in the bathroom, requesting that staff and visitors would kindly refrain from giving sweets to the children, however kind they were trying to be, because the children all had such bad teeth to start with. It was like notices in the zoo. *Please do not feed these creatures!* But we are *not* a children's zoo. We want all our children to be guided by us towards having freedom to take control of their own lives.

How the summer term dragged on. We'd known him now for four-and-a-half months and he'd lived here for eight weeks. It seemed a long, long time. Some new neighbours moved in next door, and I overheard them asking Donald over the fence, how long Sang had been here. I heard Donald's reply: 'Oh about twelve mumfs.'

The downward spirals continued. We wanted to do as Hannah and Lawrence had said we should and encourage, even if not always expect, the same standards of behaviour from everybody. It was not easy.

One evening, when an elderly neighbour passed by along our street, Sang deliberately stuck out his huge tongue at her and laughed. There seemed no way she could have failed to notice for, with his big deformed mouth, crooked tombstone teeth, and broad inflamed gums, he could indeed make some terrifying faces.

'Mum,' said Hannah afterwards, 'you can't let him get away with it. You must tell him not to do that sort of thing.'

She was right of course. Since any of the others would have been sharply told off for being so rude to an old person, to ignore it in him was indeed to condone the double standards.

So, in a quiet moment, I took Sang on my knee for physical contact and hugged him and kissed him.

'Sang,' I said. 'The people who live round here are glad to see you and have done nothing to hurt you so I hope you'll try hard to be as polite as you can when you meet them.'

He knew what I was talking about for he said, 'She stupid old lady. I hate her,' and struggled to get off my lap. I let him go. But he didn't move away, and continued to stand so close to me that he was pressing my leg. I went on with my talk.

'So people living in this family, which includes you, will not make rude faces at old ladies out in the street. OK?'

Oh dearie me, did it sound like an ultimatum . . . if you make faces, you can't live here? I didn't want it that way. I went on holding on, trying to keep him safe physically for

84

physical contact is what he craves. 'I know sometimes we forget and are rude. But we all try to be polite, and try not to go out of our way to upset each other just for fun.'

'Can't care. Hate her.' He crawled back on to my lap. 'She schupit.'

'What did she do?'

Silence. Sang keeled over sideways off my lap and crumpled into a ball on the floor and began keening. I picked him up once again and held on tight and hugged.

'We love you Sang, love you. You don't need to do all these silly things to be loved. We love you anyway.'

But how can one, and why does one love this hopeless bundle of hate and self-hate and aggression? Is love really this inexpressible surge of feeling, of pity, of concern at his total helplessness in the world?

'You're such a nice boy. Inside you're a kind sweet boy. And it's because we love you so much that we feel cross and want you to be the nice boy always.'

He stopped struggling at last and snuggled instead, and then suckled at the bare skin on my wrist. He stayed on my lap while he drank his tea-time mug of coffee and ate his syrup sandwich.

Though there were still times when his dark roaring anguish came from nowhere, out of nothing, more of his outbursts were now conscious and directed deliberately at other people. After the old lady, he began constantly to bait Lawrence, poking and jeering at him. Lawrence tried to take no notice. As he sat reading, he refused to show that he minded or even noticed, though I saw that his eyes were brimming up with tears.

It seemed as though his policy of tolerance was working and that Sang recognized he'd gone too far for, just as I was about to intervene, Sang suddenly left Lawrence alone and came instead to hug me.

'Mum, I lob you. I want you. What matter him?' he asked cheerily. 'He so sad now.'

'Yes, he is, isn't he? Because you've been teasing him. So

you go and give him a nice hug too and say sorry to make him feel better.'

As soon as we grew to anticipate one kind of infant-toddler behaviour, this strange child unpredictably did something else.

Amiably enough Sang said, 'All right,' walked over to Lawrence, grabbed him by the hair, and jerked his head down in a sudden thrust, more like a mugger than a toddler.

What did these acts of mindless aggression mean?

Now Lawrence did cry, from the unexpectedness of it as much as the hurt.

'All right then,' I said crossly to Sang. '*Don't* be kind to Lawrence if that's what you feel like.'

I led Lawrence, blinded by his tears and by his confusion that his pacifism should be returned by hate, up to their bed-room, settled him on his bed with his animal book, and closed his door so he could be left in peace.

Sang, interpreting my nurture of Lawrence as rebuke of himself, instantly curled up in fetal position on the floor and roared unstoppably like some primeval monster. As before, to reprimand him in even the mildest tones had sent him into a pathetic rage.

'I not care!' he sobbed. 'I not stay!' he roared. 'I not you fren here,' he screamed. 'I not you fren again,' he howled.

Yet he didn't resist when I sat down on the floor beside him. It seemed important for him to know that, in a fam-ily, parents go on loving and accepting whatever anybody does, so I hugged him but without saying anything. There wasn't anything much to say, except perhaps, This is all much more difficult than any of us anticipated, isn't it? Or, Why do you scream so very much and so very loudly? Or, I was, as a matter of fact, trying to cook supper. Oh well, oh hell.

Would the roaring ever stop? Would David ever get back from work? Would we ever get the next meal cooked?

After a bit, above the noise, I said, 'D'you know what I keep in a secret place in a drawer in my desk?'

86

I did not intend to reward Lawrence-baiting and scream-ing with the treat of a secret, yet I wanted to forestall him tumbling into one of his uncontrollable rages with, if possible, some input about how very precious *all* our four children are to us, not any of them more precious than any other.

Lawrence was right. The antidote to aggression had to be tolerance. Screaming and violence had to be countered by love, and more love, and more. And in the end it would have to win.

'Something,' I went on, 'very important, something I love most in the world.' Interest faintly aroused. A secret to be shared?

Sang, reluctantly and in spite of himself, roared a bit less loudly because he wanted to listen.

'And I look at them whenever I'm feeling sad. Like now I'm feeling a bit sad because two of my children are unhappy. So it would be nice to look.'

In the drawer was an envelope of photographs we'd taken on Sang's many visiting weekends. He'd seen them all before. Slowly and carefully, I took them out. He slid on to my lap. Together we looked at a picture of him on his own, of him on David's lap, of him with Hannah, with Lawrence, with Donald, of all of them with their new teddies.

Gradually he began to smile again.

But what a long slow business it is turning out to be! Some-times it seems he has made no progress at all in his sense of security. Sometimes it feels as though we are entirely deluding ourselves if we believe that he will ever be more than a noisy passenger on this craft, that he'll never put back, of his own initiative, anything into the family, let alone the world, for it is all take, take, need, take. Can we ever help him become a whole person, a complete citizen?

What a relief to get away from home! We stayed in my mother's cottage. Donald and Sang shared a bedroom. They were enormously joyful, waking us early with cheerful noise games, and bouncing bed-springs. We listened to a game of 'teddy-rescue' as teddies were thrown from bed to bed. Sang's machine-gunning noise and military exercises took over but, though loud, were joyful. After breakfast, they played outside on the lawn, making a camp with rugs and cushions, chairs and lengths of rope.

They used to play *near* each other but rarely together. There had to be two brick castles, two encampments of little plastic knights, two sets of cars. It must be a step forward that these two could now play together in the same camp? Thank you God.

As Sang, with Donald and all the little cousins, gambolled on the grass, he looked for a moment quite ordinary and I could see him not as the dark clinging extension of myself that he was so much of the time but at a distance from myself as a small, happy little boy, grinning and running. *My* boy. *My* child.

'Oh isn't he *sweet*!' I cried aloud. 'Look, Mum! Isn't he adorable?'

'Really, Rachel,' my mother laughed. 'You're just like someone with a new puppy to look after! And as for these terrible rages you and David say he has. *I've* never seen him having one. I think you just make it all up.'

Was it some innate wisdom that made Sang reserve his more bizarre behaviour for the privacy of home?

On the car drive home, Sang swayed joyfully from side to side chanting his self-composed pop song, 'We're Japanee Soldier! Dah! Dah! dah-dah-dah!' repeated endlessly in shouted sing-song. The other three, squashed up beside the chanting Sang and the yowling cat joined in with good humour. 'Dah! Dah! dah-dah-dah!'

We can do it. We can! We can can can.

7

MUDDLING ALONG

Hannah asked anxiously one morning, 'Did you know about Sang — in the night?'

We knew that he woke often, that he had nightmares, or was angry, or wet, and so made his way down to our room. And sometimes he came for none of these, but just to look at us lying in bed.

'No, not any of that. I mean, the rocking?'

'The what?'

'It's really weird. I went to the loo in the night and as I went past the boys' room I heard this strange noise. So I looked in and Lawrence and Sang were both fast asleep, but the whole bunk bed was shaking, almost as though it'd tip up. Sang was rocking, I mean really rolling himself backwards and forwards, from side to side, his whole body turning. But he was quite asleep. I made sure. I thought it was because his covers had come off and he was cold. So I put them on again, but he still went on like a kind of machine.'

No, we hadn't known about this sleep-time rocking, only about the swaying from side to side on journeys in the car when he was singing, and sometimes when he was watching television.

'It's a wonder Lawrence isn't woken by it.'

A few nights later I was up myself in the dead of night, worrying about things that couldn't possibly be resolved, when I too heard the noise and went to investigate. Both boys were asleep while the entire bunk bed, just as Hannah has described, swayed vigorously from side to side. I tucked Sang in, at the same time trying to move his position in bed so that, like moving a snoring person, it might break the cycle. It didn't wake him. It didn't stop the rocking.

Next morning, we noticed for the first time the big bags under Lawrence's eyes, like owl eyes.

'Sang rocks in his sleep,' I said. 'We didn't know.'

My elder sister had told me how her foster son of fifteen used to rock so much that her other children eventually all moved downstairs on to the sitting room floor because they couldn't stand it.

'Yes,' said Lawrence.

'Doesn't it disturb you?'

He shrugged as though it wasn't something he wanted to talk about. 'He's always done it.'

'What d'you mean — always?'

'Since he got here.'

'Every night? All night?'

'Baby monkeys and chimps do it if they're taken away from their mothers too soon. I read about it. They rock like that all the time and they don't develop.' What does a primary school boy know about child development? 'Old people do it in mental hospitals too. I saw it on the telly.'

He mumbled about how, at the beginning, before he realized what it was, he kept having nightmares that he was in a boat, rocking about on the waves. Later he realized that it was the continual movement of the bunk bed that caused this repeated dream.

'Why didn't you tell us before? We'll move the beds.'

'You and Dad worry about everything too much already. Anyway, there's nothing much anybody can do about it. I've tried. Waking him up. Or telling him. But he doesn't know he's doing it. He can't help it. Anyway, I suppose I mind him shouting at me in the morning when he gets up much more.'

Droopy-eyed Lawrence quickly sidled himself out of the discussion.

We separated the bunk into two free-standing beds.

Lawrence was very annoyed. 'There's hardly enough room in here anyway. Now we can't move at all.'

We re-assembled the bunk bed.

Donald, who shared their room when anybody came to stay, also knew already about the night-time rocking. 'I quite like it,' he said. 'It's friendly. You know someone's there.'

Sang himself seemed totally unaware of what we were talking about. It was the same with the day-time rocking when, though he was apparently awake, he seemed oblivious of what he was doing for the repetitive movement seemed to thrust him into a trancelike state.

A very pretty, very young woman with fair fluffy hair appeared at the front door. She'd come to visit Sang, she said. She was disappointed to hear that he was out for a walk in the country with David and Donald.

'I *did* so want to see him again. I'm on holiday, just passing through.'

She was Sang's teacher from his old school. I asked her in for tea. I too was sad that nobody was at home but me.

'If only you could have . . . '

If only she'd *said* she was coming, we'd have made sure that Sang was home.

She had with her all Sang's old drawings and workbooks, and a bundle of goodbye letters from each of his former classmates. I felt, somewhat irritably, that these letters might have made more sense to Sang at the time he actually left that school rather than nearly three months later.

'But you see, he went so suddenly. No one told me he was going, or where. The other children in class wondered what had happened to him.'

She also brought a battered plastic Weetaflakes bag full of eighty or ninety used felt-tip coloured pens. It was the first personal possession of Sang's from his former life that we'd seen.

'Are they really all his?' I wondered. There were so many. I suspected that perhaps he'd had a touch of kleptomania?

'Oh yes! Definitely his. He used to walk around school everywhere with this bag. Never left it alone. You'd always see him with it. I was so glad when I heard he'd got a family. He did so want parents. For a long time now, he's been saying it. Maybe a year back or more.'

It was reassuring to hear. But I wanted to know more. Like whose idea it was that he wanted parents. 'It can't have been his own entirely? Somebody must have suggested it to him?'

She didn't know. 'It was a *dad* specially he wanted. He often used to tell us how he was going to get a dad of his own one day.'

I wanted her to tell me as much as she could remember about his past.

'Well, when he first came to us, how long ago would that have been, about eighteen months, or two years, he wasn't really speaking, only one-word sentences, like he could say, 'table', or 'window'. I used to give him a little bit of homework every day to bring home, maybe a little list of spellings to learn. And the next day he'd say, "Yes, I learned them." But of course he couldn't do them on his own. He'd have done better with more time. I asked if he could have reading help for ten minutes every day at home. The people there at the Home were always very co-operative. But they said he couldn't have extra attention if the other children weren't getting it. It wouldn't be fair to single him out for special treatment.'

Why, I thought angrily, had he not been allowed this so-called 'special treatment' when many of the others had extra attention for their caliper-fittings and their leg exercises and their horse-riding? How could Sang have been denied the right, every child's right, of the chance to learn to read? He was my child now and I seethed with fury on behalf of any hint of neglect. Yet this was precisely the reason why he, and children like him, needed to be in families rather than institutions, so that they could have the attention they'd missed.

The young teacher asked, 'Does he still scream like he used to? He'd lie on the floor. We couldn't do a thing with him. We had to just leave him there roaring and kicking. He wouldn't want anyone near him. No one was to touch him. He was in a world of his own.'

So the account we'd been given of the previously well-balanced little boy was not accurate, and the current rages were not just the result of changing homes or of the way we treated him.

I had a feeling that the pretty teacher was relieved not only that Sang now had a family, but also that he was no longer in her class.

When prompted to remember a few details about him she went on to recall that Sang used to like going to the swimming pool, and an anecdote about Sang and wasps.

'He used to think he could catch wasps by their wings and kill them. The funny thing was, he was never stung.'

She'd brought a present of two wall posters of chimpanzees drinking tea.

'I thought he might like it for his bedroom. And the other's for his new brother. He's got a brother now, hasn't he?'

It was kind of her to have made the effort to visit and I begged her to come again when Sang was home. Yet to my surprise something inside me kept saying, You didn't want him then so now he is mine, he is mine, he is mine. I had a sense of maternal owning far stronger than I'd ever allowed myself to feel for the other three. Previously, I had insisted that children belong equally to, and are the responsibility of, all caring adults. Now I felt myself becoming obsessively possessive about this Nobody's Child and Everybody's Child.

Sang wasn't back in time to see his former teacher. When I told him all about her visit, and gave him the letters and pens, he seemed confused. 'What she look like? I not know her.'

Can he really have forgotten? Or is he blotting it out?

Though we didn't at the time realize it, the other children's attitude to Sang and to the disruption to home life that his arrival had caused was remarkably tolerant. Perhaps, as children themselves, they were fundamentally more able to be compassionate about another child's needs. Perhaps they

93

were able to obey without quibbling the commandment to love one's neighbour. All too frequently I wondered if we were really doing the right thing. I cried with exasperation, fatigue or fury at least once a day. Meanwhile my children, whatever they were thinking inside their heads, seldom expressed resentment about Sang's presence, or suggested that they wished he were not here.

They seemed to regard him as just as much their responsibility as he was ours and their interest in his welfare, their involvement in trying to make him happier, was not merely passive and theoretical but active, vociferous, and highly critical if they felt that we parents were doing it wrong. As Sang lay screaming one day, Donald rebuked us, 'You must hug him more. He needs it.'

Hannah, when asked by a well-meaning acquaintance the all too-familiar question, 'And what do you think of this little boy your parents have found?' replied shortly, 'I don't think anything. He's my brother.'

We went for a family outing to a seaside pub for a supper of fish and chips, beer and lemonade. The four children jumped and romped on the shingle and skimmed stones along the water while David and I sat on the sea wall admiring them and congratulating ourselves on how well Sang was coming on. This particular family treat was like a yardstick for measuring progress, for we'd come here during his very first week with us, and several times since. At the beginning, he'd been afraid to venture more than twelve inches away from our side, had been unable to jump down the steps on to the shore, to walk along the wall, to run beside the breakwater. He had been alarmed by the seaweed, worried about the lapping water, and terrified of the approaching tide. On each successive visit, as we now reminded each other, he had seemed a little bolder, a little better able to control his gangly limbs, a bit more daring about jumping with the others off a low wall. He was less clinging, more cheerfully relaxed.

It had been such a happy summer's outing. Yet as soon as we reached home something unaccountably burst inside

94

Sang's soul. Suddenly he slumped on the stairs, limp and glowering in the shadows of the corridor.

'Come on darling, cheer up. Let's all go up together.'

No response. He dragged himself along the landing like Nguyen without using his legs, which trailed lifelessly behind him, and lay like a corpse. The low animal roar was beginning in his throat. It was getting late. Everybody needed to get to bed. I decided to ignore him and just carry on calmly with the bedtime routine.

But Hannah, also coming up to bed, found this moaning corpse blocking her way. She saw neither David nor me doing anything about his terrible noisy distress, and when he didn't respond to her either, she lay down along the floor almost on top of him, enveloping him in her whole self. With her long yellow hair draped over him, mingling with his dark hair, with her arms around his hunched shoulders, she seemed to be trying to absorb his grief. She stroked his nose, and murmured endearments into his ear, not entreaties as I did, but loving nothings which required no reply. Again and again, she softly told him of her intent to love him. 'Dear little Sang, my little baby Sang, you're so sweet. I love your little nose. I wish I had a dear little nose like yours.'

Within half an hour, she had calmed him enough for him to be able to sit, then to stand and to be led to the bathroom to be washed and changed for bed. And when he spoke it was to think of somebody beyond himself. Though we'd often talked with Sang about Nguyen, about how nice it would be when Nguyen was living nearby, though we'd sent cards to Nguyen and phoned him, Sang himself had never done so. Now for the first time, he expressed concern for his friend.

He said, 'Where he Nguyen? What he do now? Who look after? Who mum he have?'

The first three months of a child's placement were known, so we'd learned on the preparation course, as the honeymoon period, a peaceful interlude when things go exceedingly well and everybody gets along splendidly. Both child and parents are likely to be on best behaviour, still enjoying the novelty

95

of each other. Only after this happy three-month stage do the behavioural problems, if any, begin to emerge.

Either the honeymoon theory was wrong or else Sang was not a usual case. For if this first three months had been the easy bit, what on earth was the rest of it going to be like?

We wondered how the staff at the Children's Home had coped with these demanding days and busy nights without cracking up from sleep deprivation. They coped, we discovered from Sang, because of a night warden who sat up, in an armchair on the landing, while the day staff slept. Sang told us about her as though she had been some kind of ogre lurking in the dark.

'Oh yeah, she dere wait other side door. You get outa bed in night, she very angry! She say, go back bed!'

So this was maybe why he enjoyed being able to wander freely about in the night and look at us in bed?

'But what if you wanted to do a pee and had to go to the lavatory in the night? She must have let you get up then? Or did you have a potty by your bed?'

No, he didn't have a potty. He told us he wore a nappy. We were astonished.

'A nappy!'

'Lon tine ago, when I bout eight. I have wear nappy, plasty pant.'

Nobody had mentioned that our big boy, who had all his back teeth and wore huge size 12 walking shoes, had been pinned into nappies until so recently. If it were true, perhaps it was not, after all, so odd that he was still wet night and day?

However, the tentative suggestion that he might prefer to go back to a night-nappy rather than the nuisance of all-over wetness each morning was instantly rejected.

'I hate nappy! I gotta wear nappy because I wet alltine. Not wet now. No more. I hate nappy! Other children laugh me! Nguyen not have weara nappy!'

It was clearly a matter of dignity. Better to be sodden than look silly in plasty pant.

A friend of a friend, working in a children's psychiatric

unit, took a brief interest in Sang's placement with us, and asked one day if the boy suffered from 'encopresis'. The word was new to me. I quickly gathered it was a close relation of 'eneuresis' which we knew only too well.

I liked the sound of them both, like a pair of tropical twins. Our son has eneuresis and encopresis sounded much more interesting than our son can't help wetting and pooing himself. I chanted these pretty words to myself as I sorted the clothing which was engendered by this condition.

We had, in part, resolved the problem (which so embarrassed Donald even when he wasn't there to see) of me carrying vast quantities of laundry past his school gates to the local launderette. Now, one afternoon a week, an impoverished student came in to be the adult at home to welcome the younger boys from school and give them tea. Meanwhile I drove our dirty linen to the university to put into the college machines. They were meant to be for the use of college members, but none of the boys and girls busy ironing crisp creases in their Levis seemed to mind. I became quite fond of the steamy youthful atmosphere. In between loads, I went and drank coffee in David's office. Student Alison, who'd previously been washing floors in Tesco to make ends meet, seemed happy enough with her poorly paid role as home teatime person. Hannah and Lawrence, too, liked her company.

Sang was quite amenable to Alison. He was, after all, used to being cared for by an ever-changing rota of young women. But he was usually extremely unmanageable when David and I returned at six o'clock to take over again as parents.

We had to face up to the fact that we'd taken on a child we couldn't cope with. Yet we didn't quite know why we couldn't cope. We knew we couldn't blunder blindly on forever like this, from one day to the next, from one moment of crisis to the next moment of elation. Somehow, we had to try to think about what was going on.

We knew so little about him, and the small amount we had been told didn't match up with how he actually was. It wasn't just the screaming and uncontrolled behaviour. It was also the general inability to cope with even the basics of normal everyday life.

Perhaps the expectations of staff in a Children's Home of what a child of nine-and-a-half might be able to do by himself were very different from the expectations of ordinary people.

He wasn't able to dress himself without help. Buttons couldn't be done up, garments went on in random order so that sometimes a small vest would be tightly dragged on over a huge jumper, or trousers on back to front. Even after being shown, he seemed unable to select for himself appropriate school clothes from the drawer. When he was left to dress by himself, it was a bizarre get-up that he struggled into. One morning he appeared for school in green towelling toddler rompers, part of his original trousseau, a tiny Aertex shirt inside-out and back-to-front and nothing else, except of course his much loved walking shoes on the wrong feet. Another morning, it was shoes and swimming trunks, though with no trace of self-consciousness.

Though he loved to wear his walking shoes, he left the shoe-laces trailing. When shown how to tie them so that he wouldn't trip over them, he managed to arrange them like a ballet-dancer's ribbons, wrapped round the ankles, then drawn to the front and knotted in five or six granny knots so that it was impossible to get them off again.

He could not wipe his bottom, nor use the lavatory without leaving smears on seat and floor to greet the next user. It seemed, at first, positively impertinent for me or David to go into the lavatory with him and demonstrate how to sit effectively over the pan, afterwards how to wipe oneself and finally how to wash one's hands. But since he wasn't the only member of this family and we all used the same facilities, any such sense of impropriety on our part had to be overcome.

He could not handle a knife to cut up his own meat and preferred to use a spoon. When left to cope without adult interference or help, he often seemed genuinely perplexed about how to deal with food on his plate.

We struggled to teach him such essentials of caring for

oneself as mattered for getting through a school day. Shoe-laces, washing hands, getting clothes off and on again in the right order. But no sooner had he learned than he seemed to unlearn and had to be taught over again. It was very odd.

We had learned on the course how children may need to regress. But was this continual unlearning in fact part of the necessary period of regression, or was it a kind of eccentricity, incompetence, bloody-mindedness, confusion, culture shock, ignorance, or what? Sometimes it seemed like a lazy helplessness induced by the fact that at the Home there had been plenty of young helpers around to look after the physically handicapped older children who'd had to have everything done for them. 'You do, you do!' he said when faced with the awesome task of those shoe-laces.

Later, much later, I felt deeply ashamed when I remembered how many times I had said, 'Oh really! don't be such a lazy baby.' Or, when seeing how he'd put his shoes on the wrong way round yet again so that his funny-shaped rickety feet seemed even more deformed than ever, I became annoyed because I thought he'd done it deliberately.

So why on earth did we go on trying? Partly because his need was so blatantly, patently there. Also there was a kind of pride in not wanting to be beaten in the same way that our predecessors had been. We knew we were not the first people to have been moved by his obvious need and his utter helplessness. Dozens of people had already passed through his life — carers, sponsors, visitors, social workers, staff, charitable volunteers. Yet none, so far, had stuck with him long enough, had hung on tight enough. Eventually, somebody had to hold on and go on holding on, even if it killed them. In our arrogance, we believed that we were going to be able to do what no one before us had managed.

But how were we to know that *he* really wanted to stay with *us*?

When one has recently given birth to a new baby, occasionally, when engrossed in reading or when woken from deep sleep, one completely forgets about it so that, on recalling its existence, one is shaken by a tremendous lurch of excitement. With stomach-churning excitement, one remembers that the vital new person is here in one's home, alive, in its crib, one's own fresh, untarnished person in the world.

It was much the same with Sang. Momentarily forgetting about him because one was absorbed in work, the remembering again of his presence in our family brought a similar frisson of delight. Every morning, whatever time he woke up, he always came stumbling uncertainly downstairs to our room and checked up on us. And though it was a rude shock to find oneself being inspected at four or five in the morning, it was also an uplifting pleasure to be greeted (when he was not angry) by that darling face, which was growing more and more familiar, peering round the door.

Joy said, 'Of course there's been a honeymoon period. You've fallen in love with him. Both of you. It's quite clear you have. That's all that matters.'

It was true of course. We had.

Joy said, 'And now he's got to fall in love with you.'

Sang frequently told us how, 'One day I gonna go find myself good mumdad. Give me feeties all tine.' But there were signs that he wanted to stay, not so much from what he said, but more because of what he did.

Though he couldn't read, though he found remembering people and place names frustratingly difficult, he discovered the significance of the name tapes which were sewn into everybody's coats. Laboriously he copied the family surname, learned to say it and more or less to spell it. Then this new name began to appear on the walls in the house in tiny spidery pencil writing at exactly Sang-height. It next appeared, scratched with some sharp instrument into the surface of our one piece of antique furniture, an elegant wooden table given to us as a wedding present by David's aunt. Just as in marriage, the commitment to the relationship had to be made and re-made. Every time the name was recorded in a new place, it was like a re-affirmation of his intention to belong.

He looked at the five volumes of photograph scrapbooks, repeatedly asking who this person was, or that, as though trying to memorize each face and its place in the chronology so as to learn to distinguish between David as a small boy on a beach and my brother as a boy on a beach. 'Dat Dad little boy gonna sea side. Dat Mum Eddie (Mum's brother, Eddie). Dat MumDad marry. Dat Hannah baby. I not here when Hannah baby.' He was disappointed that there were no pictures of him in any of the early books. I explained how we had only one picture of him from before he came to us.

The first time he saw that the pictures we'd been taking since his arrival were now stuck in the scrapbook with all the rest, he said with an expression of amazement, 'Dat me! Now I dere too! Look, dat me dad!'

Perhaps he hadn't believed us when we'd said he was staying forever. Perhaps he didn't know what forever meant?

8
COMMITMENT

When Donald came and told me that Sang had disappeared I wasn't alarmed.

'He's probably just hiding in a cupboard somewhere, or under a bed,' I said. But we both searched and he wasn't.

From other parents, David and I heard frequent scare stories how adoptive children run away as a means of 'testing out' their new home. One of the films we'd been shown on the preparation course had been a melodramatic reconstruction of the searches in dark car parks and empty building sites which a mother had to make each time her new son disappeared. He always wanted to be found. This hide-and-seek was a part of their bonding process. Only after he knew that however often he ran way, however efficiently he hid, she would always come looking for him, did he begin to feel that it was safe to stay.

When Sang disappeared, Hannah was out at Guides, Lawrence was at a music lesson and Donald was absolutely distraught.

'He's probably just outside on the pavement,' I said reassuringly. 'Waiting for Dad to get home.'

When he wasn't there either, I began to fear abduction.

If he seemed so pretty to us, maybe he was pretty to others too? Donald, with tears streaming down his face, hurried with me round the nearby streets, all of which seemed unusually quiet. Surely, in our small cathedral town, he couldn't be far away. He was, after all, so distinctive that surely someone must have noticed him?

We knocked on doors. We ran along calling out his name. After thirty minutes which seemed like days, we found him, two streets away, standing sullen and silent by the river. It was on the route which we took to go to the dentist once a fortnight. He didn't seem very pleased to be found as he said he'd been having a nice time outside a pub talking to a dog. He was obviously telling the truth because there, lying asleep on the pavement outside the nearest pub, was indeed a large black dog.

'Then I listen all happy people have nice time in pub,' he said.

Taking him to the seaside pub must have given him the idea that pubs were good places to be.

Donald put his arms round Sang and stroked him. 'Please stay with us,' he said. 'Please don't go away again. We need you here.'

'All right, maybe,' Sang muttered. 'But soon I gonna good mumdad buy me present all tine.'

Gradually it transpired that he hadn't intentionally gone away, merely wandered out through the front door which was rarely locked, turned a corner or two and then found he didn't know the way back and panicked at finding himself lost.

We had no 'rules' in the family, only mutual agreements and understandings. Now, some of these 'understandings' needed voicing clearly. 'If anybody goes out of the front door, they must always tell someone else in the family where they are going.'

Sang took the making of this rule as a positive recommendation to go out and would announce solemnly, amidst a lot of farewell hugging, 'I gonna go out now.' Then he would step outside the front door, walk three steps along the pavement, wait a moment, turn round and come back in, whereupon he would call out, 'I been out. I back now,' and wait to receive his hugs of welcome.

The fact that he didn't attempt to hide or run away even when angry, and that he repeatedly re-enacted this daring drama of departure and safe return, we interpreted as further signals that, despite our shortcomings as parents, he wanted to stay.

Though we didn't, as my mother suggested, put any announcements in *The Times*, (Sang wasn't legally adopted yet anyway) we did send out to long-standing acquaintances *It's a Boy!* birth announcement cards, crossing out 'date of birth' and substituting 'date of arrival'. Naively, we expected an enthusiastic response to this proclamation, just as there would have been if it had been a 'real' birth. The fact that our new 'baby' was extremely difficult to cope with shouldn't detract from the fact that his arrival in the family was a matter of general rejoicing.

From a small handful of friends and relations we received affectionate and encouraging letters. One old friend sent a Lego car for our little boy. Another, having not noticed on the card where it said, 'Sang, now 9½ years old,' sent a little blue matiné jacket. David's unmarried aunt, whose elegant table had been permanently marked with her newest nephew's name, wrote a letter of welcome enclosing a cheque for a hundred pounds because, as she said, 'I dare say having children these days is rather an expensive business?'

These windfalls were a lovely surprise. The approval was even more valuable, for elsewhere there was at best salacious curiosity, at worst, positive hostility. Not everyone shared our belief that adoption was a good idea. An elderly neighbour (and not even the one at whom Sang had stuck out his tongue) strode up to us in the street and, entirely unprovoked, said in Sang's hearing, 'That's a perfectly disgusting-looking child. I hate children like that. Why doesn't he go back where he's come from?'

Our pathetically innocent views were further shaken the first time we had to take Sang to a doctor.

We still had no records of Sang's health but we were beginning to be convinced that he couldn't see properly.

He watched television from so close to the screen that no one else could get a look in, and always with his head turned sideways so that he was squinting at it out of the side of one eye. When drawing too, he peered with his head at right angles to the paper.

David is short-sighted and had worn glasses since he was eleven. Without them he sees the world 'as a soft pleasant blur'.

'The day I first got them was extraordinary. Everything, my whole life, changed. At last I could see what was going on.'

Might clearer vision have the same radical effect on Sang, clarifying the blurred edges, sharpening all the senses? In due course, an eye-test would be part of the routine medical required for adoption but the legal proceedings were being slow. If having an eye-test would make even the slightest difference to Sang's prospects, it seemed worth a try. And sooner rather than later. But because the only official paper we so far had relating to Sang was his NHS medical card, we decided it would be best to start by going to see our GP. It was a bad decision.

Sang and Donald raced happily along to the surgery. Donald had been watching the Olympics on television and explained how he and Sang were being the runners, Ovett and Coe. Sang seemed happy to co-operate. Both boys pounded breathlessly into the waiting room. It seemed such a long time since David and I had been here to discuss adoption with our GP and to have the medicals for Mervyn's agency, and I felt pleased that I was now going to be able to show off Sang as the positive outcome of all that effort.

Unfortunately, our GP was away ill. In his place behind the desk was a fatherly-looking locum with pink cheeks and silver hair. He glanced up at Sang, then at Donald, then back to Sang. I explained that we were there because Sang, my adoptive son, seemed to have something wrong with his sight, we weren't sure what, and weren't sure how to go about getting an eye-test for him.

The first question the doctor asked seemed a bit odd. 'How long has he been in this country?'

'We're not quite sure,' I said, unwisely answering an irrelevant question. 'About five years, we think.'

Sang, who'd been sitting beside me, now crept on to my lap and nervously clutched my hand. I'd explained to him that the doctor wouldn't be going to do anything, except perhaps look into his eyes.

I reminded the doctor that we'd come about Sang's sight.

'And where did you say he was born? What country?'

I hadn't said, and I shouldn't have answered that irrelevancy either.

'The other child,' he jabbed his pen towards Donald beside me. 'Is he adopted too?'

At the sound of the word 'adoption' Sang's arm went round my neck so tightly I thought he'd throttle me.

But why these questions which had nothing to do with Sang's eyes?

'No,' I said. 'He's home grown.'

'What?'

Perhaps I was too flippant. 'I had him myself,' I stammered. But no, I knew that wasn't right either because I had had him, not by myself, but with the help of husband, midwife, trainee nurse, and the GP whom this man was temporarily replacing. 'I gave birth to him myself. He's natural.' But I had not come here to discuss Donald's method of entry into the world.

'How old?' The locum pointed again at Donald. Now he too began to huddle on his seat looking worried. The locum's eyes were light blue, and pink-edged. He seemed less fatherly and silvery-haired, and more sinister.

'Six,' I said. 'And Sang's nine. And they get on very well together.' I wondered if I should tell him, in fond motherly tones, how they'd been playing at Ovett and Coe. I decided not to.

'I do not advise you to hurry into having this eye-test done,' said the doctor flatly. So far, he'd asked no questions

106

about why we might consider that Sang had poor sight. 'In fact, I advise you just to see how it goes.'

What did he mean? 'What?' I asked.

He began to talk in vague terms about 'the great difficulties of this unusual situation'. At first, I thought he meant bureaucratic difficulties about Sang not being adopted yet already having our surname on his medical card. He didn't. He meant having two children of different abilities and different races in the same family. He obviously hadn't been reading the back page of the *Guardian* lately where such children were now being advertised for adoption every week. He obviously didn't know that in that year alone over 1200 older children of 'unusual situations', aged between five and seventeen and of various racial origins, had been adopted and that, after their disrupted childhoods, most inevitably had some degree of disability — whether, like Sang's, emotional, or mental or physical or even all three.

'Moreover,' the ignorant doctor went on, 'since the er, the child goes to a special school, then the matter of his eye-sight is not in the hands of the National Health but with your local education authority.'

I asked why. He just said, 'I advise you to leave it up to the special school.'

'But it's summer holidays,' I said. 'He won't be going back to school for another six weeks. If he does need glasses, he ought to have them as soon as possible.'

Ovett and Coe were growing restless so I told them they could go and look at comics in the waiting room.

'Ah, I'm glad they've gone. Now we can have a proper chat,' said the doctor. 'My dear, you must see that five years is a very long time. Since the boy hasn't caught up in five years, there's no chance he will.'

I found this unknown, unknowing man's attitude frustrating and enraging. Just when we most wanted encouragement and a bit of help, this prophet of doom was, uninvited, predicting nothing but disaster.

'Caught up?' I said.

107

'He's never going to develop.'

'Yes, he's very backward,' I said, adding, 'at the moment. Most children are from Children's Homes. And they usually regress even more when they get adopted. We know all that.'

'Since he has not reached normal behaviour for his age by now, it's quite clear that he'll remain retarded. You'd do as well to send him back. You'll only harm your others.'

This stupid old pink-eyed man had never met Sang before, had scarcely looked at him, yet after two minutes was daring to tell me there was no hope when all we'd come about was an eye-test.

'He's had severe emotional deprivation for the first half of his life in an orphanage, and been living in a Home with profoundly handicapped children for the other half of his life. He's picked up lots of their habits and behaviour. How could he have developed normally there? That's why we're adopting him, so he can have a better chance.'

The doctor cut me off. 'That's all as may be. But you must see that forcing an, an, an er er child like er er,' he groped to remember Sang's name and failed. 'Forcing a child like that into glasses wouldn't be very er, er, very kind, and not very helpful.'

'But just supposing my son really can't see properly?'

My granny, I wanted to tell him, was so blind that she hadn't known that trees had leaves or tables had legs till she was prescribed glasses at the age of three. If they could arrange glasses for a three-year-old last century, surely they could manage something for a nine-year-old this century? And just because he was backward, did he have to be denied vision to add to his backwardness? I explained yet again that the whole point was to get glasses made up, if needed, so he could start benefitting right away.

'You must realize, that he won't ever be the same as, er, same as er er normal.'

I should have been angry. Instead, I actually thanked him for his help, and left in a confusion of overwhelming dismay. According to this man, we had taken on a complete non-starter and there was no point in going on. But what on earth would it do to our other children if they saw that all non-starters were ejected?

At home, David said, 'You're just going to have to develop a thicker skin, darling. People are going to say things all the time. More and more.'

Then he phoned the education authority and was told that any person, brilliant or daft, unmanageable or calm, with round eyes or with epicanthic folds, is entitled to an annual eye-test if he or she holds a valid medical card.

So Sang was tested, coincidentally by an Asian optician who was charming, affectionate and gentle with him, who diagnosed astigmatism and extreme short-sight and said he should wear the glasses not just for watching television and drawing but all the time.

'Oh no,' groaned Sang. 'Not the glassy!'

Yes you will, because we love you, and we're going to fight all your battles for you and you're going to wear the glassy, and learn to read and write and count and dress yourself and do all sorts of things you don't yet know about.

'I hate wear dat glassy again.'

'Again? Have you worn glasses before?'

'Yeah. Got broke.'

The housemother confirmed that Sang had indeed had glasses before but when they'd got broken, it had seemed too difficult to have them replaced.

'You can imagine what it was like going for an eye-test with a child like him. He was very uncooperative.'

The person we'd found uncooperative was not Sang, but the doctor. When, some weeks later, Sang developed more bald patches of alopecia on his head and Donald got nits, we were relieved that David had already had our cards changed to another more broad-minded practice.

Sang stepped out of the opticians wearing his newly pre-scribed glasses for the first time, and shouted out, 'Yeah, yeah! merm. Look! Look, I can see!' and darted along the pavement to gaze into the window of the toyshop. He looked like a dear little Vietnamese intellectual.

Our own generation had no problem in accepting Sang. When I asked each of my three sisters if the informal agreement we'd always had about caring for one another's children if any of us should die prematurely was extended to include this new nephew, they seemed almost affronted by my doubt.

My eldest sister said, 'He's so sweet! And I'm sure there's nothing really wrong with him. It's just the language problem. He seems quite bright. He comes out with the funniest things, and you see him watching all the time. He's taking it all in.'

Whatever they may have felt about it before, David's brothers and sister showed a similar matter-of-factness in accepting Sang as a *fait accompli* and our seven-year-old niece, an only child, was brought to stay with us for a week so that she 'wouldn't feel left out of the fun'. On the first meeting, Sang's oriental appearance provoked her to practise all her recently learned judo thrusts on him. But when this didn't get any response, not even retaliation (he didn't then know what judo was), she changed her tactic, clasped him to her tummy declaring, 'My dear darling best new cousin!'

Having an extra small niece added to the general feeling that we were running an overcrowded summer ark. But, as we already knew, once one has over two children in a house, they have a way of multiplying spontaneously. The new neighbours' tiny tots, for example, spent a great part of their lives in our house rather than their own. The havoc they caused reassured me, when I could remember to laugh about it, that any child, not just the adoptive kind, is infinitely demanding. After the next-door toddler had creatively scattered salt all over our kitchen floor, walked through a saucer of yellow poster paint, then across the carpet, and majestically unrolled twenty-five feet of silver cooking foil round the kitchen, all the other children, believing that I'd suggested it as a new kind of entertainment, joined in spreading foil over the entire kitchen. The next-door tot's mother

110

came to look for him and remarked how pleased she was he should be able to play in our house because I was 'so much more liberal' than she could ever let herself be and she was sure it must be good for him.

While the plans for adoption had still been merely theoretical, some of our elderly relations had been much against it. Without considering how difficult it must be for people brought up on different values to accept ours, we optimistically hoped that now Sang was in the family, the reality of him would reverse their feelings. Alas, this was not always so. When we accepted a Sunday invitation to some elderly cousins, there was a tenseness throughout the visit. Our cousin wisely announced that, since Sang didn't know her and she didn't know him, she'd decided 'not to fuss him and to take no notice of him and wait till he's ready'. But then she didn't seem able to ignore him after all and, although Sang seemed to be trying quite hard to be on best behaviour, he was constantly reprimanded for doing things which were tolerated from the other children.

'Oh no, no, no! Don't do that, please dear. Oh don't let him do it!' she shrieked at him as we walked round the front garden for Sang was standing on the edge of the flower bed which, with his ignorance of the world, he didn't realize was a no-go area. He stepped off the flower bed and bent down to pick up and rather short-sightedly inspect some mouldy bread crusts put out for the birds and was again shouted at.

'Don't touch. Put it down. It's for the birds, not for you!'

He was ticked off for touching the rocking horse in the library even though Donald was offered a ride, and most surprisingly of all, he was told off for romping on the lawn with our cousin's grown-up son, a tall athletic man in his mid-twenties who seemed quite big enough to protect himself and had in fact initiated the romp-in on the grass.

'Get off him, get off, you'll hurt him!' our elderly hostess called desperately from the verandah in an attempt to protect her adult son who was carrying Sang piggy-back.

Several times during the afternoon, I noticed how, in-between the numerous tellings-off, Hannah and Lawrence took Sang into the rose garden and gave him surreptitious huggings. I wished there'd been a more understanding welcome. But he was not a same-blood cousin, or even a cousin at all. We could not demand that our extended families love him as we did.

Meanwhile, the two grandmothers each revealed, over Sang's physical appearance, more about their own proclivities than about his. Treatment hadn't yet begun on Sang's teeth and gums so that the dark and crooked teeth were perma-nently bared in a strange rictus grin since he wasn't ever able to close his mouth fully.

One granny said, 'It is a pity about his mouth being such an awful shape. I suppose there's nothing you can have done about it?'

The other, who always rushed with cries of delight to admire the most hideous, spotty and overweight babies in their prams, said, 'Teeth? Mouth? What's so wrong with his teeth that everybody keeps going on about? He looks perfectly all right to me.'

The paternal grandparents were taking their grandchildren to the seaside as they had been doing every year.

It was an athletic, outdoor fortnight involving long-established traditions of daily swims, rugged rock-climbs and day-long cliff-path walks. The grandparental cottage, in an isolated Welsh village, had no luxuries such as a fridge, let alone a washing machine or spin dryer.

Without hesitation, Granny said that of course they'd take Sang too, but cautiously adding, 'if it seemed wise'.

It didn't.

The grandparents, though vigorously energetic, were, as they occasionally admitted, 'not quite as young as we were'.

Besides the screamings and those fearsome twins, eneuresis and encopresis, there was Sang's lack of physical co-ordination and balance to consider. He came down the stairs one step at a time holding on to the banister with both hands. The thought of him being expected to scamper down vertical cliff paths carrying a picnic basket was impossible. And he couldn't swim.

He accepted with surprising equanimity the explanation that in Wales the cliffs and rocks might be too difficult for him to manage. Perhaps he was only too used to being left out, whether it was a hospital visit to have calipers fitted or a cliff walk.

'Yeah, yeah,' he nodded his head in agreement. 'Danger, very danger me dem rock. I not like sea.'

The housemother was urging once again for him to go back to see the other children at the Home where, she insisted, he was still, as he always had been, part of their group. Nguyen would be there, having not yet moved into his permanent family.

I was once again strongly against this visit. He didn't yet see himself firmly enough anchored in our home to know that it was acceptable to live in one household and go visiting to a former one. To return so soon would throw him further into confusion about where he belonged. However, Joy said it couldn't do any harm, insisting too, that it was just as important for us to get a break as it was for Sang to have unbroken stability. So, with the utmost reluctance, we agreed to take him back for one week's stay. Sang seemed eager at the prospect of seeing 'his' Nguyen again and we reminded ourselves that our own possessiveness over Sang oughtn't to get in the way of that friendship which was of much longer standing than Sang's relationship with us. But first, after our other three had been sent off to their hearty cliff walks in Wales, we had time on our own with just Sang.

We'd always tried to provide the children with periods of being a single child when they could be spoiled and given a sense of their own importance, not merely as members of a sibling team but as individuals. It was just as important for Sang, we thought, to have this chance to be the only child. We could consolidate our parental relationship with him. The

113

screamings might even abate when he didn't have to be in competition with the others.

We explained what being an only child meant, and how nice it was, sometimes, to be in such a situation, with both parents all to yourself for a while.

'You me Dad hab lobly tine,' he agreed amicably. 'When dey come back?'

After the exhaustingly full household we'd just had, I persuaded myself that we'd be able to get on much better with a single child and a single cat. If we had ever suspected that he would have been better placed with a childless couple without the threat from siblings, how wrong we were. During that week he suffered even more descents into his places of uncontrollable darkness, though balanced by no periods of noisy exuberance.

As usual, he came down to our bed, wet or dry, cross or cheerful, for early morning hug-ins when he either suckled my arm or snuggled into the hair on David's chest with exclamations of, 'Aah, I like nice furry.' Or sometimes he tried to do both at once.

But most of the time, he was desolate. Even while he was getting our undivided attention, he was thinking about the others. 'Dey wanna hug you all tine. I know it. I know dey wanna hug.' Twenty times an hour, forty times an hour, he asked, When were they coming back? Were they coming back? Where were they again? What time did their train get into the station? What if we missed it? How did we know they were coming back? What would happen if they didn't come back?

We realized how much he was picking up, intuitively, in speech and behaviour from being with other ordinary children. We realized too how much they did for him, in entertaining him, looking after him, absorbing him. Caring for Sang was not a job for two people, but for five.

After we'd driven Sang to the Home, we'd intended to stay 'on holiday' at home. But our chaplain friend from the London Hospital rang unexpectedly, offering us, while he was away, the use of his house if we needed a change of scene.

He was right. We did. If we stayed at home, we'd only spend the time clearing up the mess and missing our children. So we packed the mewling cat into a basket and went to relax in the East End of London in an elegant Regency town house right beside the hospital's laundry and mortuary.

We hadn't been alone together for months. We hadn't made love for weeks. I wasn't even sure if we still knew how to. We were always so tired. The nights were always so interrupted, the days of such an undiluted intensity.

On our arrival we slept like exhausted corpses for twelve hours, the next day we slept for thirteen hours, and the third for fourteen. On the fourth, we revived, re-found our lost libido, and David went to an off-licence in the Whitechapel Road and bought back half a dozen bottles of red wine and three of Dubonnet. For the rest of the stay we lay in bed drinking and watching old films on the colour television.

On each of those nights that Sang was away from us and we from him, I dreamed strange honeylike dreams in which he was the honey, stuck into my hair and my brain, clinging to my mind. His curious speech patterns, his curious needs were sticking to me so I couldn't get rid of them. All night, dreaming these honey-Sang, honey-sweet dreams, I knew, even when asleep, that I had to get rid of them, get them and him out of my head because this was meant to be husband-and-wife time. But every time, in my dream, that I clawed at the honey-sweetness inside my head, he stuck instead like syrup to my hands. Was this, I wondered, what bonding was?

When we went to collect Sang, it was not us but the cat he was most pleased to see, the same cat that he had so often kicked and squeezed by its neck, but which now he stroked tenderly in its basket in the car and asked me to carry all round the Home to show to the others there. When Nguyen somewhat imperiously demanded that I carry him, Sang explained to his friend, 'She not helper. She my merm.'

9

ONCE UPON A TIME

When you take as your baby a person with nine years of living behind him, there are so many things you want to know. What illnesses has he had? What inoculations? What was his mother's name? What was his favourite toy as a baby? But we had no facts, no anecdotes of infancy to be told and re-told to build up his past. How can one give a child a sense of himself when one knows nothing?

To make more room on the landing, I took the old cot out from where it had been folded up beside a chest-of-drawers. Before offering it to the Scout jumble sale, I started to put it up to make sure that all the rods and screws were there. On seeing it assembled, Donald asked for a last turn, clambered in and said, 'Look, I'm a baby going to sleep.' He pretended to suck his thumb, then jumped out saying, 'Now I've grown into a big boy!'

Sang, seeing the cot, at once became extremely agitated and waved his hands about and made repeated little mouse noises. He kept calling it 'the cage' and asked why I wanted 'the cage'. When he got into the cot for his turn, he lay down flat on his back with his legs bent at the knee and immediately, as though activated by the sides of the cot, began his rhythmical side-to-side rocking while, as though the cot were giving him electric shocks, started a hysterical and incomprehensible shouting, interspersed with crazy machine-gun noises. Ack-ack-ack! T-T-T-T!

The moment I got him out to dismantle the cot, he stopped

as though the electricity had been turned off.

It was eerie. Would we ever grow used to the strangeness of his ways?

The only two documents we had about him were his current NHS medical card and the houseparent's hand-written account of the things he could do which, as we were discovering, had been an idealized rather than actual assessment. Though the houseparent was the obvious person to ask about his past, she had clearly found the whole business of his departure from the Home painful to bear. She was busy preparing to retire from the post and had neither the time nor the inclination to answer our queries. Even such banalities as whether or not he was known to have had chickenpox only added to her anguish. However, she promised that, after retirement, she would sort out some photos.

When we asked direct questions about Sang's life before he came to Britain, she said she thought it was much better that he should never know, since conditions had been very bad. She would never tell him, or any other child, about such things as it would be too upsetting.

Sang himself showed no curiosity about his origins. He knew he had no mumdad, though did not wonder why, for neither did Nguyen, nor any of the other young people at the Home.

Beginning with, 'Long tine go', Sang would occasionally relate some incident from his former life. But these memories always referred to something which had happened quite recently. 'Long tine go, me Nguyen run away across road,' or 'Long tine go I have rabbit,' 'Long tine go, you come see me, have tea.' It seemed as though his consciously remembered past could extend back only as far as the last year or so.

He knew he'd come from somewhere on an aeroplane but didn't respond with recognition to 'Vietnam' or to being 'Vietnamese'. In fact he claimed, most vociferously, that he came from Hong Kong. Believing that this connection had some historical importance for him — perhaps he had relations in Hong Kong? perhaps he had stayed there in a reception camp en route to Britain? — on an outing to the Commonwealth Institute in London, while the others dashed about inspecting Canadian Mounties' hats and New Zealand plants, Sang and I made eagerly for the Hong Kong section.

'Long tine go, I bin there!' Sang told me firmly. 'Look, dey like me. Black hair.' Some of the happy Hong Kong people in the glossy posters demonstrating trade, tourism and education in the protectorate did indeed look a bit like him, certainly more like him than David or I. Still keen, Sang and I sat stolidly through the first three minutes of a promotional film but he quickly became bored. Maybe he had expected to recognize something specific.

At the medical centre where we were now registered, following our escape from Dr Pink-Eyes, I asked if I could see Sang's medical file so we might at least know what inoculations he'd had. I was told that all patients' files are strictly confidential. However, the receptionist agreed to 'take a peek' on my behalf. She discovered that there was nothing whatsoever on Sang's file. Had he lived for five years in Britain and never once been seen by a doctor? Had there been no medicals when he arrived in the country? No polio or tetanus jabs?

So we wrote to the practice with which Sang had been registered while at the Home. A personal letter from a doctor came back saying that if he remembered anything, he would tell us, but unfortunately couldn't even recall this patient. However, by chance, he'd come across a file with Sang's name on. He enclosed it with his letter and, despite its supposed confidentiality, left it conveniently unsealed. Inside were details of two disorders — a minor skin rash between the toes which, from the fungal cream prescribed at the time, sounded as though it had probably been the same athlete's foot from which Sang was now suffering. More alarming was a separate note stating that, as an epileptic, the patient must continue indefinitely with the prescribed dose of anti-convulsant. We were startled. Could Sang really have been having major epileptic fits without us noticing? Or was

118

it petit-mal? Or had the housemother's reluctance to talk about Sang's past included this detail as well? Or had he been wrongly diagnosed as epileptic in the first place and the chance of coming to us had saved him from a routine of inappropriate daily drugs? Looking more closely at the note, I recognized that the scribbled name on the top, though similar to Sang's, was not Sang's but that of one of the teenage girls at the Home. These unfamiliar foreign names had, no doubt, confused a filing clerk into believing it was the same person, especially as the address had been the same. In a bureaucratic slip-up their notes had become muddled.

So the conclusion of following that particular trail led to little more than the confirmation that, during the past year, Sang had had athlete's foot.

It was not Sang but Lawrence who first asked what had become of Sang's parents. 'His mum, where d'you think she is? Is she dead?'

'Nobody knows. I wish we did. But we don't.'

But slowly we were accumulating enough scraps and rags to make up a patchwork sort of life. We heard from people who'd visited the Children's Home, from students who'd done voluntary work there, from people who'd worked in Vietnam. As a result of an article I wrote about Sang we heard from several nurses who'd been in Saigon, who claimed that, from the picture of him in the magazine, they were pretty sure they'd known him and even looked after him in the Hoi Duc Anh.

Sometimes information confirmed what we thought we already knew. Sometimes it conflicted.

One of my cousins who had been on a diplomatic visit to Saigon described having seen rubbish tips where small children and babies were living on their own, unclaimed by any adult. 'I met two kinds of religious attitude,' he said. 'The Buddhists who respected all forms of life but didn't feel they had to do anything about human babies, and the Christians who didn't necessarily show respect for life but always rushed around gathering up the babies.'

119

We were told that, despite fighting out in the countryside, Saigon itself had been relatively quiet at night because of the curfew, so our child would have heard nothing of the bombing. In contrast, we were told by a friend who had been a correspondent in Saigon of bombers flying in so low over the city at night that the windows rattled, and of night-raids which shook the earth. How could we know which was the truer account?

There were also two versions of how Sang came to be in an orphanage. One told how he had been picked up off a pavement by a passing policeman, the other that he had merely appeared one day in the office of the orphanage but nobody had seen who brought him in. Once there, there were no reports of any relative visiting him.

There was not even any certainty that he was Vietnamese, only the knowledge that he had been found in Saigon and that he did not appear to be Eurasian or Afro-Asian. One seasoned traveller, an American, told us that she'd been astonished to hear us refer to him as Vietnamese since she'd known, from the moment she first set eyes on him, 'by the shape of his head' that he was obviously of Chinese origin. Another person who had worked for several years as a missionary in China told us the exact opposite, that from Sang's appearance, it was clear he wasn't Chinese.

The housemother's affidavit required for the legal processes of adoption described conditions similar to those we had read of in Liz Thomas' book, of squalor, poverty, lack of food; of local helpers stealing orphanage rations for their own hungry children. There had been feuds between helpers and favouritism over orphans. Sang himself had been used as a pawn in one such conflict, being retained by one woman in the babies' room long after he had outgrown the cot in which he lay to prevent him from moving on into the care of the woman's enemy who was in charge of the toddlers' dormitory. It was to an orphan's advantage to become favourite not of a poor, widowed, indigenous helper, but of some Western outsider, who might bring in vitamins and dietary supplements. To stand a chance of being favoured by such a visitor, it was better to be healthy, pretty, and female.

In the babies' room, instead of being weaned on to solid food, Sang continued to receive as his only nourishment bottles of watered-down powdered milk. Since there was not time for each of some thirty inmates in the care of one woman to be fed individually, the bottles were propped up against their mouths. It was this that had caused the distortion to Sang's mouth as his gums, upper lip and teeth would have been constantly pushed upwards and outwards by pressure from the weight of the bottle. The back of his head was mis-shapen and flattened, presumably because of always lying down. He still seemed to have difficulty in being able to chew solid food. His method was to put as much as he could into his mouth and then give one almighty swallow. Sometimes this worked and the food went down. Sometimes it didn't.

David's mother, on hearing of Sang's early life, asked why he hadn't tried to climb out of the cot in which he had been imprisoned. As she pointed out, 'Most toddlers, if you put them in a cot, pretty soon find a way out.' We conjectured some possible reasons. For convenience and lack of anywhere else to place them, the babies were kept in low-sided cots twenty-four hours a day except when taken out to be hosed down. To ensure that there would be no danger of the babies tumbling down on to the floor, every time they tried to sit up, they were pushed back down into a lying position by the helpers. After a while, Sang was presumably conditioned into staying down. In addition he would have been weak from malnutrition and apathetic from lack of stimulation.

He was not the only orphan. By 1975, there were said to have been over 800,000 abandoned or unclaimed children.

Sang's connections with Hong Kong turned out to be of an ephemeral nature. The jet in which he had been brought to Britain had landed there for refuelling. Neither Sang nor any other passengers had come off.

His interest in Hong Kong remained. He liked the sound

121

of it, though after seeing the film *King Kong* on television, he began to fuse the two. Soon, he liked 'King Kong' even more than 'Hong Kong'. Then the mere mention of King Kong, or even of 'chimpanzee', 'gorilla' or 'orangutan' sent him into ripples of happy giggles.

Eventually such incidents came to occupy the empty place of the lost anecdotes of an unknown infancy, so that where we might tell, of one of the other children, the tale of the day he fell head first out of his pram, or the day he dropped his teddy in a canal, for Sang there was re-telling the tale of the time he fell over laughing whenever we said the word 'orangutan'. Then he could shake his head knowingly and say, 'Ah, that a long time ago when I very little.'

One morning Joy rang to say she'd discovered the date on which Sang had arrived in Britain, the night of 5/6 April 1975, on a plane paid for by readers' subscription and organized by a London newspaper which, over the next fourteen days, had carried pictures and articles of the arrival.

David and I shared her excitement at the prospect of seeing what Sang had looked like as an infant.

'You were a journalist weren't you?' said Joy. 'You might see if you can get the paper to pay something towards these legal costs. After all, they're responsible for bringing him over here in the first place.'

I suspected how unmoved they were likely to be over the fate of a child who'd come off a plane five years earlier. Vietnam was old news. However, just in case, I contacted the newspaper and felt quite hopeful when they phoned back, asked for more information, then said, 'Maybe, we'll see.' But when they phoned back again it was to tell me that they didn't have copies of any pictures they might have taken, they were not a cutting agency, they didn't keep back numbers beyond four weeks. However, they suggested that if I knew the references I could go to the British Museum and look up the microfilm to see if my little boy was in any of the pictures. I felt disappointed and humiliated. Most days there wasn't even time to walk to the end of the road, let alone get to spend a day in London. We later discovered that the newspaper had centred its orphan-rescue story on the fate of a single child, a baby girl whose adoption had been arranged before she left Saigon. There would have been no published pictures of Sang. Another dead end.

Then a librarian friend searched out and sent a wide range of relevant cuttings which offered a broad perspective on the airlift. Not all the British press shared the view that these waifs had been dramatically saved from certain death at the hands of the approaching communists. Some suggested that the exodus had been a badly planned emotional over-reaction. For some of the children there'd been no plans about what to do with them once they were landed in Britain. A number of over-speedy adoptions took place of children whose natural parents were desperately searching to find them.

Removing children in need from their place of origin and transporting them halfway round the world to such a different climate and country at vast expense and to no certain end began to seem suspect as a worthwhile enterprise. Sang, without any documents to his name, was accepted into Britain by the Home Office on a 'block-booking' stateless person's entry permit and went with the group of severely handicapped older children, who were considered 'unadoptable', to the Children's Home of the charity which agreed to take responsibility for them. Here he stayed until, four-and-a-half years later, plans were finally begun to find adoptive families for him and for Nguyen.

While at the Home, Sang had had a number of sponsors, referred to as his 'friends'. Sang seemed vague about them, couldn't remember any names, couldn't remember if he'd ever met them. Sometimes he said he had, sometimes he hadn't. As far as he was concerned they'd all blurred into one unity covered by the phrase, 'Yeah, dat my friend, give me present, better'n you.' At first, David and I weren't clear what their function had been. We thought they were perhaps some kind of legal guardian or trustee and, believing

123

that their former donations to the charity might have given them some permanent proprietorial rights over Sang, were alarmed when one of them announced she was coming to visit. It sounded like an inspection. The morning she was due, we frantically painted over the damp patch in Sang and Lawrence's bedroom where the roof had leaked in case she should think ours wasn't a fit house for him to stay in and decide to have him removed.

In fact, she merely took him out for the afternoon and bought him a mass of presents and sweets, thus proving to Sang's total satisfaction that his friend was indeed better'n us. Her visit was out of curiosity, and any systematic interest in his welfare petered out.

Most of the sponsors staked no claims of ownership, and once their sponsorships had been transferred to other children, saw any involvement beyond remembering him at Christmas as now over. A few of the sponsors, however, proved to be a useful source of information about Sang's former life for, in return for their covenants to the charity, they had received reports of their sponsor child which they now let us have.

Compared to the utter confidence with which we knew the exact day and minute of births of three of our children, the shifting uncertainty over Sang's felt strange.

When we first met, he was said to be aged nine years and three months. Like a number of the orphaned children, he had no precise birth date so this was, we were told, only an an approximation. The Children's Home staff had purposely staggered birthdays through the year so that celebrations could be enjoyed at all seasons.

After a few months, it was revealed to us that there had, earlier on, been a slight adjustment made to Sang's age. An educational psychologist was told or persuaded that, since Sang's early development had been so stunted, it would be in his best educational interests to have his age 'lowered'. Thus he was in reality some six months older than we'd originally been informed. Though it wasn't very important in itself, after all, we'd known all along that his birthday wasn't his 'real' birthday, it felt peculiar to consider that all of a sudden our little boy wasn't nine-and-a-half but somewhere over ten.

I rang Joy to unload on her my sense of disorientation over this latest curious piece of information. She said she had known all along but had decided it would be easier for us not to be told. 'We thought it best if you didn't know. Actually, we didn't think you'd ever find out.'

I felt irritated by this deception. If we had been trusted with a child's whole future life, surely we could have been entrusted with a detail about how old he was estimated to be. So if we'd been kept in the dark about his age, what else was there being deliberately withheld from us?

David said, 'Oh well, he's small for his age, so it doesn't really matter, does it?'

Joy's keeping quiet about a mere six months turned out to be only the beginning. Gradually, it transpired that, in order to make Sang appear more able, his official year of birth had been brought forward and thus his age reduced on several occasions, his small size making it possible for him to pass for much younger. When we received from one of the sponsors a bundle of back reports on 'their' child, including one which stated that Sang had been brought into the Hoi Duc Anh as early as 4 April 1969, we realized that, by the time he left Saigon, Sang could well have been not a babe-in-arms but at least six years old. And how old might he have been on 4 April 1969? One day old? One week? A month? A year? Two? In any case, he would now be at least the same age as Lawrence, not nine but going on twelve, and possibly even older.

It made the amount of time on the preparation course devoted to the study of the age of the child at placement and the ages of the other children in the family seem ridiculously irrelevant.

Since Sang couldn't count beyond four or five it didn't bother him. The one thing he minded about was being older than Donald.

'Nine bigger six?' he would ask, and when reassured that it was, would chant it happily. 'Nine bigger si! Nine bigger si! Donald the baby. I nine.'

The first time Sang went to the dentist, she asked how old he was and we told her that he was nine. After making her inspection inside his mouth, she said, 'Are you sure?'

'Yes,' I said, because at the time I was. And anyway, one should never look a gift horse in the mouth.

Then, at Sang's first school medical, the doctor too asked him his age.

Sang looked at me. 'You can talk for yourself,' I said.

'Nine,' said Sang.

The doctor glanced at the record sheet which had come from Sang's previous school. 'Funny that,' she muttered. 'He was exactly the same age last year.'

The affidavit proposed a much later supposed date of birth than any we had so far had, the end of 1971, making Sang now officially only eight-and-a-half. But we were fed up with all these changes. It was important for everybody's stability to stick with the first age we'd been given, which placed Sang two years younger than Lawrence and three years older than Donald.

Though the houseparent had felt that the truth of Sang's origins was too much for a child to bear, we instinctively felt that any child's past experiences, good and bad, belonged to him, and that he had a right to them. In Sang's case, never to speak about where he came from was to leave him to cope entirely alone with his devastating past.

With our other children there were no storks or gooseberry bushes. We'd always tried to be honest, so it would involve a great deal of deception and counter-deception if we were now to start insisting that, after all, nothing was known of Sang's background, or if they were to be told what we knew while Sang was not.

Besides, it was not a simple issue of telling him something, or not telling him. The truth was already there in him, half buried in wordless depths. So it was more a question of revealing to him what he already, at a subconscious level, knew more about than we did.

The houseparent was not the only member of the older generation who advocated a policy of letting the past lie like a silent dog. My mother, even though she had expiated her own wartime experience in the London blitz by constantly talking about it, telling stories, and writing a very funny and positive book about it, felt it was unnecessary, indeed wrong, to discuss the war in Vietnam with Sang or the others. 'You'll only stir things up for him just as he's settling.'

But the implication that 'he was only a baby then, wouldn't have understood anything, won't have remembered anything' became less valid the older we discovered he was.

His often violent behaviour when he was awake and his noisy nightmares suggested that those years of lying on his back in his cot, even if he hadn't understood what was going on around him, had not been passed in some safe cocoon of oblivion. His drawing, too, indicated something different. When requested to draw he produced tiny cramped little pictures, but for himself, he drew obsessively and repeatedly, wild scribbled scenes of destruction, chaos and violence in which there was always a tiny figure at the bottom which represented himself. When he realized that the computer print-out paper in the toy cupboard could be used whenever he wanted, as could the pencils, his daily output of drawings increased to eighteen or twenty. His teacher at school wanted one day to show me one of his paintings. All around the class were pinned the other pupils' visions of trees and fields, colourful flowers and smiling suns. I recognized Sang's at once. It was all black, black, black with a tiny bit of red which was Sang himself. 'I knew you'd want to know what it's called too,' said the teacher with a wry smile. 'When I asked him to explain it, he said it's called "people killing".'

Sang had already heard, many times, a dramatized account of how David, Hannah, Lawrence, Donald and I had been searching for a little boy of his age and size, shape and appearance, not too big, yet not too small, whose name began with

S, how we had set off in the red car one Sunday in March to meet him for the first time. He liked the details of Lawrence being car sick on the journey and of Donald having an attack of tonsillitis.

So, in the same cheery, matter-of-fact tone, hoping that it was less what you told, more the way in which you told it that mattered, one evening instead of their usual bedtime book, I told Sang and Donald a brief story of an earlier finding: of how, in a faraway land which was even more distant than Ireland where we'd all been to visit the cousins, in a large city with red flowering trees along the main street and palm trees in the parks, a little child had been found on a hard pavement alone and hungry, and how, because of his pretty face and happy smile, people had always liked him and wanted to help him.

Donald, listening enviously to this glamorous, yet true-life tale, said, 'I expect he looked a bit like a rat.'

'A rat?' I said.

'Yes. A drowned rat. Babies never look pretty, specially not hungry ones.'

Though interested in the story, he was extremely miffed that in no way did he feature in it. Donald's annoyance added to Sang's sense of self-esteem. It was Sang's own story and nobody else's.

Next night he asked for it again. It became a bedtime regular.

Gradually a few distant bombs were added in, plus the policeman who may or may not have picked the abandoned child off the street and who may or may not have been the person who handed the foundling into the orphanage office. And eventually it was firmly established in all our minds how and where Sang had come to be, with warfare and street markets, and flower sellers and tanks and tropical sunsets all joined together with 'ifs' and 'probablys' and 'maybes' and 'I expects'. Sang was happy if new details were added in from one telling to the next, dismayed if too much was left out or words changed. I recorded it on to a cassette so he could listen to precisely the same version.

'But how did they know his name?' Donald asked when we got to the story of little Sang having his bottle in the orphanage which, even though it was only watered-down milk, he was pleased about and smiled and gurgled.

'I expect,' I said, 'someone said, "That little boy in cot 29 doesn't seem to have a name." And I expect probably somebody else said "You'd better ask him what his name is so we can write it down," but then somebody else probably said, "He's too young to talk," so it's quite likely that someone else came along and said, "Well, he looks just like a Sang to me." And the first person might have said, "Yes, you're right, very like a Sang. Perhaps he'd better have a surname too. What sounds good with Sang?" And, as they were Vietnamese people, they probably knew all the best surnames and decided that Nguyen Thanh was the very best surname a little boy could possibly have.'

Had his mother cradled him tenderly in her arms when he was born? Had she cared for him as long as she was able and died still loving him? Or had she run away from him and was still alive and trying to forget his existence?

Sang was less concerned by his motherlessness than I. Even though we'd talked about the fact that she might be dead or she might be alive but either way we'd probably never find out, he seemed pleased with a newly coined phrase, 'my mudder dead', almost as though it were some kind of positive achievement.

'We don't know for sure,' I insisted. Many miraculous trans-global reunions of Boat People and other refugees from the South-East Asian conflict were still occurring. Secretly, I liked to believe that there was still a million-to-one chance of Sang's mother appearing, especially if she were to discover that Sang was now attached to middle-class Europeans. I'd read of a case in Switzerland in which, a year after a professional woman had adopted a Vietnamese toddler, a poor, sick, but *bona fide* mother had materialized. To the credit of both, they reached a happy arrangement in which the natural but homeless and stateless mother moved in and they both cared for the child, who thus received literally the best of both worlds.

Sang preferred the dramatic finality of maternal death. At school he repeated, with some pride, his new phrase to one of the bigger boys, 'My mudder dead'. The boy responded in a way that Sang had not expected and began chanting it tauntingly in the playground.

He began to grasp the reality of his condition, to see how this recent gain of us as new mumdad was balanced out somewhere back down the line with having mislaid the originals. We were only replacements.

When we visited friends with babies, Sang, though reluctant to touch, would stand and stare with a voyeur's fascination. If a baby burbled, or dribbled, or yelled, or ate a biscuit, he would ask me, 'Do I do dat?' The answer was, 'Yes, of course. All babies are like that.'

When a friend was breast-feeding her new baby, Sang asked, 'Do I do dat? Do my mudder do dat me?'

'I expect so darling. If she was able to look after you, she probably did. It's the best way of feeding babies. Though of course we don't know, do we?'

A few months later, we went to tea with the same breast-fed baby, now sitting on a rug on the lawn while her two adoring sisters and her besotted father entertained her. Sang stood and watched but without asking the usual, 'Did I do that?' Instead, tears welled up in his eyes and dropped down his cheeks. It was as though he'd just seen the huge gulf between his own babyhood and that of this cherished other baby and he hadn't got the words to express the magnitude of what had been lost.

10
THE SAUSAGE WAR

The sausage war re-erupted. He was angry as angry could be because there were no sausages at breakfast. We had been out the night before and not checked on the sausage state of the fridge. On and on he nagged about this shortcoming. Four, pink, fatty sausages on a plate represented love. No sausages meant non-love. David cooked breakfast, so he bore the burnt of the morning rage. For his sake, I minded about the grinding complaints. Had Sang the right to tyrannize his father by his sausage moods?

Sang was in the bathroom, growling and thumping against the walls. I slammed the door behind us, as loudly as his own fruitless wall-banging, and scolded angrily for the selfishness of thinking only about what he wanted, for the greed when I had managed at least to get bacon and eggs, for the unkindness to David who worked so hard to cherish and care for us all.

'I love David very much. I cannot bear to see you abuse him like this.'

If Sang was a chosen child, David was a chosen husband.

After two days of retrospective sausage anger, suddenly, magic day. Sang gave David a big sorry-hug and beamed.

'I maka shar,' he announced cheerfully. He stopped moaning and set about making his shop.

'How you wry "ope"?'

'O.'

'O for orarsh?'

131

'Yes. That's right.'

'Wha' nex?'

'P.'

'P poleesh?'

'Yes. Then E for egg, then N for no.'

'N for, er, N for? Ah, that beer difficul. Ner for "mum"?'

'No, N for no.'

He wrote out the letters for OPEN on a scrap of paper, handed it over for approval, then asked, 'How you wry clo'?'

So the shop was begun, a constructive game in imitation of a Peter and Jane picture in one of the Ladybird books. And I thought I recognized, in this re-enactment of one of the vividly coloured illustrations of suburban life, an attempt to win parental approval, perhaps to apologize for the two days grinding, by becoming a Peter and Jane type child, fair-skinned, perfectly behaved, gently absorbed. Toys were selected and set out along the bench which was the shop, and peculiarly priced. I showed him how to write the pound sterling symbol so he could stick a tag to each item. A toy ambulance was priced at ££0000p, other items priced with only p, or with only a strange number. And at least it wasn't war.

His drawings continued to be about violence — houses on fire, with people burning up, car accidents with police and fire engines, people drowning at sea. There are so many ways to die. And chiefly chaotic scenes of war with tanks and soldiers covered in bright-red felt-tip scribbles.

We had long ago committed ourselves to being responsible for the legal fees. As there were no contesting parents, the adoptions of both Sang and Nguyen would pass easily through the local magistrates' court. The fees were expected to be not above five hundred pounds.

Then Joy had news. The case was turning out to be a bit more complicated than it had first seemed and was having to go to High Court in London. She'd already been to Chambers to visit a young barrister, keen to take on the case, and who was, Joy assured us, terribly nice. Unfortunately, costs were mounting, just a bit. No longer five hundred pounds but perhaps a thousand, or maybe two thousand.

We didn't dare admit that we hadn't got even five hundred pounds of savings, let alone a thousand or two, in case it sounded as though we were saying Sang wasn't worth that much. Luckily, a friend offered us a no-interest loan while another said she'd start a public fund to raise the money as soon as we needed it.

The postmaster at the sub post-office where I cashed our weekly child benefit always asked after Sang ever since the Tuesday when he'd noticed our benefit go up from covering three children to four without any visible signs of pregnancy on my part. 'How's your little laddie, then? Not playing you up too much? Got your adoption through then?' He was extremely sympathetic when I moaned about the latest hold-up.

'Blimey, dear, you'd think they'd be paying you for taking care of their misfits, not expecting you to pay them. I really take my hat off to you.'

Though I didn't like his word 'misfits' and wasn't sure who he meant by 'they', I was cheered by his other words of encouragement and repeated them to myself all the way home. 'Somebody is taking his hat off to us.'

The keen barrister rang to question me on the details of Sang's former life. It was, she said, all extremely interesting, wasn't it? She'd never handled anything quite like it before and as it was so unusual, with 'no evidence of birth', it was going to be a test case.

I felt intimidated by the legal talk, much of which I couldn't understand though I gathered that, as a test case, there could be no guarantee that we would 'win'. What, I wanted to know, would happen to Sang if we 'lost'? I suggested she rang David later but she was in a hurry to get her facts. I began to feel alarmed by the crisp hectoring tones, then annoyed by the breezy dismissal of what we'd pieced together about Sang's life as worthless, not evidence, only hearsay.

133

I didn't like her voice. I didn't like her bullying attempts to get me to 'try harder' to remember. I felt insulted on Sang's behalf by her repeated insistence on referring to him as the interesting case.

'He's not just an interesting case!' I snarled. 'He's a human and interesting child! And my chief concern for him right now is what sort of mood he's going to be in when the bus brings him home, so why don't you do what you're good at and see to the legal technicalities and we'll go on caring for the interesting child.'

We tried to get in touch with Nguyen's parents-to-be to find out how they were coping with this part of the process. Maybe we could pick up some tips. They were away. We talked to one of their children who told us Nguyen wasn't living with them yet.

'I think he's getting his own family now.'

Did this mean Nguyen's long-lost real family had turned up with some of the Boat People?

Joy didn't know but said the appointed barrister really was very good and we must trust her and be co-operative.

The legal technicality over whether Sang had really been born or not seemed like some strange existentialist parlour-game. Finally, as though proving definitively that Sang did not exist, when I went along to the sub post-office to collect the weekly child benefit, I discovered from the friendly sub postmaster, that benefit for all four children had been stopped. The DHSS attempted to clarify the situation by explaining that since the child, Nguyen Thanh Sang, was not resident with us, we were not entitled to receive any benefit for any of our children until the amount we had been fraudulently claiming over the past nine months had been repaid.

We didn't understand what was going on. It was like a Kafka nightmare. If Sang hadn't been living with us, who had been?

I shrieked a bit down the telephone and a lady at the DHSS patiently explained that if we wished to make a claim, all we had to do was to send along the child's birth certificate or his adoption certificate.

Since we had neither, nor indeed any written proof that Sang was living with us, or was living at all, I suggested that the only sure way of proving he existed was to put him into an envelope and post him first class to the benefit offices in Newcastle.

Donald thought I was serious. 'Oh no, you can't do that, Mum!' he said. 'He wouldn't like it at all.'

We appealed once more to Joy who discovered that, despite Sang's departure from the Children's Home, child benefit had continued to be claimed for him in his name.

Not to worry. Only another small bureaucratic mistake. Or was it? Our confidence in Sang's security with us was being constantly eroded. We began to suspect a plan to receive him back into the Home which we weren't supposed to hear about until it was too late to do anything. Our trust in the professionals was further undermined when we heard that the housemother was in a long-standing dispute with the charity over whether Sang and Nguyen should have been placed for adoption in the first place. The committee wanted all the children to remain together in a national group in case there was ever a chance of them returning to Vietnam.

Joy was becoming irritated by our constant wails for help as well as our bouts of uncertainty over how to cope with Sang's behaviour.

'Normally,' she said firmly, 'parents get three months' supervision after a placement of a baby, and for an older child, six months. You've already had far more than that. You ought to be settled by now. I'm always popping in to see you.'

'I've got to get away,' I told David one morning as he was leaving for college.

'Oh yes,' he said calmly. 'Where?'

I didn't know. 'Just somewhere that isn't here. I don't think I can cope with any of it any more.'

He drove me to the station. It wasn't David I wanted to

135

escape nor the children. It was our inability to handle any of this huge muddle. God wasn't listening any more either because I'd tried. It was as though, having answered our prayers of getting Sang into the family, we were on our own.

I caught a train for London, and as it trundled over the River Medway, I had an overwhelming desire to throw the contents of my bag, driving licence, cheque book, banker's card, diary, out of the window and into the water below. Sang had no bits of paper to prove who he was, yet he existed. Perhaps if I too had no papers, I could make a better job of looking after him. I wanted to affirm my identity with him. We would both be marginals.

In a kind of trance, I crossed London without thinking what I was doing, so was surprised to find myself arriving at Norwich from where it was only an hour more by local train to my stepfather's house.

My mother's reaction to find me walking in at the back door was rather sharp.

'Does David know you're here? You can't possibly stay until he knows.'

I rang David. He seemed pleased to hear I was about to sit down by a big fire and drink a glass of sherry with my stepfather. He probably knew instinctively long before I did where I'd end up.

'The two big children are being so helpful,' David said. 'I wasn't very good with the washing so all the pants are pink but otherwise everything's fine. So don't come back till you've had several good nights' sleep. Wednesday at least.'

Only after I'd made it clear that I'd not run away from marriage was I allowed to be welcomed and cosetted by my mother and stepfather. Unwisely, I began to try to explain our anxieties concerning Sang's emotional distress, the extent of which we were only just beginning to understand, as well as the ambivalence about his status.

It might have been easier to define the Holy Spirit to an agnostic.

'But he's a darling a little boy!' said my mother, getting

136

completely the wrong idea. 'Though if he really makes you so unhappy, I suppose you'll just have to send him back. After all, nobody's making you keep him, are they?'

I shouldn't have expected them to understand that as far as we were concerned Sang already was our own son and that the problem was not about how to send him back but how to hang on to him.

My mother and father, when rearing five children on not enough money and too much ill-health, had had a saying, 'When things get bad, go to the pub. When things get really bad, throw a party.'

Sang's given date of birth was in December. Coincidentally, all three other children's birthdays were, through careless planning, also in December.

'Hannah, Lawrence, Sang and Donald invite you to their combined 43rd birthday,' said the invitations, with a drawing of them gathered around a cake and in a whirl of balloons and streamers and holly — Hannah with her flying frizzy hair, Lawrence with a wry grin, Sang cute and oriental, Donald grinning as the gap-toothed youngest.

They approved the idea of the shared party. Lawrence said he'd only got two friends anyway and it'd look silly having a party with just them. Hannah said one definitely needed boys as well as girls at parties because they were more adventurous about joining in games. Sang minded only that he should still be 'Bigg'n my licker Donna?' Since Donald was six about to be seven, while Sang was nine going on twelve-and-a-half, about to be ten, that was no problem.

Donald thought it was all fine so long as they didn't have a shared birthday cake. On this point he was insistent.

'We ought each to have our own separate cake. With our name and the right candles. My friends from school wouldn't understand otherwise.'

All the talk of birthdays and cake jangled a few memory bells in Sang's mind.

'Yeah, we do dat lon tine go. Have own birthday cake own name. And lotta candle.'

I encouraged the children each to colour in the invitations that were for their own friends. Donald coloured in a black balloon.

'Oh, that's a funny colour for a balloon!' said Mama jokingly. 'I don't think I've ever seen a black balloon.'

Then he coloured in a black birthday cake, then a black-faced Sang.

'Sang's face isn't black,' said Mama gently.

'Yes it is.'

'It's more a sort of pale brown.'

'We haven't got that colour in the box. It looks all right.'

'People'll think he's a negro.'

'No they won't. Anyway, these are for my friends.'

Meanwhile Sang, colouring in his invitations, had taken a bright fluorescent-pink felt-tip pen and coloured in all four children's faces a pinky purple, as unlikely a facial colour as Donald's heavy wax black.

'And anyway, if Sang has to give me that purple face,' said Donald, 'I don't see why I shouldn't draw a black one.'

We printed, coloured-in each to their own view of things, and sent out fifty invitations. We got back acceptances from nearly twice that number of guests for brothers, sisters, parents, friends and aunties wanted to come too. I felt buoyed up by this new interest. When Sang first came, people had kept so discreetly away there had been none of the razzmatazz, well-wishing, and general enthusiasm that surrounds a real birth. Now it seemed people wanted to come and inspect us, perhaps even cheer us on.

It was originally going to be a kids' tea-party. Now we decided to make it a truly wonderful, no-expense-spared event. If we were going to have to find a thousand or two to pay for the adoption in the new year, we might as well spend a hundred or so right now on some visible celebration.

We could probably have fitted fifty friends into our house if they were all prepared to stand still with their arms down.

We could not fit in fifty assorted-aged children, plus fifty adults holding wine glasses. So we arranged to hire the Junior Common Room in David's college and to have the college chef do the party jellies, fancy cakes, rolls, crisps, tit-bits, sandwiches, eclairs, soft and alcoholic drinks.

Meanwhile, we went and ordered the birthday cakes which, as Sang said, had to have 'lotta candle' and as Donald said, had to be personalized, from the smart cake shop in town in whose windows were displayed fabulously made cakes for celebrating all occasions which we had often admired.

From the selection available, Sang chose the lemon flavour, yellow colour; both Donald and Lawrence rather wanted the chocolate so, amicably, Lawrence opted for the white vanilla and Hannah took the pink. Each cake was, in traditional manner, to have the child's own name in icing which, to forestall any problem over incorrect spellings, I wrote out, and of course 'Happy Birthday' iced on and the appropriate number of candles: seven for Donald, ten for Sang, even though he wanted nine because he said, at Chillen's Home, everybody always had nine candles, twelve for Lawrence and fourteen for Hannah.

Then we had doughnuts from the same tea-shop to give a foretaste of the delights ahead. As I paid I thought, even though each cake was costing as much as a pair of school shoes, how pleasantly trouble-free it was to order ready-made cakes instead of the usual last-minute making.

On party day I collected the four cakes in their four quality cake-boxes tied with festive ribbon. Each of the boxes had one of the children's names, correctly spelled, pencilled on the lid. Without looking inside, I drove them up to the college JCR where David was getting the room organized and the glasses and bottles set out. The boys had arranged a line-up of four separate tables, rather as though for a trophy-awarding ceremony, on which to display the splendid cakes. Donald was decorating his cake-table with

139

pretty paper and streamers while Lawrence helped Sang to decorate his.

But where was Hannah?

'Still at home,' said David. 'She seemed a bit frantic. As she wasn't quite ready, I said you'd go and pick her up in the car as soon as we'd seen to the cakes.'

From the moment that we opened the cake-boxes, everything about the supposedly perfect, no-expense spared afternoon seemed to fall apart. Out of the four boxes, came four beautifully made Christmas cakes, each of the chosen colour — the pink, yellow, chocolate and vanilla and with 'Merry Xmas' lavishly iced on to the top plus a snowman on the white cake, a Christmas tree on the yellow one, holly on the pink one and a horrible brown santa on the chocolate one. There were no candles, no names, nothing birthdayish at all.

'No candle!' observed Sang. 'Chillen home we have *candle*.'

Donald stared dolefully at his. 'None of my friends are going to know which one's mine. They won't know which one to eat. I wanted them to eat my cake. They won't know how old I am.'

Lawrence, manfully cheerful, said, 'I've always wanted a little white snowman of my very own.'

It was too late to do anything about changing the cakes but at least we could rush to the nearest newsagents' to buy candles, though the icing was of such superior quality that the candles had to be forced through it by which time each cake looked as though it had been dropped upside down in mud.

'It's really nice now,' said Donald, delighted that his friends would see by the candles, how extremely old he was going to be. 'And you can see the good cakey bits sticking out.'

Sang didn't mind the ruined crazy-paving surface to his either because already the first guests had begun to arrive. Lawrence was fixing up Louis Armstrong on the record-player.

I drove home for Hannah and found her ready and dressed

in her new glittery party outfit, her hair all prettily frizzed, but lying on my bed with clearly little intention of moving.

'Come on, party time,' I said.

'I don't think I can make it.'

'But you must darling!' I urged. 'Your friends are expecting you. Some of them are already there.'

One really shouldn't let adolescent moods dominate everything, I thought.

'I've got a terrible headache,' said Hannah.

'Pre-party excitement,' I said briskly. 'It'll probably go the minute you have something to eat.'

Reluctantly, Hannah let herself be led down to the waiting car.

The party was in full swing by the time we got to the college and Hannah put on a smiling face to greet her schoolpals and bravely joined in helping the younger children with the paper-hat making competition and pouring sherry for the adults.

Several of the children's teachers came, including Sang's class teacher and her husband. Although Nguyen's adoptive parents-to-be weren't able to come, he had been driven over from the Children's Home and he and Sang fell into each other's arms with delight to squeak and grunt together in the ritual of some long-established private language like a pair of excited little mice.

Many birthday presents were brought for the four children, as well as advance Christmas parcels to take home to put under the tree. Sang, not able to read the labels, assumed they were all for him and, even when I explained that some were and others were from the other children's friends, he still wanted them all. So did Nguyen who was able to read and was loudly upset to find that there were none with his name on. In a frenzy of united over-excitement, they tore round searching out and tearing open any wrapped parcel they could find. Like some curious variation on pass-the-parcel, they discarded with disappointment each one the moment the wrapping was ripped off to go in search of new

141

ones. When they came upon a pile of brown packets containing review journals which a colleague had left for David in the cloakroom, they tore into the wrappings of these with the same enthusiasm.

I tried to suggest to Sang that rather than unwrapping presents which were anyway addressed to other people, Nguyen might find it more interesting to join in with the funny-hat games, but immediately I felt shame for trying to halt their harmlessly destructive activity. We all had so much already. Nguyen had so little so why shouldn't he be allowed to unwrap parcels if that's what made him happy? Whether or not he understood any better than Sang the curiosity of his situation, it must have been painful for him to see Sang already absorbed and surrounded by new family and new friends while he was still waiting for the finalization of his move-in to his family.

Besides, what Sang and Nguyen were up to was nothing compared to some of the other guests. It was almost as though the worst aspects of student behaviour had seeped out of the JCR walls and into their bloodstreams inciting them to behave like drunken members of a rugby team celebrating victory. Perhaps they were drunk on the Amontillado intended for the adults? Or perhaps the age-range of children from five to fifteen was too broad? Since many of the guests were not our own children's friends but the friends of friends and thus unknown to us, it was difficult to know how to encourage them towards constructive rather than destructive fun. Lead by a hard core of sub-teens with anarchic tendencies, every game quickly disintegrated towards jelly-throwing, hand-to-hand fighting, sandwich pellet-making, and a new invention — crisp jumping, which meant flinging the contents of all the crisp packets on to the wooden parquet floor and jumping on them — all of which the younger six- and seven-year-old friends of Donald's were only too keen to join in with.

Though it was good to notice many of David's and my friends chatting away at the adult end of the party, there was no time to talk to any of them as David and I were permanently occupied preventing the larger boys from causing structural damage to the college.

At least Lawrence, who had been the most apprehensive about this party, appeared to be smiling when, flanked by his two guests, his cake was lit. 'Happy Birthday to You' and 'For He's/She's a Jolly Good Fellow' were sung four times over, cheers were cheered four times over and soon after, Hannah disappeared. I found her lying in the darkened cloakroom under a row of coathooks and realized that the earlier pretty brightness of her cheeks and sparkle in her eyes had been induced not so much by the excitement of a room crowded with happy friends as by an excessively high fever.

David got her down to the car park, and I drove her home, somehow supported her up three flights of stairs and into bed, and left her with a glass of water while I hurried back to college to help David clear up the party mess, hoping that Hannah wouldn't die on us while we were all out.

She seemed to be delirious by the time we got back and we had to phone the doctor to come. She turned out to have acute bronchitis.

Nguyen's adoptive parents-to-be hadn't got any room for Nguyen at their house that night as some of their children were ill, so they suggested that, rather than being driven back to the Children's Home, Nguyen might come and stay the night with us. It seemed a strange and sudden request for, up to now, our house with its perilously steep stairs and first-floor lavatory had been considered unsuitable for Nguyen. Moreover, we hadn't got any spare beds either. But for Sang's sake, we agreed, and Nguyen managed to slither up and down stairs using his powerful shoulders without needing any help. He assured me he didn't need a potty under the bed or a rubber sheet as he hadn't wet his bed for years and anyway could easily get to the bathroom by himself. Despite his severe physical disability, he seemed much more in control of his life than Sang was of his.

Sang was overjoyed by the unexpected visitor and

Lawrence moved out of the bunk bed so that Sang and Nguyen could sleep together in the same room just as they used to in the old days. They had a strange relationship in which Sang was obedient and willing slave to Nguyen's mastership. Nguyen could speak normally, though in a high sing-song way, but when playing with Sang, both fell into the mysterious language of their own consisting of grunts, squeaks, low intonations, and machine-gunning dah-dah-dahs, which both clearly understood. This kind of communication however, excluded all others, especially the disgruntled, over-tired Donald.

He resented Nguyen's visit. It usurped his own position as Sang's best companion. Nguyen doubtless felt much the same about Donald.

'How long's he staying?' Donald asked as the two other boys scattered PlayPeople cowboys across the floor. 'Why can't he stay with his own new family?'

'Can't,' said Nguyen. 'No room.'

'She my mum, not helper, she mum,' Sang explained of me in case Nguyen had forgotten. 'And Donna he my — he my — ' But in the excitement of Nguyen's visit, he himself had suddenly forgotten the word for brother. 'When you gonna lib new mumdad?'

'Next month,' said Nguyen. 'After half term. Next month.'

When my mother rang to find out how the party had gone I told her about Hannah busy being extremely ill in one attic bedroom and Sang and Nguyen engrossed in their strange magic-speak game in the other.

My mother, as usual, got quite the wrong idea.

'Rachel, you are not, absolutely not to adopt this other little boy as well,' she said. 'You really can't. You won't, will you? Do you hear? It wouldn't be fair to anybody.'

'Of course not! He's Sang's old friend. He's only here for the night. He's got a family all lined-up for him. It's just that there's no room for him there tonight because all their other children are ill.'

'From the sound of things, you've got plenty of illness in

your house too,' said my mother shortly, as though Hannah's bronchitis were somehow my fault which, on reflection, I could see it might well be. If only I had recognized the signs and hadn't urged Hannah out to her party, she might not have deteriorated so rapidly.

Provoked by my mother's suspicion that we were considering adopting another child, David and I discussed whether we should indeed propose that we foster Nguyen on a temporary basis in order that he and Sang could renew and maintain their relationship until the other family were ready to receive him permanently. But, though I could see the logic and usefulness to Nguyen, of his lack of mobility being linked up with Sang's willingness to fetch and carry for him, I felt that ultimately it might well become crushing to Sang's own development and I was pained to hear 'my' little boy being so peremptorily ordered about by another.

The Monday following the party was Sang's birthday day, 15 December. His first birthday in our home. With one's own born, their birthday always evokes a memory, however fleeting, back to their first moment alive, how it felt, what the sky looked like, what one said on first seeing the new little face. Sometimes, one feels a pang of self-congratulation that one has reared them so far, with not too many mishaps. And sometimes, this memory is furthered by the birthday child asking what time they were born so that the day really does seem like a re-living of a birth.

'It's always my birthday the minute I wake up,' Lawrence used to say, who knows he was born at 6.00 a.m.

Hannah has to wait till 3.45 in the afternoon to gain her new age.

'What time was I born, Mum? What time?' asks Donald.

For Sang there was none of this. He didn't even seem to understand, though we had explained it, that there is a time, an o'clock, for a birth.

I wanted to be able to tell him how, on this day more than most, I was thinking of that other woman, the real mother, the physical mother, from whose womb he had

145

been expelled. I wanted to explain to Sang how close to this unknown person I felt, how I could almost see her, how I felt grateful to her for giving him up if that was indeed what she had done. And if she had had to abandon her baby boy-child, I wanted to be able to grieve with her and for her. I wanted to share with him the sense of this being a mother's special day too, for no woman, surely, ever forgets giving birth, however unwanted the child? Where was she now and how was she bearing it, to think of her boy-child and not to know how he was?

If this had been a novel, my empathy would have reached out across the limitless oceans to touch her heart and somehow we'd come to some understanding of each other's existence, perhaps even reach some wonderful coincidental meeting.

This wasn't a novel. This was a dark December morning and I was trying to get Sang's shoes on while the smell of frying sausages floated up the stairs. Why should he have to be burdened with my grief about the first mother as well as with all the other things he was burdened with? My emotion was stupid and misplaced. This wasn't even the real anniversary of his birth. It could have been any other day in the entire year that his natural mother remembered giving birth to him. And maybe she didn't care anyway.

Most days I was too tired to cry even when I wanted to. But on Sang's so-called tenth birthday, after everybody had left for school and the house was empty, I did a lot of crying by myself. For tea-time, I bought a swiss roll and stuck ten candles in it, half hoping that having a second birthday cake might somehow make up for some of the many failures.

I bought a packet of paperchains for the boys to make up after tea.

'You can divide the packet,' I told Donald. 'Between you and Sang.'

'Sang won't want to. He never does,' said Donald. 'He always says he can't do things. But really he can. Like at Granny's we were all up on the high wall, even little Marky.

146

Sang wouldn't come up. We had to persuade him he could. In the end he did but Lawrence had to hold him.'

'Well, we'll persuade him he can do paperchains,' I said.

'But if he really doesn't want to, can I do them all?'

Donald's prognosis was correct. When Sang saw the coloured paperchain pieces, his reaction was an instant no thank you.

I persuaded.

'Oh all right.'

'I'll show you.'

'No. Can do. We do it Chillen.'

Donald got in a muddle. His chains wouldn't stick or else stuck to the wrong places. Sang needed little reminding of how to link, fold, lick, stick, and link, fold, lick and stick again. His chain got longer.

'Look, up to my ches!' he said, holding it up to himself.

He was doubly pleased, for not only was his chain nearly as tall as himself, but he needed so little help while Donald had to keep asking me to staple his failed strips.

When bored of paperchains both boys ambled off to watch Laurel and Hardy on the telly instead. Suddenly there was an ear-splitting shriek from Donald who leaped across the room and kicked Sang twice in the leg very savagely. Sang was standing, quite absent-mindedly, on all Donald's paperchains, squashing them flat.

Sang, stunned at being kicked, screamed, 'All right. You kick me! Kick me. I go way. Not lib here you. No.'

'Yeah, that's right. You go. I don't want you here. I never want to see you again,' said Donald.

'No! not want see you!'

The flare-up was sudden, unexpected, and very bitter. Sang was shocked. Never had he been threatened like this by Donald. Despite the apology which Donald was made to make, Sang remained grumpy all evening, and with good cause. His confidence in his nice little brother was shaken. I too was startled by Donald's outburst of such negative feelings towards Sang.

147

Was it just simple seasonal over-tiredness? Or was it because of his own failure with the paperchains? Or are we deluding ourselves and there was far more bottled-up resentment in all the children than we could allow ourselves to see?

Joy rang to tell us that Nguyen's adoption wasn't going ahead after all. The other family had had to pull out. Their children had found Nguyen and his physical handicap too difficult to adjust to. Nguyen had said he did not want to stay at the Home and was being moved to a professional foster home in a different area.

We dreaded having to tell Sang that his long-awaited friend wouldn't be moving to live nearby after all.

To our astonishment, there was no wailing and yelling of 'it's not fair'. Instead, Sang cried quietly, not roaring, just real tears, then said, 'Poor he. He my fren. Now he got no family lib with. I got family.'

It was another step forward in Sang's own commitment. He was seeing beyond himself to feel compassion for his friend, and to see his friend's situation in comparison to his own. Those dreaded twins, encopresis and eneuresis, increased.

A short while later, Nguyen's would-be adoptive parents separated and their five children were dispersed between the two parents' separate homes. It was shocking to be bystanders to the collapse of such a long-standing marriage involving so many people, and to be reminded of the fragility of even the most stable-looking households. Half-heartedly, we tried to reassure ourselves that at least poor Nguyen hadn't had to go through the divorce of his new parents as well as all his other difficulties. From the outside, it wasn't possible to know if he had been part of the cause of the breakdown or merely the last straw.

Every afternoon at 5.30 there was choral evensong in the cathedral when one could sit in the security and anonymity of an ancient choirstall participating as much or as little as one wished. Leaving Hannah, Lawrence and Donald at home looking after each other while David was helping at Cubs with Sang I took my sadness and despair and anger out to the cathedral.

It was now so hard to accept, to believe in the rightness of what we're doing. I felt such anger with Sang for being like he is, with the world for letting it happen, with God for not keeping up our spirits and sense of joy. And the day's psalm began,

'Save me, O God. For the waters are come in, even unto my soul. I stick fast in the deep mire, where no ground is: I am come into deep waters. So that the floods run over me.

I am stuck in deep mire. Will God save me from the deep waters?'

11
MENCAPPED

As the months passed, the erratic patterns of Sang's behaviour didn't alter much. We just grew more used to it. And the more we learned about disturbed children, the more we saw how his behaviour matched it. Sometimes it seemed as though he too had been reading up on maladjustment as he worked his way with ferocious tenacity through periods of self-mutilation when he sliced through his index fingers with the kitchen knives, picked open sores on his body till they became infected, face-slapped, head-banged against the walls. He tried to strangle the cat with his hands. She was too surprised even to fight back. He ate his poo-poo.

In between, he was funny, affectionate, generous, lovable, noisy and often apparently happy. And he never stole, and he always told the truth, or as much of the truth as he understood.

After the collapse of Nguyen's placement, a secretary from the charity which supported the Children's Home rang and asked if we were sure we still wanted to keep Sang.

'You don't have to you know dear.'

I felt furious. Didn't she understand? He couldn't possibly leave now, not after being with us for nearly a year. Apart from anything else, it would be disastrous for the other children. If they were feeling suppressed resentment, his abrupt removal might seem like their doing and leave them feeling responsible for it. They might believe that any child who became unmanageable risked being thrown out.

'We just thought that, after what's happened to Nguyen, you might feel it'd be for the best for him to go?'

Nguyen wasn't Sang, or vice versa. What had happened to Nguyen wasn't at all the same as what had happened to Sang. Nguyen had never actually moved in with his new family. But perhaps she was trying to say that the new administrator at the Home wanted Sang back?

No, it wasn't that. It was just the lady in the office trying to be helpful.

'Specially as it's all proving so tricky for you with his papers.'

She didn't understand anything. 'Just because it's difficult,' I said archly, 'doesn't mean it's got to be abandoned. As a matter of fact, we're just about to celebrate his first anniversary.'

I was merely seizing an excuse to open a lot of bottles, eat a good meal, and go on pretending we were a happy ordinary family. It wasn't in fact a year since he'd come to us, only a year since we'd first met. The day we'd driven over to the Home and all first set eyes on each other had been a bit like a birth in that it had marked a beginning of something. It was like a difficult premature birth and we still weren't quite sure if the infant would pull through.

It would have been more productive, I realized after ending the phone call, if instead of getting cross, I had thought to ask if her office would provide us with some kind of certificate or letter to prove that Sang was actually living with us. This would at least have resolved one of our worries.

We were suffocating, drowning, floundering about in so many problems we didn't seem to know which one to try to grab at first. There was Sang's disturbed and disturbing behaviour. There was the administration about legal status. There was trying to help him integrate into the family and into normal everyday life. There was the uncertainty of who he was inside, and who he wanted to be. There was the constant fear that he could at any moment be taken away just as we thought we were beginning to own him. There was the sensation of having been totally abandoned to cope on our own. For now God obviously wasn't watching any more, let alone giving directions.

We were inexperienced circus performers who'd been thrown too many raw eggs to juggle with. We were only just managing to keep them all in the air. Then another egg was thrown to us. Or perhaps we'd had it all along but it had been invisible.

While waiting for David in the university bookshop with my load of clean laundry in two big plastic bags I found myself staring at a display-table carrying a selection of recently issued titles. This literary castle was surmounted by a paperback called *Parents and Their Mentally Handicapped Children*, a worthy-sounding topic, probably put out to attract the Social Science students. There were some twenty copies. Parents and their mentally handicapped children, parents and their mentally handicapped children, parents and their mentally handicapped children, twenty times over. They were all mouthing it out, and seemed to be talking directly to me. Picking up a copy and flipping through its pages with detached interest was the first step.

But then I rebelled against it. Mentally handicapped was what happened to other people's children, not to ours. Even to think such a phrase was a betrayal of parental trust. We were the parents of four much loved darlings, the youngest of whom needed to be picked up from school very soon so I wished David would hurry up, and the second youngest of whom was an emotionally disturbed, possibly traumatized, adoptee with a language problem.

To consider buying such a book was likely to bring bad luck, havoc and destruction into the house, as though there wasn't already enough of it.

An Indian colleague of David's saw me as she was leaving the shop and came back in to say hello.

'How lovely to see you!' she said with genuine friendliness. 'What have you been up to? We haven't seen you about for ages.'

152

I felt embarrassed to have been caught fingering *Parents and Their Mentally Handicapped Children.* There might seem to be something voyeuristic about my interest. I moved my hand and pretended it was a new novel I'd been looking at.

We chatted politely about our respective families, then she invited us over to Sunday lunch.

Sang's behaviour when under the strain of 'going out' even to people he knew and liked wasn't reliable enough to know when he might have an unexpected turn of temperament. I didn't want to risk our friendship, so I turned the invitation round so that she and her two girls would lunch at our house.

As soon as she'd left the shop, I bought a copy of the new paperback on the table and stuffed it down inside one of the laundry bags where no one would see it.

Sang came bouncing in from school and began to tell us all about his busy day.

'Im hoyidaye I gonna go fmimi an I gonna *die!* yeah I gonna *die!*'

He was so pleased about it, whatever it was. Ya, terrific kiddo. But whaddaya mean?

He meant that in the holidays, he wanted to go swimming and learn to dive.

Breathlessly he went on, 'Todda saw fil schoo fil you see it you know fil hou maka hou ver dange. Ooh, ah, um naught boy men say wen. Dange. Big. Big say keep off. Dange. He ger squash mud. Big whee. Ver ver big whee.'

What he meant was, 'Today we saw a film at school. Did you see it? Do you know it? Film about making a house, very dangerous. A naughty boy, men say don't, went (into the) danger. Big big (notice) says Keep Out Danger. He gets squashed, yes that boy gets squashed in mud. (Under) big wheel, very big wheels.'

We were able to decipher this exciting piece of accident-prevention propaganda about the dangers of playing on building sites, because both Lawrence and Donald had seen the same film at their schools and filled in the gaps in Sang's narrative for the baffled parents.

'It's really funny, Mum. You and Dad sometimes don't understand Sang. But I always can.'

To understand, one had to know him well, know the kind of thing he might be talking about, interpret his idiosyncratic vocabulary. One had to know, for example, that 'gonga', 'konging', and 'go-go' all meant the same thing: 'donkey'. However, one had to be aware that the word for 'Goldilocks' was also 'Gonga' or 'Go-go'.

'No wonder he finds the story of Gonga and the three bears so confusing,' I said. 'What's a donkey doing eating porridge?'

'Though one might just as much wonder what in heaven's name three bears were ever doing eating porridge?'

Despite an inability to use language the way the rest of us did, Sang talked a lot. As we all watched a nature film which Lawrence specially wanted to see Sang chattered merrily throughout. Failing to say and remember dolphin satisfactorily, he referred to the creatures leaping about across the screen as 'gogi', a word which sounded very like 'gonga' and 'go-go' (donkey) but which for Sang had the meaning of 'goldfish'. Towards the end of the programme, seeing that these gogis were of a very different size from the kind of goldfish one knew in glass bowls, he began to call them 'way', which was his word for 'whales'. The comprehension of language by the dolphins seemed at times rather greater than Sang's own.

Perhaps he found talking difficult because he didn't *know* anything? Children from institutions could be totally ignorant about the most commonplace facts that any home-reared child of a similar age would know.

Sang didn't know how to tell the time, or even what time was, didn't know about the days of the week, nor the names of those days. He didn't know that there were named months in a year, nor when his own birthday was.

We often played the Pavement Game with the children. You run along the pavement and guess what's going to be under each manhole cover. The aim is to get to the next

154

manhole cover first and get it right. WATER? GAS? ELEC-
TRICITY? or GPO? It's not really so much a guessing as a
pre-reading one. When Donald was first learning to read,
sometimes we played it blind-folded. Then, the service hidden beneath the cast-iron lid had to be worked out by feeling
the shape of the raised metal letters.

No version of the game worked with Sang for not only
could he not distinguish the difference between the shapes of
'GAS' or 'WATER' but more significantly, he had absolutely
no idea what gas meant, or what electricity was, or what the
Post Office might be. He didn't know that wasps sting, an
ignorance which seemed to be confirmed when he caught and
played with one and wasn't stung. Donald, who had initially
warned him of the danger, was greatly impressed.

But the next time Sang played with a wasp and tried to trap
it between the bare palm of his hand and the window-pane, as
is the way of wasps it stung him. He roared for half an hour,
not only with pain but with outrage that the insect should
have done something so unexpected.

'It was a bit silly to play with it, wasn't it?' I said rather
firmly.

'Not know it crickle!' Sang sobbed. 'I not know! Why you
not TELL me?'

He wore a bandage and a sling for three days which we
hoped would help confirm in his mind another bit of useful
information about the world, that wasps do crickle.

The occasional difficulties in understanding appeared to
be drawing to an end when, on returning from school, he
announced, 'Today I see spink terrapin!'

'You did what?'

'You know merm!' When one didn't understand first time
he was annoyed. 'I see her, schoo. Her spink terrapin.'

Eventually we caught on. He had been seen by the school
speech therapist.

This seemed like good news. His name had been marked
on a list and stored in a file. Another useful confirmation that
he existed, though only later did we begin to discover that

being diagnosed as in need of regular speech therapy was no guarantee that a child would get it.

She was a gentle greying woman in late middle-age who called to see me at home. I responded to her warmth. I talked too much. Here was a person who wanted to hear me talk and talk about him. She explained how she encouraged the children to draw while they were having their session with her. It helped them relax. Sang had done her several nice drawings of his new family. She had them in her file, along with a report of initial findings. The file, I noticed, was marked 'Private and Confidential', not for my eyes. I want to read the notes. He is *my* son. I want to know what she thinks.

But she isn't here to give me progress reports, rather to try to establish possible causes of Sang's defects. She asks many questions, few of which could be answered. Is he deaf? Has he had any serious illnesses? Has he had measles? Does he dribble a lot? How does he eat his food? Can he chew with his back teeth or does he have difficulty? What strange questions. I recall a spastic three-year-old I once knew whose mother had to manipulate the food to the back of his throat because he was unable to use the movement of his tongue or mouth to get it there himself. I realize with horror that there is some similarity between that and Sang's method of pushing food haphazardly into his mouth and swallowing it whole or letting it all fall out again on to the table.

The inability to use consonants, to say certain sets of words, the immaturity of sentence construction, all pointed, says the speech therapist, towards a simple lack of development rather than to any physical defect. However, she is going to confer with an oriental colleague to see whether there is anything in the Vietnamese language which might have had some effect on Sang's present inability to speak normally but she doesn't sound optimistic that early passive exposure to one language could prevent a child creating the correct sounds of another.

'And of course one never knows to what extent any damage at birth, or soon after, might affect a child's ability to

156

develop intellectually,' she says thoughtfully. 'Undiagnosed brain damage is the cause of many cases of failure to develop.'

Damage? What does she mean by damage at birth?

Her summary is that, while she will investigate all possible causes, it seems that Sang's language is entirely compatible with that of the other retarded children she teaches.

'We don't ever hope for very much back from mentally handicapped children like your little boy, do we?' she said, as though expecting me to agree. 'But we try to do as much as we can.'

Hearing her use that phrase was as though this otherwise civil woman had leaned forward and slapped me across the face. I tried to protest, to explain that Sang's unusual speech was the result of being born in Vietnam. She pointed out that it was now six years since he'd arrived in Britain and began to tell me about her Down's syndrome niece, a dear girl of seventeen. 'These children bring so much love into the world.'

How dare she suggest that our darling is anything like some dappy dum-dum relative of hers?

'Well as a matter of fact,' I say defensively, 'Sang's had quite a rough life up to now. He was very deprived but he's going to catch up on everything as soon as he's settled.'

'Yes, of course,' she said kindly. 'Even so, he's not very, well, very bright is he?' She took out of her Private and Confidential file a picture which I recognized as one of Sang's. 'I mean, his drawings for example, are hardly the work of a mature boy of his age, are they?' She was right. Though vivacious and active, the picture was more like a three-year-old's scribble. 'But he's a very sweet child. And he's very very lucky to have found you.'

Afterwards, I went and lay down feeling sick and seething with fury at the interfering woman. And then I did some crying.

In the evening, David and I talk talk talk. We had sincerely resolved not to talk all our time away, always about one particular child. But we can't help ourselves. There is so much to say, groping round and round in circles.

Until now, the mentally handicapped have been other people, another group, nothing to do with us, but now images of handicap come crawling back.

'D'you remember seeing *A Day in the Death of Joe Egg* in Glasgow?'

We both remember it, and how, at the end of the play, the father of the irreversibly retarded child, who was never going to grow up, leaves. It is the only logical thing to do.

Our Indian friend came, as planned, with her two young daughters. Sang behaved impeccably. Perhaps he recognized how her hair was like his, black and glossy, how her complexion and black eyes were more like his now than mine. He stood by her chair and stroked her arm.

Little Aysha soon grew bored of the long relaxed meal with the adults talking and slid down from her place to play with the toys I had put out on the floor. Sang got down too. Aysha decided on a big wooden puzzle. She hadn't seen it before. She stared carefully at the pieces, then within a few minutes had done the puzzle and was showing it proudly to her mother.

Sang wanted his turn with the same puzzle. He'd done it many many times before with my help but always fumbled with the pieces and could not work out how to put them together to make the picture of the tree with the eggs and the nest and the birds. Now Aysha showed him where each piece fitted in. Still, he couldn't do it. Aysha trotted round the room to find other toys. She did all the jig-saws from the cupboard, did them again, then moved on to the brick box. She balanced bricks on top of each other into a tower. She made a complicated and imaginative castle with cantilevered steps.

It wasn't bloody-mindedness or emotional instability which prevented Sang from putting together a baby wooden puzzle, which prevented him from learning to put his shoes on the right feet, to know the days of the week, to dress himself. He wasn't learning like other children learn. He wasn't learning at all. He might never learn.

158

Aysha went back to the tree jig-saw on the floor, contented and absorbed. I watched her with envy and hatred in my heart. How dare she, at three years old, be able to achieve instantly what our ten-year-old, after a year's practice, still could not do, what our ten-year-old might never be able to do? I wished and wished that they had not come. I wanted everything to be like it had been, when there was still hope. But how could I hate Aysha whom I had known since her birth? It wasn't her fault that she was normal.

Once the idea of a mental handicap had been implanted in our minds, there seemed to be confirmation of it at every turn.

Watching Sang, at how he grinned aimlessly at nothing and laughed inappropriately, one saw it was not because he was insolent but because he did not understand. There was no cause-and-effect in his life. He learned nothing by experience. He had to be taught everything, everything. How to eat, how to hold a spoon so the food didn't drop off, how to drink from a cup so that it didn't pour down his front, how to do up a button, how to open a door. And then, willing and eager though he was to learn, he unlearned and next day, had to be taught again. And again. And his slow slow progress was matched by our slowness in recognizing his handicap.

No! he will not be handicapped. Deny the handicap and it won't be there. The reason he can't learn is because he is a traumatized war child. But how about if he is a traumatized war victim and a mentally disabled child? If one, why not the other? Because we can't bear it that way.

Furtively and obsessively, I read *Parents and their Mentally Handicapped Children*. I had expected a cheerful practical manual telling what fun it can be to build a treehouse for a Down's syndrome daughter, a mobile for a paraplegic son. Instead, I found an often cheerless record of a dozen families about what it felt like to be them, how they coped and didn't cope. The interviews were conducted and edited by a man whose own firstborn was profoundly mentally handicapped so there is an inside understanding. This father wrote

159

of the sense of 'shame' of having an imperfect child, and his continuing pain seeps through the pages of the book like a weeping graze.

The book gives a view of a society which had little space and no compassion for mentally handicapped people. A solicitor protesting about the proposal to build a long-stay hostel in a smart residential area is quoted as saying, 'It is a well known fact that all grades of mongol have committed murder or other criminal acts.'

It could have been depressing reading. In fact, it was a relief. These families were like ourselves. We were among colleagues. The turmoil and uncertainty so many parents described reflected our own turmoil over the past year. The odd behaviour of some of their children reflected that of Sang.

When I showed the book to David, he noticed, with surprise, that he had been taught by the author of the book many years earlier.

'You met him once, too. He gave a tutees' lunch at his house.'

Dimly I recalled our uncertainty about whether, as the wife, I was supposed to be invited. David had been the only married student on his course. I remembered a calm academic house with tidy rows of books, white walls, red roses in a bowl on a low, uncluttered coffee table. There had been no outward signs of any kind of family life, let alone signs of a severely retarded, wildly unmanageable eight-year-old whose problems, according to the book, had dominated and eventually broken the household.

How could a family cover its pain so well? Or perhaps there had been signs but we innocent newly-weds had been too naive to perceive them.

It was impossible, too, to reconcile the memory of the unruffled host with the chaos and mental anguish I'd just been reading about. And where had the demanding son been hidden during that quiet lunchtime? Perhaps the author had exaggerated for the purposes of Social Science? Or maybe he had invented the interviews with the other twelve families? Or perhaps mentally handicapped children are themselves merely a figment of improper parents' minds? Or possibly he was not even the same man as David's former tutor?

I wrote to tell him, whoever he was, how useful his book was in expressing for us those things which we were still too afraid to say ourselves. The author replied by returning, sixteen years late, a student essay on education written by David. He added a note explaining how he and his wife had recently separated, both having become simply 'worn out' by the needs of their handicapped child.

12
SORTING IT OUT

Sang was seen by a local educational psychologist who, assuming we'd demanded the assessment because we were pushy parents wanting our child to be cleverer than he actually was, told us curtly that the boy was correctly placed and would not be moved to mainstream schooling and that we were fortunate he had a place in special school at all.

When asked what Sang's IQ was estimated to be, he replied scathingly that Intelligence Quota was an outmoded way of assessing or describing intellectual ability and was no longer in use, though he didn't say what system was now used. When asked how far we might expect Sang to develop, he said that it would be extremely slowly, that currently he had no quantifiable reading age, that he might eventually learn to read simple tabloid headlines in *The Sun*, or that he might not learn to read at all, but that luckily, like all Chinese, he was very polite.

The psychologist seemed so bored, uninterested, and anxious to get us out of his office that it didn't seem worth pointing out that his last comment was a racist generalization and that anyway Sang wasn't Chinese. We came away from the meeting knowing little more about Sang's likely prospects.

Meanwhile the speech therapist sent a health visitor round to us with a heavy-duty waterproof mattress cover which would not be as crinkly and noisy when Sang rocked in his sleep as the lengths of greenhouse polythene we'd been

162

buying from the garden centre. She also brought a first delivery of 'Inco-pads' — incontinence pads like sheets of blotting paper to put under the bottom sheet. We had had no idea that such things existed, let alone that we were entitled to a limitless supply, free, from the local health authority. Somebody knew how incontinence in a large child can be more than just a minor daily nuisance. To be offered such basic practical help was like a wonderful gift.

Though Joy was no longer officially supervising us, she kept up an unofficial interest in Sang's progress and was extremely upset when she heard about the so-called 'mental handicap' and said she hoped we weren't going to accept this verdict. 'If people go round telling you he's mentally disabled, I suppose you'll want to send him back?' she said wearily.

Why did everybody always keep talking about 'sending back'?

'Mentally handicapped!' she repeated with distaste as though the word were dirty. 'I shouldn't say too much about it if I were you. D'you want to label him for life with that?'

Of course we didn't want to abuse him, but if he really was mentally handicapped, to keep hoping that he wasn't didn't seem to have much point. And everybody pretending he was going to 'grow out of it', and lowering his age so that he seemed more able than he was, quite apart from the dishonesty of it, didn't seem an appropriate way of helping him.

Hannah's reaction was the same as Joy's. The first time she overheard us use this new expression, 'mentally handicapped', when referring to Sang, she was shocked and upset.

'He's not!' she said as if defending him. 'He's not. You know he's not. You shouldn't say it.'

There was scrambled egg for breakfast, cooked by me because David was away at a conference in Germany.

Sang: (*complacently eating scrambled egg without even mentioning the lack of sausages*) Why I not got lar' clo' (alarm clock)?

Rachel: (*drinking coffee half asleep*) I dunno. People save up

163

and buy them if they want them. Hannah bought that big tin one with her birthday money. She has to get up early for her paper round.

Sang: Why I not go one own?

Rachel: (*shrugs, it being too early in the morning for a debate on possessions*)

Sang: Anyway, I gonna say (save) my mon (ey) get dog.

Rachel: Ah. Ahm. That's good.

Sang: Big dog how much big dog cost?

Rachel: Dunno.

Lawrence: (*joining in because infuriated by mother's lack of interest in this important topic for he too has always wanted a dog and finally found an acceptable way of having one on a temporary basis*) You can't really have a big dog, Sang. It wouldn't be fair on the dog.

Sang: Lon tine go, I hab big dog, other home.

Lawrence: But you see, Sang, there's lots of space there. All that garden and woods. But it's not kind to keep large dogs in a town.

Sang: How much him cost?

Rachel: A pedigree dog? About £150.

Sang: Wha'?

Rachel: A pedigree dog, that means an alsatian or a labrador.

Sang: Wha' bout dog Rumper him? (*he refers to Aunty Alex's red setter, Rumpus*) I get one. I gonna hab puppeeeee. I gon take him walk schoo. My dog.

Lawrence: You know Sang, you really can't. Our garden's too small. The puppy that we're going to have here one day maybe, we'll only be able to look after it while it's little, while it is still a puppy. Then it goes back to the Blind Home to be trained to help somebody.

Sang: Wha'?

Lawrence: And when a puppy's going to be trained as a guide dog, it's all right to have it in town so it can get used to pavements and small homes. We'll get it used to city life. But it won't stay here.

164

Sang: (*gradually realizing that though it seemed at first that Lawrence was showing positive reaction to the desire for a dog, was in fact pointing out the disadvantages*) Aw, shudup you.

Lawrence: Don't say shudup. I'm just telling you so you'll know.

Sang: (*in frustration that conversation has become too complex to follow begins to hit side of marmalade jar with spoon*) I can't care! Shud up you!

Lawrence: Don't do that Sang. It'll break, the jar.

Sang: Donna, he do dat.

Lawrence: Well it's silly him doing it too. It's glass. It'll smash.

Sang: Why you talk me? You shud up. Not argue me.

Lawrence: I wasn't arguing. I was just explaining to you about guide dogs.

I was tempted to intervene, to advise Lawrence to lay off a bit, when I realized that this kind of silly bantering was an essential part of family life. To tell Sang things about guide dogs and the vulnerability of marmalade jars was to respect him as an ordinary brother.

Donald was wetting with increasing frequency. So now there were two sets of soggy bedding every morning and two boys to be bathed. Donald was also finding himself wet during the daytime and, just like big brother Sang, coming home from school wet. Angrily, he would strip off his clothes, stamp naked upstairs to the bathroom. Even if it was a cry for attention, he refused to be helped.

'It's all right, Don. It doesn't matter. It's only wee.' Soothing words were no comfort. Of course it mattered.

Hitherto so cheerful, so happy to go to school, Donald began to dawdle in the morning when it was time for us to leave, to walk stiffly like a wooden doll, refusing to hold my hand, dragging his feet almost as though he too had had rickets. He slid reluctantly in through the gate. There were tears at the back of his eyes. He began to poo in his pants. Two soiling schoolboys.

The teacher was nagging at him, he said. 'She says I've got

to work harder. She says I'm not trying. She says if I don't work harder, she doesn't know what'll happen. She thinks I'm stupid because I don't do all the sums. I don't want to go to school any more.'

It was a cosy relaxed church primary. We'd known most of the staff for ten years.

Could it be that Donald wanted to be more like the brother who never had to do sums, who didn't have to work at all, who had specialists inspecting him and everything difficult done for him? Or could it be that he feared becoming like that brother? Or was it that there were too many demands on him at home? Were his needs being overshadowed by Sang's screams? Was he worn out by the time he reached school? Was he getting enough sleep? Was he getting enough attention?

Our new handbook, which I read till I knew it almost by heart, advises that where a mentally handicapped child has brothers or sisters, it is important to involve, or at least inform, their teachers of the fact.

The young headmaster was always available to parents at going-home time when he was organizing his own small children, who were among the pupils. But I feared having to talk in so public a place as the playground. I feared exposing Donald's misery and incontinence to the scrutiny of other mothers. I dreaded admitting that Donald's brother was mentally handicapped. Nor did I want Donald to think I was interfering in his life. Home and school were, for him, separate worlds. He didn't seem to want any overspill from one to the other. So, I made a formal appointment with the head, didn't tell Donald about it, and crept in the front door so there was no chance of him or any of his classpals noticing me.

I found myself trembling. Why had I wanted to come? Why did the headmaster need to know about our domestic set-up? I kept *Parents and Their Mentally Handicapped Children* clutched in my coat pocket like a magic talisman to give me strength to make my statement, to try to explain how the

166

needs and conditions of brothers are inextricably bound up with one another.

I was unable to begin speaking. What was I ashamed of? I took out the book, flapped it about and launched into an incoherent ramble about how Donald didn't want to ask his friends home to tea any more, how we didn't know what was going on inside his head, how he seemed to be unhappy. Then I thought, Isn't being unhappy a condition of life? especially at just seven, the beginning of the age of reason. I tried to explain how he seemed to see the world distinctly separated into two, the clever achieving half which was at school and the other one at home where people don't manage to do things, and he didn't know which half he belonged to. He seemed to be under pressure trying to keep them separate. Being told by his class teacher that he was stupid increased his confusion.

The head listened, reassured, said he'd advise the teacher to take the pressure off, treat Donald more carefully, expect less back. He promised that he himself would keep a special eye on my child's welfare.

'As a matter of fact, I've always thought that we ought to do something to bridge the gap between mainstream and special schools, some kind of integration to prevent the special-school children being so isolated. We're a happy school here. We've a lot to offer each other. They're all children, after all. I wonder what we could do that would be useful.'

I suspected that this unexpected interest in the social isolation of handicapped children was merely an attempt at solace for a worried parent. It turned out to be sincere. His first step was to make a point of personally welcoming Sang whenever we came to school concerts or met in the street. Many people asked me how Sang was. This man thought to ask Sang how he was. His more official action for integration took longer to achieve, though was again commendable in its apparent simplicity, and a first of its kind in the area.

Eight years on, when head at a larger school, he initiated a weekly lesson of music, singing and percussion which a class

167

of nine- and ten-year-olds shared with a group of profoundly retarded pupils from a special school. By then, Sang was no longer a schoolboy. I went at the invitation of a little girl I knew. The normal schoolchildren, in pairs, each befriended one handicapped child, welcoming him or her at the school gate and taking personal care of their special contact during the visit. The music session was disciplined and matter-of-fact while at the same time joyful and celebratory.

We realized that the complexities of life with Sang were not going to dissolve spontaneously. From now on we had to concentrate on what we could do for him, rather than on what we couldn't. In fretting over the delay in getting him adopted, in worrying about our failure to achieve normal behaviour, we'd been wasting energy on the wrong things. We had to concentrate on his needs rather than ours.

Since he didn't have proper papers, we set about inventing substitute papers, making sure his name was recorded in as many places as possible. We enrolled him at the library, we opened two Post Office savings accounts in his name, we began the long-winded process of getting him an international travel document (though without birth certificate, or entry-into-Britain certificate, this proved nearly as protracted as trying to get an adoption).

The legal process was still lumbering on and getting nowhere. We wrote to our MP, to other MPs, we wrote to the Home Office, wrote to anybody who'd ever had a finger in this pie. We dispensed with the costly services of the lady barrister, and the agency which had placed Sang with us paid off the remainder of the fees which we couldn't afford. Later, when we learned from another agency that they discouraged all attempts at legal adoptions of refugee children who were without papers because of the high cost and unlikely outcome, we knew we had done the right thing. When we heard of a probable change in the law whereby, after a child had lived for five or more years in a family, the parents would be able to secure an adoption at magistrate court level rather on the grounds of 'squatters' rights, we decided that this was what we must wait for.

Meanwhile, to see if we could make sense of Sang's peculiar and still very uncertain situation, we arranged a meeting at our house with representatives of the adoption agency, of the Children's Home, of the charity which organized the Home, with a friend who was a social worker and had known Sang since his arrival in our family, and with Sang's class teacher. She gave an account of how she found Sang to be to see if it matched up with any previous account and, since the representatives of the charity gave the impression that they had come to our house to take Sang away, we were glad when she also insisted that to move him would be very detrimental.

Throughout the meeting several of the participants got Sang's name wrong and referred to him by the name of one of the other children who still lived at the Home.

'We aren't talking about any old child who might've once been in care,' I said angrily. 'We're talking about this one particular one. So let's at least all be consistent in getting his name right.'

I fetched a photograph of Sang and propped it on the table, with a card with his name on underneath. The confusion over who was being discussed and the curious absence of any documentation or medical records from before he came to live with us became clearer when we were told that there had been a fire — nobody knew whether deliberate or accidental — in the grounds of the Home. Many of the children's notes had been destroyed.

Sang, returning from school and realizing that all the people gathered round the table were expressly there to talk about him, began to behave abominably, flinging himself to the floor for a good roar, squirming on to my lap, sucking the table, and when taken by his teacher into the next-door room for the supposedly calming effect of listening to his favourite record, suddenly turned the volume full blast so that floorboards and walls reverberated and nobody could hear anybody speak.

169

The conclusion of the afternoon was that a plastic dust-bin liner containing some of Sang's toys, a biro pen, some drawings, old postcards, and workbooks from his previous school was handed over to us. Though this delivery of personal possessions was a year overdue, at least it was a clear recognition that Sang was finally with us to stay. From then on, we accepted that he had an adoption by dictionary definition: *adoption* to take a person into a relationship he did not previously occupy, especially as one's child.

Whichever way we looked, the world was filled with mentally handicapped people. We had joined a great big club.

The house next door was sold and new people moved in, an elderly widow and her daughter, Jane, twenty-nine years old, four feet tall, and with Down's syndrome.

Now why had God decided that this was the moment to remove the silver-foil spreader and instead send a mongol to live next door to us?

A new man delivered the coal. He was a mute who made snorts and strange guttural grunts, but was exceptionally strong as he silently heaved the heavy sacks of coal through the kitchen. Why did God send this strange dumb person streaked with coal dust?

'How's the little boy?' an acquaintance asked.

'Which one?' I said, so often feeling prickly these days. 'I've three little boys, not counting David.'

'You know. Ching. Your little boy, the new one.'

'Oh fine.'

'Things going all right now?'

'Sure.'

'You sounded so low last time I saw you. There's a girl in our village, well you know, not a girl, a woman. She's got this child. I thought you'd be interested to meet her. God, I don't know how she does it. She's got three or four of her own already. Then she took on John. He's brain-damaged, been battered by his parents. She's extraordinary. Poor kid. He's appalling. I can't look at him. Well, he was on a bean-bag, just left lying in one of those Homes, on a bean-bag for eighteen months because nobody could think what to do with him. He was a bright little chap before. But now Carrie's been doing so much with him. I just thought you might be interested. I've got her number, if you like? I felt sure you'd like to see her.'

Hell, would I? No I wouldn't. I had no interest in wonderful women coping with other people's brain-damaged monsters.

Two days later, I found the number, rang, was invited, and set out, wondering as I drove along the leafy green lanes how I should explain my desire to visit. Excuse me Carrie, I'm a friend of a friend and I rather want to inspect your brain-damaged child. I've been told that he's very macabre and you're very brave.

I didn't have to explain anything, least of all that I was finding myself drawn inexorably towards an interest in mentally handicapped children. There were half a dozen other women there.

John was put straight on to my lap while his mother served coffee and cakes to everybody. He was five, an exceptionally handsome and large five, but floppy as a rag dolly. His eyes swivelled in his head and he dribbled constantly. He was in nappies and stank. How could his mother, his new mother, love him? How could she bear to think that another woman, the first mother, had done this to the child?

My arms were already aching from the weight of holding him after only five minutes.

'There's my beauty,' said his mother. 'Isn't he gorgeous?' She gave him a smacking kiss and John smiled and gurgled with delight.

'They say he's blind too. What rubbish. He's not blind, are you my pet? He can see when he wants to. Watch this.'

She put a red Smartie on the coffee table.

'Now John, find your sweetie.'

On cue, John found it and ate it.

'They say he's been made deaf too by the blow. They say he'll never learn to speak. It's rubbish. Listen to this. John,

171

Ba ba black sheep, come on, and then you'll have another sweetie.'

The supposedly deaf John crooned the required nursery rhyme and was rewarded. Then he was passed on to be cuddled by another mother, and it was my turn with a tiny Down's syndrome baby. If big John had felt limp, this little girl felt so lifeless it was more like holding a folded cotton handkerchief. Her first mother had rejected her soon after birth, her new mother was hoping to adopt her as soon as possible. The hold-up was because the baby had a heart defect.

'Ridiculous, isn't it!' said her mother angrily. 'Making us wait till after her operation. If she needs parents, she needs them before she goes into hospital, not after.'

Every woman had a similar tale to tell of some injustice done to her child by a social worker, or a committee, or a high-up decision-maker, or a health visitor, the very people who were supposed to be bringing welcome support.

Each of these amazing women had specifically set out to adopt or foster a mentally handicapped child. The love each one expressed for her received child was probably of the same force as ours for Sang. What was different was their combined toughness, the fury of their determination. They were a terrifying bunch. I felt almost sorry for their social workers. I wondered if this intense distrust — even dislike — of all professionals was a necessary part of the bonding process? Did we each have to convince ourself that we were the only person in the world who truly understood the needs of our child?

My own tale of woe, that we had set out to adopt a bright child with prospects and were turning out to have an irreversibly retarded Asian one, was received with reverent and sisterly sympathy though no understanding.

One mother said, 'Oh I do think you're brave. I don't think I could love a non-white. I couldn't ever bring myself to touch it.'

172

I said, 'I didn't think I could ever love a mentally handicapped one.'

'Oh, but that's quite different! Kids like ours, they're so lovely, they're the best of the lot! You get so much love back. They really do need us.'

Our sixteenth wedding anniversary and alone in the house I wept uncontrollably. So little progress in so many months? Or so much in so short a time? It's a question of perspective. It feels, from here and now, like an unchanging situation of hopelessness. But are we here for progress? Dear God please help me. I am so lonely. I am angry. I am bitter. I have fallen out of love with the child. I have lost sight of the husband I married.

This time, I turned not to the Samaritans but to my new neighbour, mother of a Down's daughter, who has survived over thirty years of this desolation. I felt an intruder, to go weeping with red eyes to her front door.

I knocked and entered.

'Can you help me?' I said with bold firm voice. Try to make it sound as though you want to borrow a pound of sugar.

'Yes of course my dear. Look we're just having lunch. My younger daughter's here too, with her little boys. Do come in.'

I came in.

'What can I do for you, my dear?'

I need, I need, what do I need? I just need somebody. Because I can't bear it any more.

'Oh my poor dear. What is it? Have you had any lunch yet? Let me get you a plate? We've some ham left.'

It's not lunch I need. It's a chance for self-pity. It's my turn. 'Because it's all so awful.'

How could I weep in front of those people whom I hardly know, all over their salad and ham? Have I no shame left?

I sat with my new neighbour and her elegant married daughter and her two grandsons while they ate their lunch and comforted me. The grandsons were so appallingly noisy as only toddlers can be that I was restored. And I learned from the clever sister how easy it is to hurt the whole child by caring too much for the simple one.

'I don't really like going to the place where she lives,' she said. 'I was always jealous of my sister when we were young.'

How could this young woman, so beautiful and fulfilled, possibly have been jealous of her dumpy, squashy-nosed, lumbering, loose-tongued sister?

We must not give Sang more attention in our hearts by weeping more because of him than because of the others.

That weekend, a friend's new baby was baptized into the Orthodox Church. As we have adopted Sang, so God has already adopted all of us without any legal papers. If it hurts us to love Sang with all his small imperfections, how does it feel to God to have taken on humanity with our millions of failings?

13
ADOPTION BY FAITH

Before we went to the family service, Sang had to be dressed — or redressed — appropriately. In nervous anticipation of any outing he prepared himself in an unusual arrangement of clothes. His shoes were taken off and replaced on the correct feet. His face, which had been washed after breakfast, was re-wiped because somehow he'd have golden syrup round his mouth. I knew that God didn't mind about the syrup, but I did because I anticipated receiving lots of embraces during the dull bits of the service and Sang's kisses were sticky enough without the addition of syrup. Similarly, while God probably wouldn't mind the wearing of a pink fluffy jacket with a swimming costume, or a stripy silk tie with a collarless, sleeveless singlet, I minded about other people in the congregation minding.

Sang was given collection money because he too wanted to carry small jingly objects in his pocket. The coin was wrapped in a hanky so that it wouldn't clatter when it fell to the floor beneath the pew as it surely would several times before it reached the collection plate.

We set off gently, trying to amble, not rushing to be on time because then he'd sense tension. Sometimes at the porch I realized that in trying to make him look socially acceptable, I'd forgotten to brush my own hair. David would remind me that God didn't mind that either.

Sudden distress signals in the aisle. Sang expected to sit where we all sat last time and the elderly sidesman, not understanding this desperate need for things to be the same, was showing us to a different pew.

The choir were already processing in and Sang refusing to move. Please God give me strength, grace, courage, peace. Today. Now.

A lull during the first hymn, then during the lesson he began humming and rocking from side to side as though leading a rugby sing-song. The pew and all the worshippers on it also swayed. Lawrence had an embarrassed expression as though he wished a winged angel would reach down and bear him away. While restraining the rocker, I tried to rejoice in the spin-off benefits. Already, at seven, Donald had taught himself to find his way round the prayer book and was on the right page at the right time. He'd had to. We were always too occupied with Sang who might at any moment join in the singing while the others are praying or in the praying when the vicar was preaching; who might lie on the floor and groan, or wet his pants, or hammer his feet on the wooden floorboards, or want to climb along the back of the pews chatting to himself.

The first time he went up to the altar to be blessed with the other children during the Communion, at the vital moment he had jerked his head away from the priest's descending hand. So now kneeling at the rail, one puts both arms round him, restraining, hugging, holding on, and somehow receives the sacraments at the same time. The gaze of a churchful of other families burns into one's back. Please don't stare at us. Just put up with us.

I longed for him to feel more a part of it. But how could he when he didn't know what was going on?

Sang hated it if other people were given things and he was left out. Seeing Hannah, who was already confirmed, receive Communion, he once asked, 'Why she do dat?' but didn't wait for the explanation about the symbolic re-enactment of the Last Supper and didn't pursue this issue of the unjust dispersal of bread and wine to some and not to others.

Since he wasn't beginning to initiate any demanding

theological questions on the meaning of life, God, Jesus, or even going to church, it was up to us to promote the ideas.

'Perhaps it's time for him to be christened?' one of us said to the other one day.

'Perhaps he already has been?'

We contacted the housemother at her retirement flat. She wasn't sure, but thought that possibly there had been a mass baptism in the Hoi Duc Anh orphanage by a nun.

'With a bucket of water, sprinkled over the lot of them.'

We later were told that a crash during take-off of a Galaxy freight plane laden with orphaned babies destined for the USA, most of whom died, had so distressed the Christian nurses and care-workers who'd known those children that, thereafter, all evacuees were perfunctorily baptized before departure.

Sang might have been included in a mass dousing. He might not.

'Does it really matter?' we wondered.

Yes, it did. Though we didn't believe that, unbaptized, he would burn in fires of hell, nor that, doubly-baptized, he would be breaking any religious laws, we needed to know that he had been given the same rites of passage as our other children had had.

We had often envisaged that the day we went to court to hear a judge granting a legal adoption would be the great gateway to the happy-ever-after, the public event which signified private security.

A baptism, or re-baptism, besides being an important spiritual ritual, could be a chance for the civil ceremony we had failed to secure, the occasion for making public witness to his permanent membership of this family, made not to a magistrate but to the higher authority of God.

Sang had already been to three baptisms of cousins or friends. We supposed he'd remembered a bit. He hadn't. He was alarmed.

'Well, it makes people even more part of a family,' I said. 'The family of Jesus.'

177

He didn't like the sound of that very much. He seemed to suspect it meant moving to another family. We tried a different approach. 'Christening' sounded better than 'baptism', a bit like Christmas. Sang's curiosity was aroused.

'And you get presents,' said Donald. 'I got a silver cup when I was a baby. It belonged to my grandfather, Donald Anderson. But it got stolen when I was only half. I never saw it. You get other presents too, don't you, Mum?'

'Well,' I said. 'Just Bibles and prayer books.' I didn't want the getting of tangible objects made of silver to seem like the part that counted.

We looked around for godparents. One friend whom we asked declined as she felt that the spiritual responsibility was too awesome. An Irish friend, Clodagh, had already volunteered when we went over to stay with my sister in Dublin. 'If ever he's to be christened,' Clodagh had unexpectedly said before we'd even thought about it, 'I'll come over and be godmother. I'll be giving him the silver mug with my initials engraved on it which I was given. I don't really hold with all these ceremonies of course. I'm a Quaker at heart. But I'm coming anyway.'

She sent the engraved mug ahead as a token of her intention to come in person. Uncle Jim, my eldest sister's husband, also volunteered himself. I was godmother to his youngest child, Eloise. For a third godparent, we asked a friend who was a Roman Catholic just in case Sang had previously been baptized into the Catholic Church by the nuns in Saigon.

The vicar came to discuss the service. He wasn't one of the college chaplains accustomed to bringing students and guitars round for jolly house communions so we had to explain a bit about Sang's unusual circumstances and that it might not be quite like baptizing an ordinary ten-year-old. He was a bachelor priest and inexperienced in the ways of most types of young children, so nothing Sang did surprised him.

The vicar felt that Sang should make the responses himself, as is normal in the baptisms of older people. Would he, he asked, be able to manage this? We too felt that Sang should somehow be actively involved. But with his limited vocabulary of even concrete nouns, how could he understand the meaning of abstractions like redemption, trust and believe, Holy Spirit and ways of evil?

We worked through the printed baptism card adjusting the language.

'Would he,' the vicar asked, 'understand the question, "Do you wish to be like Jesus?"'

Sang had been told that Jesus is all around and everywhere in our practice of loving other people, yet is invisible. Lately, this invisibility had been a source of endless concern to him.

'Do you wish to be like Jesus, except not invisible?' Hannah suggested.

Sang had also been showing a consuming interest in a picture book about the Christian Crusaders as they went about slaying and decapitating infidels in the name of Jesus.

'I think he'd want to be like Jesus if it meant being a Crusader and carrying a sword,' I said. 'It's all rather a problem, explaining the Crusaders to him.'

'For all of us, I think,' said the vicar.

'What about,' Hannah said, getting back to the text, '"Do you wish to follow Christ, and be like him, according to the socially acceptable principles of the times in which you live?"'

David said, 'No wonder if takes whole committees so long to write the prayer book into modern English.'

We came to the question, 'Do you believe and trust in him?'

'That word "trust",' said David, 'is a very tricky one. It's really the key to his whole life. He's never had anyone to trust in, so he doesn't know, can't know, from experience, what it means.'

After nearly an hour of tea-drinking and discussion, we had the responses in terms which seemed to be within Sang's scope.

'And, I believe, probably theologically sound too,' said the vicar.

'Does the church, or the archbishop or whoever it is, *mind* you rewriting bits of the services?' I asked.

'Hm, I expect so, but our Lord doesn't,' said the vicar.

In the room next door the children's television programmes had finished. Donald and cousin/god-daughter Eloise wandered in to listen to the grown-ups' talk. Eloise was living with us and going to school with Donald for the summer term.

Sang lurked out in the hall, peeping through the half-open door, apparently too frightened of the vicar to enter. When I tried to beckon him in he disappeared behind the coats. So I went and fetched him, leading him by the hand with what I hoped were encouraging noises. Only the day before, he had been shouting out about how he was going to be 'Christy in chur'.

Reluctantly, he came in and sat huddled on my knee, clinging tightly to my arm, and buried his face in my hair. He began to croon softly with his eyes shut. Is this child really ready to stand up in church and make public replies to questions? Yet it was perhaps reassuring that he should find the prospect intimidating for it must mean that the significance of it had come to him. Just as we longed for him to develop emotionally, so we wanted him to have the chance for spiritual development. But could one develop a spirit? Or was it there already in position like the brain, heart, liver and spleen?

'It's all right Sang, there's nothing scary. We're just talking about how it'll actually be and what we'll all do.'

Eyes more tightly shut.

He was wearing his green Cub Scout jersey and the vicar asked about being in the Cubs. At first, Sang seemed unable to understand let alone answer two simple questions about whether he'd been long in the Cubs and whether he enjoyed it.

'Did you make promises when you were invested?' the vicar persisted.

'Yeah.'

'Do you remember what those promises were?'

To my surprise, for he was still clinging to me like a baby koala, Sang opened his eyes and replied, 'Promise be good help other. Do best. Help.'

The vicar explained that the baptism would be almost the same, and how there would be some questions to which Sang, if he agreed to wanting to be baptized, would answer, 'Yes.'

'Do you love Jesus?'

'Are you sorry for when you've been naughty?'

'Will you try to be like Jesus?'

'Do you believe and trust in God who made you?'

'Do you believe and trust in Jesus who loves you?'

'Do you believe and trust in his Holy Spirit who helps you?'

Still curled up in fetal position, loudly and clearly he replied 'Yes' to each. Holding him as he lay snuggled on my lap, I noticed the shadow of dark down already on his upper lip. My baby. My man-person.

When the vicar began to explain about the water in the font, Sang began to lick my face in a strange reversion, less to babyhood than to kittenhood.

'I tire now. Go shleep,' he said, buried his face in my jersey and began to snore exaggeratedly. His escape from fear was often to withdraw into pretend, or even real sleep.

His fear seemed to be chiefly about the effect the water might have on him. At each of the infant baptisms we'd been too, the baby had yelled itself red in the face at the first touch of damp on its forehead.

'Shall we just see what it's like with some pretend water?' I suggested.

'No, no, no,' said Sang.

'Shall we have a practice? Just a little one?'

At once, the chair on which the vicar had been sitting became the stone font and he the robed priest. I stood Sang up and nudged him towards the chair. Just as at real baptisms when smaller children are encouraged to gather round to get a good look, Donald intuitively moved in close and Hannah, David, Eloise and I became the rest of the congregation. Sang cringed and held my hand tightly. Donald held my other hand equally tightly. The vicar leaned over the wooden seat of the chair and in his cupped hand scooped up some of the invisible dropless water.

'In the name of the Father. And the Son. And the Holy Spirit.' Three times, he poured invisible water on to Sang's forehead. Like the invisible Jesus, the water, though still invisible, was obviously there. As was the font. In the 30-second enactment of baptism, they seemed quite clearly to be there.

Sang giggled with relief that it was all so simple.

'And that's all,' said the vicar. 'Then I shall mop your face with a white linen cloth.'

Sang, my moustached man-baby, Christian Crusader, skipped away to play. Invisible Jebus was with him.

During the next three days, I heard him on the stairs shouting to the world, 'What day tolay? When my Christ? Only three more day my Christ!'

Yea Lord, three day his Christ.

Thank you God. You were listening after all. For the three days leading up to the baptism weekend, Sang became so happy, so relaxed, so amenable, showing an ability to love and to be loved.

'Hello Mum!' with good cheer at breakfast. 'You all right? You have nice tine shleep?' He performed his 'weekend duty' of emptying the waste paper baskets into the big bin with joy and enthusiasm. Love with responsibility. He set up a happy game of 'baysh-shit' (spaceship) in the garden.

'I reshew man. Reshew man weara boot alltine?'

Wanting to rescue somebody must be better than wanting to slay them.

He sat up on top of the garden table wearing his pyjama bottoms instead of shorts to look more like a space uniform, and his smelly old wellies as moonboots, playing inventively and happily.

Before communion one can fast and pray and confess. Before battle, warrior kings can meditate and pray. Before all great events one prepares oneself. Before baptism we had a small preparation. After picking them up from their Friday afternoon judo class, instead of driving directly home, I took Sang and Donald to the ancient church of St Martin and Bertha the Queen which stands just outside the city looking down on to the cathedral.

In the still evening sunlight, the yew trees outside were dark with the apricot sun shining on to the grass, and low sun streaming in through leaded windows. The church was heavy with the scent of massed flowers.

The interior of the church was floodlit and sombre classical music playing in the background.

'Why hab war noosi (music)?' Sang immediately asked.

'It's not really meant to be war music,' said Donald.

'It like my war noosi!' Sang contradicted. He meant his Tchaikovsky 1812 record.

'Yes, a bit. That's because it's grown-up music, with an orchestra,' said Donald, who was learning a lot from the children's 'Monday Music' club they both went to.

'Why hab noosi?'

'To give the place atmosphere maybe? Make it seem more interesting?' I suggested.

Luxuriant displays of summer flowers in the nave, chancel, vestry, balanced on the pews represented events from the city's past. Donald caught the intended mood of local history, glory to God for creation, quietness of soul, and poked around on his own, coming back to show us when he noticed some tiny detail of interest in the old brickwork, a rare strange flower in an arrangement. Finally he fetched Sang and me to see the font which he had discovered, curious and ancient, leaded inside and out, and embossed with intricate decorations and Bible stories.

But fenced off by a low oak rail and carved gate which

183

would not open however hard they pushed. Why so many barriers in churches to impede a child's progress, or rather to impede the progress of one child leading his brother towards the family of Christ? Both boys together tried to push the gate.

'No,' said Sang, giving up the struggle. 'Not allow.' But Donald went on pushing.

'He wants to see it,' he said. 'Don't you Sang? Then he won't be frightened on Sunday when he has to go to the font.'

'Yeah,' said Sang. 'Me hab got go Christ like dat.'

I tried the gate but it seemed to be locked. So I asked one of the attendant flower ladies if there was a key we could use.

'Oh, oh dear. Oh. I don't know if you can. Oh, you'd better ask the vicar.'

The vicar was chatting to festival visitors.

'But of course,' he said. 'Go right ahead.'

The barrier to the font was not locked, merely jammed. Like gaining access to the kingdom of Heaven, it was extremely easy to push open once you knew the knack of it.

So we inspected the font and Sang, in awe, touched the patterned lead sides, and Donald found the baptismal roll and counted how many children had been baptized since 1950.

Then, in the heady-scented atmosphere, I reminded them how to pray. How many many times one shows the same thing, the same gestures so that they might become as easy as skipping or teeth-cleaning.

'Whenever we happen to go into a church for any reason, what people do is to say a little prayer, just a small one like saying "Hello God", before they go out again. Kneel down, shall we, hands together like this.'

We knelt. Hands together.

'Dear God, thank you for your church. Thank you for the lovely summer flowers today. Please bless us and take care of us. Amen.'

And for Sang, an extra line. 'Please bless me and take care of me specially on Sunday at my christening. Amen.'

184

'Now we go out, hone,' said Sang.

So out we scampered into the low apricot sun, pausing in the porch to sniff at a vast bowl of huge, cabbagelike, red velvet roses.

Sang sniffed. 'Hmm. They flowertaste lobely.'

While I walked more sedately along the path, the boys chased across the ivy-covered tombs, choosing one after another to read the inscriptions.

'Who dere?' Sang asked and Donald read, 'Henrietta Woods. 1916.'

'Dere?'

'William Mount, 1902.'

'Dat dere?'

'Charles Henry Webb.'

And on till Donald finds a strange circular stone, two or three feet in diameter, and runs round and round its circumference till he's giddy.

'Who dere? What dat one?'

The inscription was carved round the edge and Donald read it as he ran.

'It says, "I am the One, and the one is Me".'

'Yeah.'

14
WIDENING HORIZONS

'What tine it gone be?'
  'What time we hab grunks after?'
  'What I say?'
  Then he began again. 'What tine it gone be?'
  'What tine we hab grunks (drinks) after?'
  'What I gone say?'
  Sang was very nervous.

The usual family service congregation was swelled by nearly thirty Sang-supporting extras, including the offspring of some actively agnostic friends who, though they felt they shouldn't come themselves asked us, please, to take their children. We were all squashed cosily into a pew near the font, Donald and Sang on either side each tightly clutching a hand, David on the end so he could get out to read a lesson.

As the pews around and behind filled up Donald whispered, 'Isn't it exciting for Sang that so many different people are here specially for him?' And then, 'I wish I could've been christened.'

'You *were* christened,' I whispered. 'And there were lots of friends came, and everybody made a big fuss of you.'

'But I'd rather have waited till I was ten.'

'The trouble is,' Hannah agreed, 'you can't remember the fuss when you're only a baby.'

Suddenly, Sang's anxiety broke loose. He raised both arms in the air above his head, clapped, twisted, slapped the side of his face, groaned low in his throat. But it was just a brief echo of how he used to be, all over within sixty seconds when he reverted to the thoughtful and solemn ten-year-old in blue shirt and long trousers, holding up a hymn book close to his spectacles.

'Would the parents and godparents like to come to the font?'

One ancient lady, short-sighted and hard of hearing, was annoyed to have been asked by the sidesman if, because of the increased numbers, she would sit in a different place from her usual one and when the vicar announced that the baptism would be next, said loudly, 'Baptism, baptism? What's he on about now? I don't see no baby.'

We parents, with the godparents and the congregation prayed, according to the texts before us, that Sang should be surrounded with God's love, protected from evil and filled with Holy Spirit.

'We welcome you into the Lord's family, we welcome you,' we all said, at which point my eldest sister started to cry, so she revealed after. 'It was just like a wedding. So many promises. So much emotion.'

Sang made his promises loud and clear as though he understood his part of the arrangement to 'Lob Jebus, be sorry when I not goob. Let Jebus God lob me.'

And perhaps he, too, saw it as not only a public statement of adoption into the family of the church, but also as his intention of long-term adoption by us for, after the ceremony, he reminded David and me, 'I lib you here all now. One tine lon tine go, not like and scream scream. Now I lib you allway.'

Sang's enthusiasm for church-going and his concentration increased in miraculous leaps and angelically assisted bounds. Now he wanted to stand when he saw others stand, kneel when they were kneeling. Eagerly he trotted forward to the altar rail to be blessed. At his school, they sang the Lord's Prayer and he was learning his own personal version, 'Our Father, Shiny Halo, Hubbledum de die day,' which he shouted out with gusto. He was joining in all the Amens and

187

at the time for the sign of peace, grinning broadly, he would turn to shake hands with all around him. During the intercessions when the priest implored, 'Lord in thy mercy,' Sang's voice boomed out, 'Hear our prayer.'

Sometimes one suspected that he had always had special protection from his invisible father. Sometimes one knew without doubt that Sang had a direct line to God.

The curative powers of the Holy Spirit didn't always seem to last through into the weekdays. Leaving for school was a struggle. At eight o'clock each morning, with enormous relief I bundled a grumpy Sang on to the minibus, knowing I wouldn't have to cope until the bus returned him nine hours later.

In some ways, the later he was brought back the better. It continued to provide a welcome breathing space for the other children to have attention and help with homework. Nonetheless, three hours a day seemed an exceedingly long time for any child to spend just sitting on a bus doing nothing. Apart from a rare excitement, such as when one of the other passengers had a fit, or when the bus broke down and they had to be rescued by the police, there was nothing stimulating about the journey.

Though Sang seemed to enjoy being at school, it was hardly surprising that he loathed the ride. Most days, he arrived home with wet or dirty pants, sometimes feeling sick, always grumpy because he'd missed out on his favourite TV programme. 'Playschool' was long over. 'Blue Peter', which he couldn't understand, had just started.

He was eleven when we decided to take a calculated risk and see if he could learn to make his own way to school just like the others.

I had noticed a middle-aged Down's syndrome man who, no doubt thanks to enlightened parents, roamed freely and safely around town with an air of jaunty liberty. If he could find his way about, then perhaps Sang could. Though he was small, poorly co-ordinated, and — so we believed — lacking in stamina, he was not physically disabled.

The school, despite the head's misgivings, was co-operative and agreed we should at least give it a try. The traffic police advised an approved route. Even so, it was not going to be straightforward. There were numerous small roads to be negotiated, a long narrow alleyway, a footbridge over a railway. At a brisk adult walk, it was perhaps twenty-five minutes. At Sang's shuffle-shamble slope it might be three-quarters of an hour. Since he couldn't read and had no sense of direction, teaching him street names was no use. And since he couldn't speak clearly, he wouldn't be able to ask the way if he got lost. He just mustn't get lost.

On non-school days we practised, time after time, always going exactly the same way. He had to be helped to memorize the way with visual landmarks, and repeated mental jogs.

'Look, Sang! See, we're going past where we bought the balloons.'

Then up the lane past the red postbox where Sang would post some letters as a practical reminder of this landmark.

Next, the fire station where a classmate's father worked, followed by the pub on the corner with the picture of a golden key, then the police station. That was easy to remember. Sang liked the police, ever since the local constabulary had taken a party from his school on a cross-channel trip in mid-December. Many of the children had been sea-sick both ways which had made it even more memorable.

When he began to seem ready, David and I reorganized life so that one of us could escort him on real school days while the other was seeing the rest of the family off. Soon after my furtive visit to the headmaster, Donald had decided he would begin bringing himself home from school, and in the mornings was now at the stage of needing only to be escorted halfway, that is, until he had reached the High Street where he was seen, but not accompanied, across the traffic.

For Sang, the same codes of behaviour had to be instated, and repeated. Always go straight to school and come straight back. Never go off and play with a friend on the way. Don't

189

get into anybody's car even if you think you know them, however nice they seem.

There were other dangers we hadn't foreseen. On one of the trial walks, he was walking ahead, demonstrating exactly what he'd do when he really was alone. He paused correctly at the dangerous crossroads where there was no pedestrian crossing. Patiently he waited, as drilled, on the kerb, watching the lights for the few vital seconds when all were red and it was safe for him to cross, making sure, as instructed, that car drivers clearly understood his intention to cross. Suddenly from behind, rushed an elderly woman who misinterpreted his deliberation as indecision, and grasped him by the hand.

'Quick dear, if we run now we'll get over,' she said and dragged him through the moving traffic to the other side.

A new rule had to be added. 'Don't let anybody try to help you across the road. Always decide for yourself when it's safe.'

He had to remember such a lot of instructions which, for a person bad enough at recalling even the days of the week, was a sign of his own determination to succeed.

We got him an orange fluorescent waistcoat to wear over his anorak.

'You're not really going to make him wear that, are you?' Hannah asked incredulously. 'It's so bright he looks like a Christmas tree. Everyone'll see him.'

We had been having some family dispute about how much illumination children riding bicycles ought to display. I was forever providing luminous arm-bands, leg lights, supplementary reflectors which were usually spurned.

'They're *meant* to see him.'

Sang thought the waistcoat made him look like a motorway worker and was proud to be leaving home in the same way as the others.

'And you'll have to keep your glasses on Sang, otherwise you won't be able to see which way to go.'

190

He had lately decided he didn't like glasses and taken to hiding them in unusual places.

The school was pre-warned that he was on his way, we kissed him goodbye and he sidled out of the house and along the pavement, falteringly at first, turning to wave enthusiastically every few yards. His stout new walking shoes seemed to make his feet look floppier and flappier than ever. He swung from side to side, seeming so small and so vulnerable to the dangers. Sending him out on this adventure alone for the first time was both exhilarating and terrifying.

What if he lost his way? What if he was molested in the subway? What if he was teased by other children? What if he ran across a road and got knocked over? And what if he never got lost and never learned to find his way? What if he never discovered how to walk along a pavement by himself? What if he never learned to grow up but stayed a man-baby for the rest of his life? Letting go of the apron strings is difficult with any child. With a child like Sang, who had not the ability to think or talk his way round a hazard, the possible dangers seemed to be multiplied.

David said, 'D'you think I ought to follow, just in case?'

But we both knew that, if we were offering Sang this chance, it had to be carried out with proper dignity.

All the same it seemed a very long wait till, at 9.30, we dared ring the school secretary to check on Sang's arrival.

Yes, he was safely in the classroom and yes, somebody would make sure he was pointed in the right direction at going-home time.

'It ver ver difficul. Hab to think ver careful all tine.'

Sang was pleased with himself but by no means triumphant, let alone confident. He was all too aware of the dangers which might, and sure enough soon did come his way. There was the dog with the teeth which, so he claimed, was set on him. There was the day, so he reported, when he paused to look at a pretty front garden and the owner shouted at him to go away and never stop near her house again. Not everybody welcomed the notion of retarded schoolboys lurching around the streets. There was the gang of bullyboys at the bus station who invariably taunted him as he passed.

Lawrence, returning once along the same route, caught sight of Sang's ordeal by the buses and at tea-time congratulated Sang for the amazingly cool way he'd handled it.

'They were really foul to him,' Lawrence said. 'Calling him names. Like "Ching Ching Chinaman" and saying he comes from the veggie school.'

'Yeah, dey do allway say dat me.'

'But you did just the right thing, didn't you? He took no notice and kept on walking straight past. They were really big boys, Mum. It must be so scary for him, going along there. I think Sang's the bravest person in the family, to put up with that. I know I couldn't.'

By having to remain alert and in control of his own destiny instead of being able to let events wash over him, he became much more aware of the town in which he lived, discovering for himself about mail collected from postboxes, about getting soaked through in rain, about getting cold if you chose not to wear your gloves, about getting cold and white in snow, about early-closing day. The first time he registered that some of the shops were closed, he came home outraged at this apparent change in the order of things for he liked looking at the brightly lit windows and seeing the shoppers and the assistants busy inside.

With the increased and regular exercise, he began to sleep better. So we all slept better. His legs became stronger and eventually even muscular. We discovered that he was quite a sturdy little boy.

Over the next year, as his confidence increased, he began to err off the strict code of conduct, coming home by different routes, or entering into illicit transactions with friends. But even these small misdemeanours were part of his growth. Only once did he fail to return at the usual time. I waited. I worried. I rang the school. No, he'd left as usual. Eventually, he was back, truculent in manner, mouth sticky and dribbling, pockets stuffed with empty sweet papers. He had discovered the prohibited pleasure of going into a sweet shop. Though he'd taken the precaution of eating most of the evidence, he'd not thought to dispose of the wrappers. For pinching small change from the dinner-money jar on the kitchen shelf and for disobeying he was suitably told off. But in fact we were pleased that he was making use of his new independence to get what he wanted.

The success of the experiment in freedom was due partly to his own courage in making a try of it, partly to the support of people out and about in town. Acquaintances and colleagues would tell us how they kept an eye out for him.

'Saw your boy today,' said the lady serving me a granary loaf in the baker's. 'Isn't he doing well? See him every day now, regular as clockwork. Always give him a wave.'

As we saw him off down the street in the morning, waving from the doorstep till he turned the corner, it was increasingly in the knowledge that he was being entrusted into the hands of a watchful and caring community.

A close family friend told me, 'I stopped and tried to say hello but he wouldn't answer and just walked past. I suppose you've told him he mustn't talk to anybody on the way?'

'Only strangers,' I said. 'Perhaps he didn't see you?'

Later, I realized that, once out on his own, such was his need to concentrate on the task of finding his way that everybody was a stranger, for when I myself met him in town coming towards me along the pavement, though I waved both arms to attract his attention, he didn't seem to establish it was me until we were nearly on top of each other.

'Don't you even know your old mum? Didn't you see me waving?'

'Yeah. I think you maybe annudder person.'

Despite the effort at school and home, he was still not a reader. He didn't even seem to like books much. As a bookish family it was a disappointment. He was missing out on so much that we saw as an integral and comforting part of childhood. But if picture- and storybooks formed a part of

193

normal childhood, surely they could become part of his child-hood too?

While he was still at his toddler stage, Sang had a chronic inability to concentrate on anything for more than a few seconds at a time without darting aimlessly about, never quite sure what to do with himself. Even asleep he moved restlessly. The speech therapist had told me that, with her very profoundly retarded clients, even training the child's eyes to rest for a moment on a brightly coloured image might be the total achievement aimed for. If it gave pleasure to the child, enabled him to focus on members of his family, to become more aware of himself and his world, then it was worthwhile.

So how to persuade Sang to stay still long enough to look at a few pictures in a short book? By bribery. There had to be the lure of milky coffee and a golden syrup sandwich, lots of kisses, and no other distractions. Even if the cat walked into the room, he would begin wriggling away. My insistence on a brief but regular routine with a picture book while the others were doing their homework was endured only because he liked being cuddled. Training him to sit still for a few moments, might, we hoped, develop better concentration, perhaps even lead on to actually recognizing familiar objects in the pictures and learning their names.

We had started with a selection from Ladybird's *First Books*. Methodically I turned the pages and talked about what we saw. They would hardly win prizes for high art, but they did show a lifelike range of ordinary everyday objects, a bed, a bath, a flight of stairs, red cherries, shoes, cotton reels. Chatting about these commonplace things, I hoped to demonstrate that all objects around us had names and that these names remained consistent, that a 'bath' was always a bath, and didn't turn, as Sang had supposed, at random, into a 'bedtime' or a 'pyjamas'.

Much of young children's fiction attempts to create a make-believe world where children can let their imaginations loose. But Sang was already living in such a world where the real, the half-real, the feared, the longed-for, Jo'

Way (John Wayne), Go-go and the three bears, Scooby-Doo, 'my-fren-I-know-him' (the six o'clock newsreader whose face Sang recognized) were all scrambled up. For him, the function of books had to be reversed. First he had to be led, even dragged, out from the seclusion of his private universe and shown the real world as represented in pictures, and flights of imagination could follow later.

Some days, even when all the conditions were fulfilled, nice drink, nice sandwich, cosy corner, no distractions, he couldn't seem to let his eyes rest on the page. It seemed to require too much effort. We had to work out what he did like, namely food and toys, and move on from there.

It was ironic that, though we had several thousand children's books in the house with fabulous new ones arriving for review every day, one of the earliest to actually win his approval and hold his interest was handmade and rather tatty. It was seven pages long with pictures cut from magazines of a tin of golden syrup, a chocolate bar, some cake and a can of 'grizzy gring' pasted into an old exercise book. His preoccupation with toys was put to good effect, if not satisfied, by going through mail order catalogues, always starting at the beginning as one would with a proper book, turning pages, my hand over his, carefully, one at a time.

During his protest stage, I had persisted with the daily routine, because we had so needed to feel we were doing something to help him. Like John's mother making blind John see the Smartie, it gave me a sense of usefulness and purpose.

One day, when an alphabet book was open at a picture of 'J for Jet', Sang sitting on my lap, suddenly seized hold of my index finger as I held the page and bent it back as far as it would go so that the pain took my breath away. At that moment I knew he was really beginning to respond to the pictures because he was terrified of jets in the sky.

The idea that one might keep a book to hear it read again escaped him for some time. One of the picture books we gave him he put in the dustbin. I suppose he thought it was like an empty cereal packet and disposable after the first look. I wrote his name in his books and we knew he'd begun to accept the concept of ownership when he began to scrawl his own *S* in the other children's books. We knew he'd begun to listen to the words of a story when he used to tug at my sleeve and said, 'Slow, slow, not stand!' meaning not understand.

Even though he couldn't follow a story-line, we read aloud to him every day and eventually there was a glimmer of a breakthrough when a story by Quentin Blake called *Mr Magnolia* actually spoke directly to him. He was still obsessed with footwear, liking to wear his wellington boots at unexpected times, on hot sunny days, in bed, out shopping. In the story, Mr Magnolia has only a single boot to wear until a friendly child finds another, unmatching, one.

'Shoe! shoe! He got one shoe like me!' Sang cried out with excitement the first time he heard the story. Tears of excitement and relief that he had made this link between life and fiction, between Mr Magnolia's footwear and his own, sprouted from my eyes and down on to Quentin Blake's nice pictures.

Despite the vast selection of pop-ups and startling modern books in the house, Sang began to show a strong preference for old Ladybird *Keywords Readers*, which he hoarded by his bed, not for their text, though I sometimes read this to him if he seemed to be in a listening mood, but for their illustrations of Peter and Jane, whose background was a 1950s suburban stereotype, whose daily activities were banal and unimaginative, and whose parents lived out rigidly defined sex roles. Once Sang had grasped that he was an adopted child, this representation of the perfect nuclear family leading ordered and unchanging lives seemed to offer him magical reassurance. However, the same type of goody-goody child in Ladybird's *The Party* distressed him. He disliked the change in routine as they got dressed up in their best. He feared the fact that they walked alone down the road to the neighbour's house.

'Dey too young do dat,' he said.

Above all, he disliked the picture of hunting the thimble with the menacing implication of competitiveness among children. Party games carried the threat of being tested, of winners and losers. The child who never understood the rules would always be the loser.

Gradually, wonderfully, more books began 'speaking' to him. Several days after seeing a clip of Walt Disney's *Jungle Book* on television, he noticed in the bookshop window the figures of Bagheera and Mowgli on the front cover of a little paperback. In that moment of recognition, a flimsy undistinguished paperback became important to him. I bought it for him and he actually asked to hear it read. Books I had paid money for were more valuable to him than the cornucopia of free ones arriving by every post. A book he had chosen himself had even greater value, though on several later occasions he mystified me by choosing from the shop a second copy of a book he already had at home.

When he liked a book, he stopped rocking. He couldn't rock and look at pictures at the same time. Another spin-off benefit was the improvement in hand movements and co-ordination. Selecting a book off a shelf, getting it the right way up, turning its pages in correct order from first to last, required a surprising amount of skill.

As his self-awareness grew, so he came to realize when he was being fed baby pap. Although intellectually he seemed to be somewhere between two and five, this didn't mean he was two, three, four, or five. The range of books had to grow with him. Many nursery picture books whose subjects covered precisely his areas of interest, toys, being baby-sat, wet beds, camping, going on a visit, proved unsuitable because even he could see that the chubby dimple-cheeked characters were pre-school tots, not big boys like himself. It was beneath his dignity to identify with these babies. The challenge was to find picture stories which, while at his level of comprehension, didn't show toddlers and didn't patronize. Stories featuring animals were one way. Not stories of creatures in the wild, but ones in which a pet, often a dappy-looking

197

dog, was chief protagonist in an otherwise human calamity. Having begun to master, roughly speaking, some of the code of normal social behaviour, Sang had a fine sense of the ridiculous when someone else, for example the dog, or a chimpanzee or an orangutan, got it all wrong. Then he would cry out in its defence, 'Not his fault! Can't help it! He only nominal!'

Like any boy growing out of infancy, he too needed a share of adventure, action. Illustrated Old Testament stories were good sources of manly excitement with all those battles and death offering a kind of socially acceptable violence, as were Edward Ardizonne's *Little Tim* tales, which show a mere boy being daring heroic and resourceful in the face of many dangers. He could see the action in the pictures, even though he couldn't always follow the plot. I became adept at sight-reading two sentences ahead and where it seemed too difficult, reducing it to the vocabulary I knew was within his reach. If one was in a hurry, one could even skip several pages without him noticing. When Donald overheard, he was furious at this short-cut deceit and protested Sang's rights to hear unabridged and consecutive plots even if Sang himself didn't mind.

15
CHRISTMAS COMES BUT ONCE EVERY ELEVEN MONTHS

Christmas and the multiple birthdays loomed ahead like a great dark mountain. If this year was to be anything like last, we were in for a build-up of distress from November onwards. For weeks now, there had been the excited handicrafting of handknitted ties, handmade matchbox holders, lino-cut cards, lovingly moulded lurid green peppermint cream mice. From the additional whisperings of secrets whenever Hannah was out of the room, and the furtive choosing and wrapping, it was obvious that she was going to be the first to be centre of attention, the initial receiver of birthday presents. Sang resisted all attempts to be drawn into the preparations. He didn't wish to choose her a present. He didn't wish to help make one.

Our tradition for the December birthdays was to start the day with a candlelit breakfast. This dawn celebration, an intimate family affair, was in addition to a more open-house tea-party later on. It was initiated on Hannah's fourth birthday when prolonged industrial strikes in Scotland with accompanying power cuts and bread, yeast and eventually even flour shortages, had obliged us, and all Glaswegians, to breakfast by candlelight on scones, flapjacks or cake through most of November and December.

The breakfast cake theme was perfected a few years later when, travelling through northern Nigeria, we were forced, by the harmattan, a Saharan sandstorm, to take refuge on the eve of Donald's first birthday as unexpected guests on a Swedish mission station. We were surprised, on the morning of the birthday, to discover that the missionaries always celebrated Sunday breakfast with candles and sweet sticky Scandinavian cake — a ready-made birthday event for his first year.

For Hannah's birthday breakfast, I found some pale roses left over from summer still flowering in the garden and put them, with winter jasmine and ivy leaves, on the table by her little pile of parcels. The gloom of a winter morning was softened by the candles standing amongst the Weetabix, milk bottles, flowers and iced ginger cake.

As soon as she began to open her first present, Sang's anger erupted.

'For me! It for me!' He grabbed at the parcel.

The parcel contained a flimsy lace teen-bra.

Sang was persuaded, reluctantly, to give the packet back. He didn't seem to recognize the garment for what it was and demanded that he must be given one like it when it was *his* birthday.

'Just same *my* birthday. Just like!' he said crossly.

Lawrence thought it was very funny. 'A bra? Whatever for? You haven't got any bosoms!'

Donald was mystified. Hannah, supposedly girl of the day, was appalled to have unintentionally been the cause of Sang's unhappiness. She gave him the offending bra, and said if he really wanted it, of course he should have it.

He already collected and hoarded by his bed some extraordinarily unlikely objects. Wanting, now, to have a pretty bra of his very own was, perhaps, not so different from keeping sixteen empty cardboard boxes next to his bed.

But of course, he didn't only covet Hannah's lacy bra. He wanted also the silver-blue eye-shadow which Lawrence had chosen for her, the coloured hair-ribbons from Donald, the RSPB birthday card from Granny and Grandpa, the embroidered namhda bedside rug which David and I had got from the Oxfam shop, and most of all, the bar of Bournville

200

chocolate which was supposed to be from himself to his sister.

Quickly, Hannah shared it out between all of us. We were all glad when the birthday breakfast was over.

Sang stomped around muttering to himself about the many deprivations he was obliged to endure.

'Chillen Home I get *good* birthday. Get lotta lotta present. Lotta stocking. I go back Christmas Chillen Home. Schoopid Christmas here.'

The memory of Christmases past seemed to be a muddle of hysterical happiness and of repeated disappointment. Like many children's home inhabitants, he'd been the victim, the passive recipient of much intensive seasonal charity and transitory sentimentality. Presents had tumbled upon him like meteorites from space. But who they came from and why was a blank. He had little concept of them coming to him from a real, known, remembered person who cared personally for him. Like many institutionalized children, his experience of getting had not been counterbalanced by the experience of giving and sharing. In some subconscious way he seemed to understand that his real needs, of being loved as an individual for himself, had never been satisfied.

His seasonal vocabulary was part of the muddle. 'Christmas' sounded much the same to him and so meant the same as 'kiss'. *To, for* and *from* were interchangeable so that the message 'from Sang' on the parcel containing Hannah's birthday chocolate bar conveyed, in his terms, 'to Sang', so how dare she share it out to everybody. 'Carol' and 'card' were the same thing, meaning something boringly connected with reading and written words. Thus, me (opening an envelope addressed to the whole family): 'Oh, look our first Christmas card this year!' Sang: 'Yeah, we done that school yesterday' (meaning we sang carols at school). 'Present' meant also 'surprise', also 'secret', which was also 'postman arriving'. That wretched postman who brought bills and work letters for Dad and Mum instead of surprise-secret-present for Sang.

Doubtless he had heard some Christmas carols because he

talked of 'icker gonger icker gonger gonna nodder day'. He believed in Santa with rather more conviction than he did in the story about the baby born in the stable. That all, adults and parents included, could give each other presents, was met with outrage. I remembered a curious day at a summer fête soon after he'd come to us when, trailing round the stalls on some Kentish village green, I'd suggested he choose something from one of the craft stalls — a lavender bag, a pot-plant, a candle — to send to his housemother. He had been perplexed.

'Not bir-day,' he had said.

'I know. But it might be nice, as a way of saying hello, just to show you're still thinking of her.'

'Schupid. Not give presents grownup. She not like it. People not give presents her.'

David had been sharing with the children the secret problem of how to care for a large pink flowering bush which he had bought for me. It had to be kept hidden from my sight, but in healthy condition. I was amazed when, finally, I received it, to hear how it had survived several days in a dark, hot, dry airing cupboard without wilting. We were even more amazed by Sang's disbelief that it really was meant for me.

'Grownup not get present! Chillen only get present. Not grownup. That schoopid. Grownup not get present Chillen Home. I go back.'

'He can't really go back just for Christmas, can he?' asked Donald, curious.

'No,' I said firmly. 'Of course not. He lives here now. People can't just chop and change about where they live whenever they feel like it.'

Nonetheless, his suggestion that he return to the Children's Home for the Christmas holiday provoked a rush of conflicting emotions. I felt surprisingly hurt that, even after all this time, he should want to go back, that the memory of better presents was still stronger than the reality of consistent people. I also felt a wish that he could go back, and thus leave us free to enjoy a peaceful break. Then I felt guilt that we weren't trying hard enough to give him everything he wanted, everything he had missed.

But helping him overcome the many disappointments in his life was part of giving him everything he'd missed, whereas promising him the moon yet never returning to give it to him was what the numerous well-wishers in his life had done. Rather than smother him with more gifts than he'd ever had before, somehow we had to involve him in the process, engage him as an active participator instead of a passive receiver. We had to force him out from his seasonal self-pity and into a creative and Christian celebration of family life.

Hardening my heart to the moans about never getting enough presents, I began our campaign for a happy Christmas. 'You've lived here,' I told Sang, 'for a long time now, haven't you? So this year you're going to have to put up with *our* kind of Christmas, even if it *is* different. And we're going to start getting ready for it, you and I together.'

Together, we would prepare a book.

'A Christmas book,' I announced. 'About all the lovely things that are going to happen.'

The Christmas Book by Sang and Rachel had lined pages on one side, plain on the other for the pictures we would draw. Its contents page listed our chief topics:

1. Christmas
2. holly
3. presents
4. cards
5. the old man
6. Jesus
7. more presents
8. birthdays
9. December
10. more about December
11. Christmas carols
12. jingle bells

For lesson one I read aloud to Sang this contents page, then talked about holly, presents, and more presents. Sang was not impressed and only half listening.

'Where the present? I not see present. How many present I get?'

He had expected something better than just talking about abstractions and words on a page.

'And see there's a little picture of a sprig of holly on the top of the page to remind us it's all about Christmas,' I persisted.

'Prickle,' said Sang.

'Yes, that's right. Holly has prickles. And red berries. See the red berries.'

'Prickle,' said Sang firmly.

Next day for our holly lesson, we drew some holly on the blank page. Or rather, I drew some holly and Sang watched crossly out of the corner of his eye.

'Prickle,' he said. The leaves were prickle, the berries were prickle, the stalk was prickle, the name was prickle. Holly always had been called prickle, was certainly called prickle back at Chillen Home and that was all there was to it.

'At Christmas,' I wrote in clear type opposite the picture, 'we have holly. It has red berries and green leaves. It has prickles too.'

Further down the page I wrote, then read aloud, 'Can you write prickle? Can you draw a prickle?'

'Maybe,' he said.

With a pencil placed in his hand, he could and he did. Hurrah. The Christmas project had begun and we were on our way. By drawing his dark, cramped, and crooked prickle, he discovered he liked hearing and talking about presents, holly and December.

'At Christmas,' began the next page of the next lesson, 'we say "Happy Christmas" and we write "Happy Christmas" on Christmas cards. Can you write "happy"?'

'happy happy happy', he wrote, copying the word as I pointed and chanted.

'Can you write "Christmas"?'

'Christmaschristmaschristmas', he copied.

'Can you write "Happy Christmas"?'

'Happy Christmas, Happy Christmas', he wrote. And 'Hap kissmore,' he said.

We practised saying 'Happy Christmas' to each other. We were different people walking about the room, round the table, greeting one another with different voices, different gestures. End of lesson.

The following day we moved on to learning about the mysterious shapes of parcels which can disguise or enhance the contents. A round-shaped parcel contains . . . a ball! A rectangular-shaped parcel contains . . . a picture book! What on earth does a teddy-bear shaped parcel contain? We practised wrapping up objects in brown paper and presenting them to each other. Hannah and Lawrence, passing through the room on their way to make hunky peanut butter sandwiches for their tea-time snack, joined in out of a sense of family support. Donald joined in out of genuine interest at the new game, enthusiastically wrapping up carpentry tools taken from the cupboard under the stairs. As we received our parcels, we practised being pleased, even when our present turned out to be a blunt screw-driver, a rusty tin of old nails or a duster.

Sang found he liked the game of giving. Unexpectedly he launched into it during Sunday lunch. He slid down from the table, took a small wooden duck from the toy box, carefully wrapped it in pink tissue paper and carried it round to David.

'For you, present.'

Then he reclaimed it, rewrapped it, and presented it to me.

'For you, I give present.'

Then again, and again, round the table, with a childish air of importance, the giver as centre of attention.

Babies and toddlers discover the pleasure of this game, tirelessly donating one of their toys to a parent or visitor before reclaiming it to offer elsewhere.

David gave me a glance of embarrassed pain. 'This is two-year-old stuff, isn't it?' he muttered, as he graciously accepted a wrapped building brick. Had our great big boy no sense of self-awareness? Of course he hadn't. And anyway, wasn't the behaviour of a generous boy-toddler infinitely preferable to that of a selfish grabbing adolescent?

Day by day we progressed with Mum's twelve-part course in Christmasology.

At school his class was learning to recite a seasonal rhyme which was apparently about money, icker money, poor old people, and big fat hen. Eventually it was revealed to be 'Christmas is coming, the goose is getting fat. Please put a penny in the old man's hat.' This, with heavy indoctrination from mother Rachel about sharing with those who are poorer than ourselves, became another lesson, though Sang showed little compassion for whoever these poor might be.

'They go get some money,' he said with perfect logic. 'Then they not be poor.'

When the first Christmas card arrived that year and we opened it, looked at it, talked about who it was from and finally hung it up on a string stretched across the room above the sofa, Sang cried out with astonished pleasure.

'We do that Chillen Home!'

He had recognized that the traditions in this household were not, after all, so very distant from the ones he had experienced elsewhere.

As his and my confidence grew, and it became clear that Christmas was not the same as 'kiss', I introduced an advanced lesson in the etymology of the word.

'"Christmas" is two words put together. "Christ" is a name for Jesus. "Mas" is a word for a party or a special day. So Christmas means Jesus' special party day.'

I wasn't too sure he'd got all that. I elaborated.

'And his special day is when we think about his birthday, as well as about presents and parties for us.'

Sang easily recognized the importance of 'birthday'.

'Like my birthday! My birthday soon.'

'Yes, like you,' I agreed. 'In fact, nobody really knows exactly when Jesus was born. Just like nobody really knows exactly when you were born. But all the best people have secret birthdays.'

Donald was still young enough to believe that the subject of birthdays was sacrosanct. He was not old enough to recognize propaganda when he heard it.

'Not all the best people!' he interrupted indignantly. 'I know when my actual birthday was because I was born here, wasn't I?'

I altered my propaganda. 'Some of the best people, such as Sang, and Jesus, and the Queen, celebrate their birthday on a different day from when they were born. And others of the best people know exactly when they were born.'

'And I was born in this house, wasn't I?' Donald said.

'That's it. And Jesus was born in a draughty old stable.'

'A bit like Grandpa's woodshed,' Donald added.

'And Christmas Day is the day we think of Jesus' birthday. And as we can't give a present to him, we give them to each other instead.'

On the blank page facing this information, Sang drew a smiling woman saying 'hoppy birthay' to a waiting crowd of tramps, pensioners and some footless dwarfs. First in the queue is a man with ragged clothes who, in a balloon issuing from his mouth, says 'No presente.' He is followed by two crippled old women on sticks who don't want, or else aren't expecting presents either. A fourth man walks away in the opposite direction. Two tiny children with canary yellow hair (signifying that neither of them was Sang) are receiving most of the presents and danced happily out of the picture.

But Christmas-Birthday-Present, that amorphous event, did not come speedily enough. Sang grew restless. Why couldn't it be tomorrow?

Granny Verily sent, as every year, an advent calendar. Now we could see that Christmas Day was a particular day, with a date and double doors, could see that Christmas Eve too, was a particular day, and that each day when another door was opened drew us nearer to those big double doors of the twenty-fifth. Getting angry about the slowness of time to proceed did not alter the numbers which were written on the doors.

Our Christmas book had a significant section on birthdays. To people asking, 'When's your birthday, Sang?' would come the oblique answer, 'Last year, I had it,' or 'Gonna have cake for birthday,' or 'Hannah had her birthday.' Even if he didn't know much about Christmas, Sang reckoned he knew about birthdays. He knew that Hannah had already had her birthday and it wasn't fair. But he still didn't accept that a person's birthday was connected with a given date in the year. In our society, date of birth governs most of the important things that happen to you.

On our advent calendar we could see the door for 15 December waiting to be opened to reveal its tiny printed picture. We wrote 'Sang' on the door, and the door already opened for 4 December had 'Hannah', and the door for 23 December had 'Lawrence'. But there was no door for 29 December, so where to write Donald's name?

'Poor licker Donna. He got no door,' said Sang.

'I don't mind,' said Donald stoically. 'It's much better having your birthday after the Christmas rush.'

In the Christmas book we wrote and then read aloud, 'Some people have birthdays in December like Jesus.

'Sang's birthday is on 15 December.

'Hannah's birthday is on 4 December.

'Lawrence's birthday is on 23 December and

'Donald's birthday is after Christmas on 29 December.'

I too was learning things, like that slow learners need to be taught the same thing many times over before it even begins to be learned. Sang did not seem to grow bored of the frequent repetition.

'How old will Sang be on his next birthday?' asked our lesson on birthdays.

'How old will Hannah be on her next birthday? How old will Lawrence be on his next birthday? And how old will Donald be on his next birthday?'

There were spaces where we would fill in the ages after

we'd talked about them. Sang had not grasped the concept that, at a person's birthday, they moved on one number, stepped forward to the next age.

But why should he have? In dealing with the other children's birthdays, this system was perfectly straightforward. But where Sang was concerned, laying down these rules was a nonsense. His birthday was not his birthday. His age was not his age. It wasn't just innumeracy which confused him. It was that his own age had indeed moved up, and down, and two years running had been the same.

They were preparing a Christmas play at school. Sang had been selected as one of the kings.

'Because I been good boy,' he explained.

It was, we gathered, some kind of reward for the fact that he no longer had screamings in class. He had a part to learn, though when we tried to ask what, he said it was too difficult to explain and we'd have to wait and see.

In the Christmas book, he drew a picture of a robed, crowned figure and asked me to write beneath it, 'This is Me. Sang is the king.'

On the afternoon of the performance, the school hall was packed, and stifling with the aroma of that day's dinner still lingering in the air.

By the time one has seen several children through primary school one has witnessed a good many nativity plays. Yet, whether one's child is a shepherd with a tea-towel, a sheep with a bell, an angel, a wise man, or the mother of God, every enactment of the story always feels like the first. I felt tense with excitement. I longed for him to get it right.

Sang processed in, barefooted, through the dining hall, with his brocade curtain cloak, his cardboard crown, his gift of Terry's All Gold studded with silver foil decorations quivering in his hands. He was a magnificent king, reverent without being pious, sombre without being sad. He had two pages to walk behind him who occasionally overtook and had to wait till their king caught up. When at long last, he reached the retarded schoolgirl with the dolly in the manger, I waited with eagerness and anxiety to hear him speak the lines he had been learning.

'I bring gold,' he said quietly but clearly.

He had got them right.

Afterwards, I talked to the mum sitting next to me. I wanted her to know, everyone to know, wanted to tell them all, 'My boy played one of the three kings, the one with the gold.' When I asked if she had had a child in the play too, she turned out to be one of the dinner ladies and seemed almost affronted at the suggestion that a child of hers should have to come to special school. Perhaps she didn't know how enormous was Sang's achievement.

The play was given a second performance in the crypt of the cathedral in the week before Christmas. As we were ushered along by the sidesmen, we caught a glimpse of the three kings waiting in a side chapel, barefooted here too on the cold Caen stone, with the shepherds and angels twittering like winter birds.

The second king wore the same NHS black plastic-rimmed glasses as Sang, had dark straight stiff hair, a neat snub noise and occasionally wore a similar, contentedly vacant expression.

'Could be twin brothers, couldn't they?' said their class teacher, patting her pew to make room for us. 'Aren't they just darlings?'

She too must have seen her share of tea-towel shepherds and tinsel angels.

Afterwards she introduced us to the second king's father. He tried to explain to us what his son's brain was like.

'You see, it's like a peeled orange inside.'

He seemed totally mystified yet fascinated by why his son should have a brain like this. At first I thought he was describing some medical abnormality.

'And it's all quite perfect inside. There's no lesions. But it's as though one of the segments of the orange isn't there. He's really very clever. He can recognize exactly where we are on a car journey, even if we've only been there once before

210

and yet, there's these gaps. Like the missing segment. Whole things simply don't add up. So strange. Our other boy's not like that at all.'

I had never thought of Sang's brain being like an orange with a missing segment. It seemed to me more like an empty jug waiting to be filled up with good things.

On Christmas morning the children climbed into our bed to open their stockings. The big ones brought us tea on a tray and a bulgy sock they'd filled with jokes and funny presents. David opened up the miniature bottle of whisky and handed it round for each child to have an experimental swig with their tangerines. When Sang began to draw out the parcels from his stocking, joyfully, he unwrapped his chocolate coins and handed them round, enthusiastically he shared his sugar mouse so that all could have a nibble. Alleluia! Alleluia! The miracle of Christmas. His only complaint was about the taste of whisky.

On Boxing Day Sang got his and Donald's teddies to perform a puppet show on the kitchen table for us to watch. By himself, he organized chairs in enough rows to seat a large audience, and cut up dozens of scraps of paper as entrance tickets.

The performance itself was incomprehensible. Nonetheless, it was a happy, a triumphant Christmas. Alleluia!

16
SHARING THE LOAD

'What's the point in having two parents if you're away half the time?' Lawrence demanded. 'Why don't you and Dad divorce properly, like everybody else? Then at least we'll know where we are.'

As some things began to seem better, others began to fall apart.

It was difficult to explain satisfactorily to a thirteen-year-old why David and I, though still claiming to be a devoted couple, were going to spend more time living separately.

One should never make bargains with God. However, I had done so. Right at the beginning, after one of the poo-and scream-ins, I had lain in a hot bath trying to recover and made a private suggestion to God. I vowed to give up committed writing for two years (innocently assuming then that Sang's situation could be tidily 'resolved' within this set period of time) if he agreed to 'make everything come all right'. These were my words, not his. I didn't know if God had even heard because he hadn't answered in any clear way.

I had, I felt, kept to my part of the bargain. I had kept my writing work to small-scale articles and reviews. I had not attempted to start anything demanding. When an editor had amazingly offered me an alluring full-time job, I had turned it down. God, if he had indeed entered into my bargain in the first place, had kept to his side of it in that we had been led to love Sang deeply and were slowly being also led to see him as the kind of person he was rather than as the kind of person we had hoped he would be. But the two years were now up.

Some people with jobs and families manage by writing all night. With Sang on the prowl, the nights were often quite busy anyway. Besides, it was more than just me having time to restart writing books. It was also how to have the time to stay married. Caring for Sang was a full-time job. He needed constant supervision if he was to be kept both safe and happy, and it was quite apparent by now that the intensity of care wasn't just a temporary necessity for a year or two but was a long-term project in which David had been taking an increasingly bigger share. We took turns with the nights, with the cooking, with the caring. Still we were physically and emotionally drained. There was a constant swing from elation to despair. We wanted the family to survive. We wanted our marriage to survive. But there seemed no time ever left over for being married, for 'remembering to care for each other' as David's colleague had advised us we should.

Many couples could, and did, cope splendidly. But many more did not. We felt hounded by the knowledge that, among families with a mentally handicapped child, marital breakdown was ten times more likely than the average. When we had been really desperate, my youngest sister had come, bringing her own two small girls, to look after our four as well, so that when David had to make his trips to Glasgow or Lyons, or Montpelier, I could go with him. On one such journey, in November, we took a night-train which delivered us at Lyons main station at four a.m., it had seemed like a curiously uncomfortable and unromantic way of trying to make time to be together. It was on these excursions from 'normal' life, that we began to realize the kind of perpetual strain we were living with. Somehow we had to change things.

If looking after each other properly was the first step to looking after the children, then choosing to live apart was our solution to looking after each other. We called the new arrangement 'flexi-parenting' rather than separation.

From my stepfather we had bought, at knock-down price,

a falling-down stable which we were doing up as a long-term holiday home. It was still in a primitive condition, but it became our second home for the away-parent to live in. Donald was nearly eight, old enough we hoped, to cope matter-of-factly with having an alternating mum and dad. Hannah was fifteen, old enough to be 'in charge' if an emergency cropped up when no parent was home by tea-time.

A fortnightly parent-shift was usually the absolute maximum that the home-parent could tolerate without cracking, but was just long enough for the away-partner to begin yearning for the demands of home life again.

Becoming a single parent was tiring and desperately lonely, with that type of desolation that comes only when surrounded by the noise and exuberance of healthy children. Each time that it was David's turn to leave, I planned daft jobs to occupy us as I couldn't bear to watch him set off with his briefcase and toothbrush. One January morning, I took the children round the streets just ahead of the council refuse cart and made them help me gather up and drag home all the discarded Christmas trees which the big shops had just thrown out and we planted them in our back yard to make it look like a Siberian forest. It was a totally useless activity but kept the miseries at bay.

Changeover weekends, Friday evening to Monday morning, began to take on all the bitter sweetness of whirlwind romances. The children entered into the spirit of these rapturous home-comings. They appreciated the novelty of the fresh, yet familiar, listener to their news of music, Scouts and school.

'Look at these. Dad's got me these new trainers while you were away!'

'D'you want to see the way I've rearranged our room?'

'Have you heard about my report?'

On my first departure, I felt as guilty as an absconding wife. But once away, the release from minute-by-minute responsibility lapped around one like limpid waves. For me, it was the repeated broken nights which were most destructive so, initially, it was always sleep that most needed catching up on. Even though the bed in the stables was damp and slightly mouldy and the room exceedingly cold, occasionally with water trickling down the inside walls, I could sleep for twelve or even thirteen hours at a time. Often I seemed to hear Sang's voice shouting out in his sleep, just as in reality he did at home. There was no phone so the away-parent had to bike off to a phone box. Once, I got through to Donald who, hearing my voice, immediately dissolved into tears. He'd just been shouted at by one of our aged neighbours about playing football near her garden fence.

'She told me to go back to where I'd come from, never come round here again,' he sobbed.

We were used to elderly people in the area occasionally being rude about Sang, either because of his uncontrolled behaviour, or his race. At least it made a change if now they were being abusive about Donald instead.

'Couldn't you have told her that you were born in this street and that it's your street too?' I suggested.

'She wouldn't understand. You don't know what it's like, Mum.'

I felt wretched. What kind of mother is it who isn't around when her child most needs her? I tried to comfort him down the line.

'Where's Dad then?'

'I can't tell him,' Donald wailed. 'He wouldn't understand either. Anyway, he's busy hanging out the washing.'

'You go and tell him. I'm sure you'll find he wants to understand.'

That call was an exception. Mostly they were all too busy getting on with their lives to talk and it was reassuring to know that they weren't missing me as much as I missed them. From David I sometimes got only a brisk, 'Can't chat now darling. Just got the supper on the table. Then there's Cubs, and then PTA meeting.'

When I was home-parent, I was often just as curt with David if he rang at the wrong moment.

For longer-term comfort, there were the children's letters. Even Sang took pleasure in sending cheerful pictures and making full use of his twenty-five-word written vocabulary.

'der mum tody I good time dad cook good food I see good tv tody I go school tody Tody I see cat I see dad I see you.'

David and I too discovered that the separation created an opportunity to express by letter the kind of loving sentimentalities that we rarely got around to actually saying. One of the older children finding one such soppy letter lying next to the cereal packets at breakfast said, 'Gosh, I didn't know you and Daddy still wrote letters like that to each other.'

We had sometimes worried that, because Sang needed so much attention, the others were becoming neglected. Under the new system, so we assured ourselves, with one parent concentrating single-mindedly on running the family, they all got a better deal. We tried not to ask ourselves if it was really good for them.

'Mum's less bad-tempered than when Dad's here as well,' Hannah observed. 'But more morose. And actually I can see more of her. I know I can have good long chats with her without thinking she's really wanting to get away and talk to Dad instead of me.'

But what about David when I wasn't there?

'He makes terrible jokes at meals to cheer us up. He watches more telly than when you're both here. He lets us stay up later too.'

Overall, David was more easy-going, though his cooking, according to the children who did the washing-up, was always greasy fry-ups or splattery roasts.

'Thank goodness for a Mum salad again,' Hannah greeted me on one returning Friday. 'Dad just doesn't seem to care about vegetables.'

Lawrence said, 'Dad doesn't bother about having baths half as much as you. But he does get very cross with the cat. He threw her out of the back door and nearly broke her leg. He takes everything out on her. It's really not fair and she doesn't like it.'

Donald said, 'It's really nice with only Dad here because he reads me really good stories.'

I had thought that I read him good stories too, but as a time-saver, I had got into the habit of reading a shared bedtime book to both him and Sang which meant always choosing an undemanding compromise. David did the bedtime routine properly, choosing each child a separate and appropriate story.

Though none of the children positively approved of flexi-parenting, they tolerated it. Surprisingly, Sang, whom we most feared would react badly, actually found it easier relating to one adult at a time. He benefitted from a highly structured day with lots of repetitive support, and it was easier to keep to the routines when one knew that time spent with him was not time spent neglecting, or feeling neglected by, one's spouse.

'You do always sometimes go away,' Sang said with a hint of reproach on one of my returns, then with unexpected insight added, 'You do get fed up. You do get tired. I been a bit a pest.'

'But I always come back again, don't I darling?' I said. 'And so does Dad.'

'I guard you when Daddar not here. I help you doing thing.'

'Yes, you all look after me, don't you? I'm so lucky.'

But the absence of Daddy somehow reminded him of his earlier reliance on sausages. When he saw boiled eggs for breakfast he scowled and said solemnly, 'No gank you I not hab no breaktis, no noth.'

I coaxed a bit about the need for some kind of nourishment to give a chap mighty strength before the walk to school. 'And I'm sure you remember how you told Dad you were going to be so sensible all the time he's away? And I expect he may even be bringing a present back with him.'

Sang decided that he would, after all, eat a bowlful of Sugar Puffs as well as the egg.

'Presents from Daddy. Hm!' Hannah muttered from behind her own cereal bowl. 'Bribery and corruption.'

David began working as a professor in a French university. He commuted across the Channel, returning in time to take over his turn of flexi-parenting. Uprooting all four children, now aged between nine and sixteen, and putting them into French schools where they wouldn't know the language, let alone have friends, seemed in some ways exceptionally cruel. But not half as cruel, according to the older two, as having to go on enduring our system of flexi-parenting. So we all uprooted together and moved to live in Normandy for a year.

The head-teacher at Sang's school was shocked at our decision to take Sang. It would be less damaging to his development, he said, for him to be temporarily fostered with somebody here in England and so continue in the same school than have to make this big move. We, however, believed that consistency of family life was more important than consistency of school life and that we should all stick together. We also felt that if this opportunity to widen their horizons was good for the other children, then it would be good for Sang too and was a risk worth taking.

As a first stage in the widening of horizons, we took the children on a four-week 'grand tour' of France, Switzerland and Italy, staying with friends or in youth hostels which, in Italy, were often disused palaces. We wrote on the back of Sang's hand in indelible ink our name, passport numbers and some contact addresses just in case he should get lost in the swirling crowds around the art galleries of Venice or Florence.

After the grand tour, Hannah and Lawrence were plunged immediately into the hurly-burly of *collège* and *lycéé* where the course controllers made few concessions to their being foreign and unable to understand French as well as their peers.

For Sang there was no equivalent in the French educational system of the special needs school he had been at. The educational psychologist suggested four possibilities. He could go to a newly opened school catering specifically for Vietnamese refugees (curiously called, even in French, *Les Boat People*), or to a college for sub-normal teenagers which prepared them for the adult world, or with Lawrence to the ordinary secondary college for eleven-to-fifteens and hope he'd survive, or, the fourth suggestion which we opted for, could go with Donald to the local *école primaire*, (primary school) where both boys joined *une classe d'initiation à la langue française*, a special intensive class for newly arrived immigrants, lasting one year, after which the pupils supposedly moved out into mainstream schooling.

Mostly, Sang was super-stoical about all the changes. He didn't actually seem to be very concerned that he was in another country, and since he had such a tenuous grasp on any language, the fact that everybody spoke French was of less concern to him than we'd expected. We soon realized how much of his understanding in English had been achieved not by listening to what was said but by watching people's movements, then making a guess at what might be going on. He applied the same method when coping with French, throwing in an all-purpose *'Oui monsieur'* to anything that seemed as though it might be a question which expected some kind of response from him.

He settled easily into class. There were few other pupils, and he was the eldest by several years. The teacher was experienced at handling disturbed, confused children newly arrived in this strange land. She was even used to big boys wetting their trousers and had a special supply of dry trousers of various sizes in a cupboard.

The school day was long, from 8 a.m. till nearly 5, with Saturday morning school too. However, there were Wednesdays off.

Donald found the first few weeks in the *classe d'initiation* terrifying. So Sang's more easy-going insouciant attitude was supportive. For the first time their roles were reversed. Sang could actually make a positive contribution towards caring for his younger brother. Their racial differences were reversed. In England, Sang had been the only non-white in his class. Now Donald was having a turn at being the only white child in their class. The other seven pupils were Tunisian, Algerian, Turkish, also a Vietnamese girl who had just arrived in Europe with her family, and three Cambodians who had spent the previous seven years in a refugee camp in Thailand. They had witnessed brutally frightening events and when they came to our flat, the eldest girl clung to the radiator with a look of frozen terror rather as Sang used sometimes to do. Their father had been shot and their tiny trembling mother was obviously still in shock.

None of these pupils were, according to a chic Parisian friend, ideal companions from whom to pick up quality spoken French. In fact this friend under-estimated the effectiveness of the direct teaching method or the determination of children who wanted to learn. Within weeks, Donald, and the eldest Cambodian were beginning to communicate with one another with reasonable fluency and soon had enough French to start real lessons in the main school.

Though he was co-operative in class, Sang was not really expected to make any progress in French. But the teacher's emphasis on vowel and consonant practice seemed to have some beneficial effect on his English pronunciation. And simply being in France was like a living Geography lesson in that he was learning about such things as coming across the sea, and how the bread came in unfamiliar shapes.

One afternoon as a particularly typical Frenchman with beret, baguette and bike pedalled slowly past, Sang exclaimed with the delight of sudden dawning, 'Mum, that a French man! This France!'

His English school had given us readers and workbooks to use during our time away and so, every evening, with weary resignation, we plodded on with our stumbling attempts to master the three R's. He learned to tell the time to the nearest quarter of an hour and to count up to ten. But we had to come to terms with the fact that, however much effort went on putting into learning to read, Sang was never going to become 'a reader' in the sense of being able or wanting to read for pleasure. However, it seemed not yet too late to give up trying to encourage him to become a user of books so that he might have some activity to fill the empty hours when there was no telly to watch, or when the others were doing homework.

We read aloud to him consistently, almost persistently, from the Grimm Brothers, Hans Christian Andersen, King Arthur and the Knights of the Round Table, C.S. Lewis. I wanted him to be drenched in words, in stories, in language. Surely some of it might stick? He responded enthusiastically to Jack the Giant Killer, the small boy appearing to vanquish all his foes by strength, in fact by stealth. But what on earth was he making of Theseus fighting the Minotaur, or of Icarus who flew over Knossos and saw below him the vast labyrinth his father Daedalus had built for Minos King of Crete? He never asked as Donald had done, 'What does "Knossos" mean?' or 'Who was Aegeus?' So did he understand anything of the Greek myths?

Sometimes as I read aloud a new story, I simultaneously recorded it on to tape so that he would have it there to listen to again. The novelty of being taught how to use a cassette player pleased him, though it was immaterial to him whether it began at the beginning or in the middle or even at the end. Stories for him didn't need beginnings, middles and endings but were a continuous stream of comforting spoken sound. With speech improvement as an end in sight, we tried using the commercially produced story cassettes, particularly those with an accompanying picture book, but the speaking voice was usually far too rapid for our slow-thinking child to follow. Besides, taped stories, even if listened to in the right order, were no substitute for the close one-to-one attention of a read-aloud story and a cosy cuddle.

Every Wednesday, the school rest-day, while the other two boys were having their trombone and French horn lessons in the Conservatoire de Musique, Sang and I went across to the public library on the other side of the road to look at books. There was another non-reading book-user we sometimes saw, a tall gangling youth, poor-sighted, inarticulate and retarded, who also spent Wednesdays crouched over a toddler-sized table, oblivious to the smaller library subscribers around him as he worked his way methodically through a pile of cowboy cartoon books chortling to himself.

The children's library was modern, attractive and extremely well-stocked with foreign titles, including many English ones. Finding the right kind of books that Sang might actually enjoy, as against endure, was largely a case of trial and error with many failures along the way. My naive belief that by reading aloud to him, as we had to the others, from such fine storytellers as James Reeves, Kevin Crossley-Holland or the Grimm brothers, the fluid language would somehow rub off on him was entirely ill-founded. Rather, he was confused by rich language. He much preferred picture books where he could see what was happening. The Asterix strip-cartoons, though no use for reading aloud since the puns, the plot, the historical ironies and the non sequiturs went over his head, were nonetheless a good source of visual excitement, especially when one character could be seen bashing up someone else. He liked any picture book to do with hospitals, dentists, operations, war, fighting and television, as well as anthologies of newspaper cartoons, for though the political or topical references passed him by, the detailed drawings of human peculiarities delighted him and seemed to be giving him an entré into the adult world.

The extraordinary gaps in general knowledge continued to open up like gaping craters. One day, in the *bibliothèque publique*, as we sat at one of the tiny child-sized tables looking at a picture storybook, I realized that he didn't understand the meaning of spring, not only didn't recognize the word, but had no idea what seasons were. We took so much for granted. Yet how could this boy be thirteen-and-a-half years old and not understand spring when outside the apple trees were laden with blossom and the grass growing lush and green? What sense could he have made of our Sunday excursions to admire the Normandy countryside in spring? Then

I felt annoyance at my own failure to notice when he was not understanding.

I fetched another picture book illustrating the seasons. Sang, immediately sensing that more pointless indoctrination was coming his way, became cross. Of course he knew what I was on about.

'Sea-side!' he said, angrily pointing to 'summer' to show he knew. 'Dat Christmastime!' he pointed out 'winter'. These two were quite enough for anybody, nor did they need to follow some repetitive rhythm. As Sang knew perfectly well, sometimes it is cold, sometimes hot. Some days there are flowers, some days snow, such changes being random occurrences in an ever uncertain world.

17
SEEKING IDENTITY

The assorted lowerings of Sang's age had made his physical development seem to begin at an alarmingly early age, and certainly well before he was ready. He was teased in the school showers because of his pubic hair and manly genitals by other twelve-year-olds who still had little-boy figures, while his deep broken voice seemed strangely out of place as he dug in the sandpile with little cousin Bertie.

My friend Pat, visiting one day, asked who was the man she could hear in the next room.

'That's Sang, watching telly,' I said.

'Yes I know Sang's there. I waved to him through the window. But there's a man in there too. I heard him talking. I wondered if you'd got a student living with you?'

Sang knew he didn't want to grow up. 'I not be man,' he said. 'I be licker baby boy.'

As his thirteenth birthday approached, his fears of growing up increased. Repeatedly, he told us he wouldn't have a birthday this year, didn't want a change. Just because his emotional and mental age was in one figure, it couldn't prevent his body age keeping to chronological and hormonal time. Yet he was already halfway to being a man. So together, we compiled a chart listing those things which I knew he admired about big brother Lawrence.

Being 13 is good because you can
a) *stay up late*

Being 13 is good because you can
b) wear size 6 shoes
Being 13 is good because you can
c) drink some wine on Sundays
Being 13 is good because you can
d) grow a beard and a woolly willy

With respect to clause c) his next birthday cake was laced with apple brandy and under clause d) he was given a battery razor to use on the beard.

He had an unusual relationship with his own body, as though he didn't quite know where it began and ended, or even if it was all his. He seemed to register little pain when he opened up old wounds, or picked at the skin till it bled. Shoes tightly laced on the wrong feet caused no discomfort. When he had an infected cut on the sole of his foot, he didn't complain; it was only through his repeatedly blood-stained sock that we realized. Sometimes, instead of picking at wounds on his own arm, he would move his attention to my skin and try to remove my freckles and moles.

'Won't come off! Get it off!' he said. Once, ill with a cold, he asked me to tell him, 'Have I got headache?'

Compared to the complexities of coping with the emotional life, seeing him through the various necessary medical processes to treat his distorted mouth and hearing was, though long-winded, all perfectly straightforward, merely a matter of making appointments, keeping to them, sitting in queues, holding his hand, explaining what was going to happen to him, and being profoundly impressed by how brave he was.

After many dreary visits and tests at the hospital hearing clinic, the consultant concluded that Sang's hearing loss, consistent with exposure in infancy to loud noises, was irreversible and there was actually nothing anybody could do about it, except to ensure that his ears were always kept syringed out.

As for his mouth, there was more scope for improvement. The orthodontic treatment lasted four years. First came a programme of straightforward oral hygiene to improve the health of his inflamed red gums. The decayed teeth were filled, and he had several taken out. Although he found the hospital atmosphere alarming, he was again extremely brave. Sometimes he fidgetted just when an X-ray machine had been carefully positioned beside his jaw, but he rarely complained about injections, pain, or indignity. Then began a programme of being fitted for and wearing a series of braces and moulds, straps and springs until, by the age of fifteen, he could actually close his lips together and his smile became endearing rather than grotesque. There were now several good reasons for him to practise keeping his mouth closed. If it wasn't permanently hanging wide open, he looked better, his breath smelled sweeter, and most important, the continuous slight pressure of his upper lip over his upper teeth would, according to one of the consultants, help prevent the newly aligned teeth from all springing out sideways again.

With vague notions of idealism and liberalism, I'd thought at first that race didn't matter, that differences were unimportant for within a short time of Sang's arrival, we had ceased to see the ethnic differences, or rather, we saw through them to the boy inside. Maybe race didn't matter to us. But it mattered to the rest of the world. When we went out shopping together, I knew that people noticed, eyes flicked from his face to ours, back to his, then away. It wasn't usually hostile, just human curiosity.

In the early days, he seemed to believe that by joining our family he would eventually develop Caucasian features.

'Wish I been born like you,' he would sometimes say. 'Wish I got yellow hair like my licker Donner.'

He would often examine himself in the mirror.

'Look merm!' he said one day. 'My face going like you now. My hair going curly.'

So we would stand together in front of the mirror admiring him as he was.

'Look at that nice thick black hair you've got. Isn't it shiny and strong?'

'See Sang's lovely skin, such a good colour. And it won't get burned in the sun, will it?'

Gradually he did come to see the permanence of his own racial identity. If we passed another Asian child in the street, he would tug at my hand and whisper, 'She look like me?' When we encountered a party of Japanese tourists going round the cathedral, it was Sang who stared back at them, open-mouthed, drawn by their similarity to himself.

When he came to understand about babies growing inside a mother's tummy and being born from her, he had to learn that, however much he wished the reverse, he had not been born from my tummy. Instead of accusing me of not giving him enough presents, he now wanted to claim me as a biological mother. Flattering though this was, it was far more reassuring when he reached a stage further and could examine himself in the mirror and say, 'I like me like this. I not gonna change now. But I wish I had that other mummy who look like me.'

As he grew to feel more like himself, so we tried to become more like him. Our interest in South-East Asia was kindled by his presence.

From many of the national adoption agencies was coming disapproval over non-white children who had been adopted into all-white families and 'turned into whites' rather than having been provided with a proper sense of their true roots and cultural identity. This was countered by unhappy reaction from long-established white parents pointing out that they might not be perfect but, at the time, they had been a darn sight better than no parents at all. The conclusion of the debate was that all parents must be encouraged to help their child feel familiar with and proud of its origins. We had to create for Sang an identity which was simultaneously appropriate to his racial origins and to his current place in a white Western family.

How to tell him in simple terms, gracefully, and without it seeming like approval of violence, that his origins lay in a country which had been chopped in half, much of whose culture had been destroyed, whose national unity had been shattered? The concept of civil war in which brothers and sisters, parents and children, end up fighting with opposing armies is hard to understand for any of us. For Sang it was quite incomprehensible. For some time he was convinced by his own catchphrase summary of the South-East Asian war, 'We Japanese. We won.'

There are many specialist or 'problem' picture books to help a child over the threshold of a new experience — black adopted baby, black West Indian older adoptee with white parents, handicapped brother, child in wheelchair. But nothing about Vietnam. We searched in vain to find the book which showed the geography, countryside, the people, the customs of Vietnam. Any book available in Britain was for adults about the strategies of war. Since diplomatic relations had been closed, and Vietnam was in no position to develop a tourist industry, there was no access to colourful leaflets which might show the prettier side of Vietnam.

So we enlarged our collection of Chinese background picture books, carefully by-passing the fact that the Chinese and the Vietnamese had been centuries-long enemies. Sang couldn't read the text and at least the children in the pictures looked nearer to himself than blue-eyed blondes. Even France, which caters for the cultural assimilation of its immigrants more wholeheartedly than the UK, offered no great surprise store. However, while living there we were able to find some strip cartoon children's books, written in French and telling Vietnamese folk stories. We went out to eat in Vietnamese restaurants and we heard Vietnamese spoken.

At first, Sang positively resisted some of our attempts at Vietnamization. When I learned to say one or two phrases in Vietnamese and suggested that Sang might like to learn them, he declined. He was not particularly interested in the Vietnamese strip-cartoon books from France, nor in the cassette

228

of Vietnamese pop music. Yet at the same time, it seemed to be important to him, an essential part of our relationship that, even though he didn't want to hear about it, we should continue to find out all we could.

Just as he had had to be shown how to conform to normal everyday ways of eating or dressing, so with the onset of manhood, he had to be led firmly towards another aspect of social acceptability.

Hannah said privately one day, 'I don't really mind hugging Sang when he's wet and I don't really mind his bad breath too much. But I don't think it's right him wanting to come into my bed for a hug when he's pee wet and sperm wet and got an erection.'

I had become aware of how Sang liked to come into our bed as usual, and now to rub himself against me. How were we to treat this delicate issue? In infancy, he had been denied proper physical contact, then in his boyhood he had been offered it. Yet now, we seemed to be wanting to discourage it. He still needed and craved the comfort of physical contact. So how could maternal and sisterly affection be offered without it being sexual stimulus? He needed to be reassured that sexual feelings were not in themselves wrong, and that a big willy in the morning was good, but not to be shared with the Weetaflakes.

'And anyway, if he's my brother, it's incest,' said Hannah.

When I overheard myself explaining in short sentences with easy words that wet dreams and early morning erections did not come down to breakfast, I felt quite embarrassed on my own behalf, yet also pleased that Sang seemed to be not only listening, but interested.

'Your willy is a very good willy. And it's all your own to take care of,' I heard myself saying. 'You already take care of yourself, don't you? Clean your teeth, brush your hair. Put on your glasses. Your willy is yours to look after too. You can play with it in your bed. That's your own private place isn't it, where you can do what you like. Then when it's breakfast time, everybody puts their willies away inside

229

their pants and we all come down with our daytime clothes on and all eat food.'

One day when Sang was lying in the bath, he called out to some of Hannah's schoolfriends who were downstairs, that they must come up and talk to him. This seemed to be an unconscious desire at sexual provocation.

We had not encouraged him to lock the bathroom door since he wasn't always adept at undoing locks, nor did we want to encourage a repetition of the time when, trying to be independent, he had decided to take a bath on his own initiative, filled the tub up from the hot tap only and, without testing the temperature, stepped straight in scalding both feet.

'OK, them girls not come and see me. What if they want to? I lock door to keep em out,' Sang suggested.

No, I said. The bathroom door need not be locked, just closed. That way, everybody would understand he was enjoying his privacy, but if did happen to need help, somebody in the family would be able to get in.

It was surely a lot less difficult than the learning that must be dished out by parents of mentally handicapped girls. At a meeting for adoptive parents of mentally handicapped children, we heard one mother explain how she had totally failed to teach her Down's daughter to manage her own sanitary towels until she began taking her into the bathroom with her during her own periods. Actions spoke louder than wordy explanations.

When he came home from school, Sang liked to come up behind me and nuzzle the back of my neck with big slurpy kisses. He was probably only imitating what he had seen film stars doing on B movies on the telly. But that did not mean that either of the grannies would know. Nuzzling necks, like erect hugs, had to be discouraged. But if maternal and sisterly hug-ins were now becoming prohibited where was he to get the physical contact he needed?

David made a conscious effort to hug him more, big friendly bear-hugs. So did Lawrence. So did our ordained friends. Donald went on romping in puppy fights on the floor just as they always had. The various uncles followed suit and also hugged more.

Not everybody approved this re-routing of hugs from the female relatives to the males.

'It really won't do!' said Granny. 'The way the uncles are always hugging Sang like that. I've already told them not to.'

'It's all quite open and friendly,' I said. 'He likes it, and needs it.'

'But don't they realize that it's going to turn him into a homosexual?'

18
JOURNEYS THROUGH GRIEF

The process of coming to terms with our son as a permanently retarded human, whose learning difficulties were not a brief and curable condition but an everlasting fact of life, was the hardest part of any of it. Other aspects of Sang's life we accepted, we adjusted to. But this one was a like a brick wall. Again and again, like an action-replay of an appalling accident, we seemed to reel from the shock and bounce back to re-live our worries over again. We argued, we queried. We saw improvement where there was none. We refused to see what was obvious before our eyes. We cried. We stopped crying.

And we learned that for other parents too the discovery that their child was mentally retarded had been like hearing that the child had died. And the stages of grief through which they had passed were often just the same as those following actual clinical death.

When Simon's mother first heard her son diagnosed as autistic, she wrote how it was, 'As if he'd just fallen to pieces in front of my eyes. Everything had just been totally and irreversibly shattered.'

And Jessie's mother, after hearing Jessie diagnosed as having Down's syndrome wrote, 'Our world collapsed about us. I remember the quiet voice talking and my immediate desire was to run — any escape — because what she was saying was unbearable.'

Hospital staff are well aware that how parents first learned that their newborn baby had Down's syndrome enormously affected how they would later cope. Yet, in the case of older children, or those with less instantly recognizable mental handicaps, the same concern was rarely shown. The professionals involved naturally assumed that somebody else had already explained. Usually, nobody had.

I met Mark's mother on a Special Educational Needs teachers' course to which she and I had been invited as 'speakers' to offer our first-hand account of the parents' viewpoint of the effects of the Education Act 1981. Mark's mother was herself a teacher. She recounted how, when Mark was five years old, by chance she had bumped into his primary school headmistress in a supermarket one Saturday. Over their loaded shopping trolleys, the headmistress casually mentioned that the meeting to arrange for Mark's 'statementing' would be taking place the following Monday. This was the first that Mark's mother had ever heard about it. She had no idea that he was thought to be mentally retarded and was to be moved to a different school. She did not know what being statemented meant. Six years later, in the seminar room with the assembled trainee teachers, she wept in the seminar chair beside me as she remembered that brutally unexpected revelation. I didn't know what to say so I put my arms round her and cried too. The trainee teachers watched.

It may be hard to understand the depth of loss felt by parents of even mildly retarded children. Even when the diagnosis is received with some kind of relief that what has been secretly suspected was being recognized, parents are numbed by overwhelming loss of the anticipated child, the abrupt ending of natural expectations, plans, ambitions. Yet since the child is still so palpably alive, grief is churned into a turmoil of concern, confusion, despair, fear. Some parents feel unable to take it in.

As shock recedes, parents grow angry that the child who might have been, the chess-player, the football player, the future producer of grandchildren and the protector of old age, has been taken away. We all want to grab back the progeny of our dreams. Indignantly, we wonder why it has happened to us. What have we done to deserve this imperfection when all our friends have able-minded offspring with positive futures to look forward to? In self-defence, we look around for someone to blame. For some, anger is turned inwardly against themselves, or even against the child.

Where a handicap is caused by some genetic fault, parents often blame the 'guilty' partner. Others say how they rail against the supposed Creator. Or righteous indignation is directed at families who have not managed to hold on to and care for their handicapped child. Publicity given to the successful adoptions of Down's syndrome babies regularly provoked my neighbour whose own, dearly loved Down's daughter was now in her thirties to rage at those 'weak' parents who had 'relinquished their responsibilities' by having their child put into institutional care or who put them up for adoption. 'I've cared for my daughter for all these years and of course it's been difficult. But I love her. How dare these people think that they can just give up?'

After I had stopped being angry with Sang's speech therapist for introducing the phrase, mentally handicapped, into our home, I shifted blame to the Americans, all Americans. I found it hard to speak to any US citizen without demanding to know what part, if any, they had played in the 1960s Peace Demonstrations. Soon, I shifted blame to the French, even though their involvement in South-East Asia had ended long before Sang was born, then to the newspaper which had sponsored the airlift bringing Sang to the UK. I blamed the housemother for withholding information about him from us. The anger of this grief was fuelled by a conviction (which at the time seemed perfectly logical) that if only she hadn't falsified the records, Sang would have been all right.

David felt the anger of grief as outbursts of fury against himself for not recognizing the signs sooner. He had been trained as a teacher, even got a distinction for his Education degree. But what had been the use of all that theoretical

234

knowledge when he couldn't even see the symptoms of learning difficulties in his own son?

'Of course I should've known!' he would shout. 'Every time I heard you trying to teach him to read. Always going over the same ground, day after day and him having to relearn the same things again and again. It was obvious!'

And then his anger would turn into rows between us even though we were both on the same side.

In bereavement, there is often a stage of refusing to accept that the dead person really has gone for ever. A widow hears her husband returning home and putting his key in the lock, sees him suddenly in a crowded street. An extensive search begins to find the missing person, to create the posthumous bond, by re-reading old letters or diaries, by experimenting with the occult, or simply by noticing vivid family likenesses in the deceased's descendants.

Similarly, parents grieving over a handicapped child deny what they have been told. They may appear to understand the irreversible nature of their child's condition, yet as soon as their anger has burned out, start to search extensively to regain the 'lost' child, by seeking out the perfect cure, through therapy, or by attributing the child's problem to some lesser and reversible disability. John's mother was always telling me that her son was deaf, and how his apparent retardation was entirely due to this undiagnosed deafness. She was immensely distressed when, after tests, it was recommended that John should go to a school for learning difficulties rather than to one for deaf children. The subconscious refusal to accept the unacceptable probably explains why even experienced parents can fail to recognize a disorder as obvious as Down's syndrome in their own child, or, even if seeing it, are convinced that their own child shall not be affected by it.

In the face of the evidence, David and I convinced ourselves early on that if Sang was given the stimulus that he had previously been denied, plus a good nutritional, spiritual and intellectual atmosphere, he would begin to catch up. After all, the housemother's report on him had said that he would catch up by his early teens. As a result of our efforts, we saw progress day by day, even hour by hour. Even after we had recognized the beginning of his learning difficulties, I still anticipated that with our support, he could take and pass public exams in English and Art.

Seven years later on, tidying his room was like going through a catalogue of our search to find the hidden boy. It was also a catalogue of the failures. Not his. But ours, for trying so hard to change him.

The Meccano Set, suitable for age nine, given to him at age fifteen: discarded.

The Duke of Edinburgh Scheme pass book: D of E scheme launched into it at age fifteen, abandoned after six sessions.

The knitting of coloured squares to make a baby blanket, no a teddy's blanket, all right, a single completed square to be a mouse's blanket: three rows completed (by me).

The jig-saws: 2-piece jig-saw, completed; 25-piece jig-saw, nearly completed. 100-piece puzzle: still unopened in its box with the cellophane wrapper. 'I hate jij-see puzzers,' he would say. So did I.

The red diary to help him learn about such abstractions as days, months and the passing of time. For him, time was never measured in books, but according to hunger. Time was those dull bits in between the last meal eaten and the next one to come.

There was also the music therapy, the canoeing therapy, the painting therapy.

Attempts to stimulate a retarded child back to normal intelligence are useful ways of making oneself feel better. There were some successes. For instance, the swing in the garden. By the age of thirteen, Sang had learned to get on to the swing by himself and to move himself backwards and forwards without needing to be pushed, a sport which became his socially acceptable substitute for rocking. There

236

was his unfaltering willingness to colour in with felt-tip pens. This we interpreted and proclaimed as artistic talent, and, as 'proof' of his ability, we submitted one of his colourings-in for a national art competition. To ensure that we weren't disappointed, I noted on the back that he attended Special Educational Needs school. Sure enough, the competition organizers decided to award several 'special' certificates with small 'special' prizes. At the time, this certificate provided what we needed — instant solace. We were able to tell the family about his achievement though we didn't tell them how I'd ensured he won. Seven years on, finding that certificate and the never-used prize paint-box in the drawer, along with the eight balls of coloured wool, the three rows of knitting, the D of E Award enrolment book, the diary, the loathed, detested construction kits (couldn't he at least learn to tighten up nuts with a spanner, we had thought), it was one more reminder of how desperately we wanted to be duped, wanted to avoid the truth that he was never going to grow up in the same way as the other children.

The normal — and competitive — world charts children's growing-up against measurable standards of progress.

'How's he coming on?' carries an implication that the child ought to be 'coming along'. One can lie and say 'Very well,' brag about art prizes won. Or one can be honest and say, 'Not at all well. In fact, it's all a big worry and we simply don't know how to cope. What on earth can we do?' But parents often find that people don't want to hear too much more about this parental anguish, specially if the child is beyond infancy. Dappy helpless babies are cute enough. Dappy adolescents likely to be roaming the neighbourhood are a threat. Parents feel judged on how quickly, and how well, they learn to accept the situation and control the child. 'She's taken it terribly well and she's so good with him' is a seal of approval while 'She's still worrying about her mongol' suggests it's time she got over it otherwise everybody will be loaded with the responsibility.

237

Acceptance is rarely made easier by the common condolences parents are offered. Well-meant palliatives, such as, 'He'll be all right in the end,' 'He'll grow out of it,' 'He's probably a late developer,' 'Lots of children don't walk till three,' encourage parents to postpone investigation, to go on denying that there's anything wrong. Cheerful encouragements like, 'At least he's alive,' 'At least he doesn't look funny,' 'At least he hasn't got a hare-lip,' 'Well, he's not as bad as some children' inhibit parents expressing real sadness about the disabilities which the child does have.

David and I found the supposed palliative, 'Well at least he's only adopted' painful, both for its implication that our anguish could be rated on some comparative scale, and the suggestion that as an adoptee, Sang was a lesser child. Another common condolence was, 'At least you don't need to feel guilty about him.' But why should any parent feel guilt?

The truly insensitive or inappropriate condolences, 'It's a pity children like that don't die at birth' or, (as a social worker acquaintance observed of Sang), 'It's a pity he looks so much more normal than he is; he really seems quite all right till you get to know him,' infuriated but were, curiously, better than nothing at all.

When, instead of seeking signs of improvement, parents say they begin to notice the benefits of the kind of child they actually have, they are nearing acceptance, even if these 'advantages' seemed pathetically futile to others. For instance, Danny, multiply handicapped with cerebral palsy, and who went to the same family support group as Sang, was always dressed in pastel shades which on any active boy would have been quite impractical. But as his father, proudly holding to those positive qualities which Danny did have, explained, 'Other parents can't let their children wear these kind of colours because they'd get so dirty. But our Danny never gets dirty!'

Some parents eventually come to regard their handicapped child as some kind of special gift or bonus.

As our neighbour sometimes told me, her handicapped daughter had more friends than almost anybody she knew because she had such a lovely nature. 'It if weren't for her, I know I'd be having a very lonely old age. As it is, the house is filled with all her young friends (the voluntary workers at her hostel).'

Another parent we knew found that even after twenty-five years, he was still only able to regard his adult Down's son as a child who had failed to come up to his own hopes until one day, taking his son out from the long-stay hostel for a treat of sausage and chips, he was caught unawares by the fact that, at long last, they were actually enjoying each other's company. 'I am surprised at the pleasure I feel at seeing David. The disappointment remains but now, once a fortnight, there is also real pleasure and enjoyment of each other.'

The stages of grief overlap, ebb and flow, so that often we regress time and again to earlier levels of despair or anger. When, finally, I began to realize that Sang's retardation really was irreversible, that no amount of tender training, patterning, caring, loving, feeding, sorting Lego men and coloured wool, could ever make any difference to his intelligence, the hurt of this secondary despair was overwhelming, like a physical pain in my side. I had migraines, piles, polyps, inexplicable pains in the legs, mouth ulcers, palpitations, cold sweats, nightmares, wrist pain. I had panic and fear, and fear of fear. There was fear of death and longing for death. Because of the confusion and clouds in my head, I couldn't see God and didn't care anyway.

'But why us? Why us?' Why couldn't we have had one of those cute little bright-eyed kids who win gold medals for sport and scholarships to college and are a credit to everybody?'

As receiving, not birth, parents, knowing that we 'brought him on ourselves', as my mother put it, didn't diminish this stupid envy of other people's clever adopted children who change and progress.

'But nobody made you have him, did they?' said my

mother. 'I really don't think you can expect to get sympathy when you never had to have him in the first place.'

Perhaps only those who have themselves sunk as low in the belief in the worthlessness of themselves and their child can empathize with the feelings which lead some people to want to reject or kill their handicapped baby.

As a way of ending my pain, I found myself dreaming of killing Sang. When I realized the utter terribleness of this dream, I allowed myself instead to think about finding him quietly dead in his bed in the early morning. It would have been easier I felt, to have come to terms with a truly dead child. Even though I knew from my sister Alex, whose first baby died, that the pain of loss through death is never healed either, I felt that at least this failed child would not be there every new day, as a perpetual reminder of what he might have been. For the ghost of the able-minded child lingers on so that the gleam of intelligence in a normally uncomprehending eye, a random expression of such apparent understanding can briefly trick one into believing that the whole thing has been a bad dream. I saw too, how it would have been easier for others to tolerate our sadness if there had actually been a funeral.

Little things continued to niggle showing how, at some levels, I still was not accepting. A friend, hearing me arranging for a baby-sitter, expressed surprise. 'Aren't your boys a bit big for that now? Surely they grew out of needing baby-sitters years ago?' And I felt unexpected rage that a) I hadn't myself noticed how odd it was to be still needing to organize a baby-sitter, b) that I should have to explain to my friend that the mentally handicapped don't grow up like other boys and c) that we would go on needing baby-sitters long after her sons were needing baby-sitters for their own children.

Before we can entirely accept, we may have to forgive who-ever we feel is to blame. The believer has to forgive God for what he has done. The genetic disability carrier has to forgive himself or herself. The professionals who may have given wrong advice, too much medication or not enough, have to be forgiven. We may all of us also have to forgive ourselves for still minding when we feel we shouldn't. I had to forgive my mother for failing to understand.

Gradually anger burns itself out. Searching ceases as the Nobel-prize winning, chess-playing, reading, thinking person is not found.

After a death, the final stage in grieving is the letting-go of the lost person, the moving forwards to a way of life which is in the present and the future, not only in the past.

For families bereaved through handicap, there is letting go both of the expectations one had for the future of an ordinary child and there is also preparing to think about the physical letting-go of the care of the child. But relinquishing such vulnerable children into what seems an unprepared and unaware world is often unthinkable.

After a decade or more of unshared care, many older people have turned into 'handicapped parents', and the dependence of their handicapped child has come to give them their entire *raison d'être*.

However positively the bereaved approach re-growth, an underlying sadness remains which can be rekindled by significant anniversaries.

For some mothers, it is the subsequent arrival of another child which revives the latent grief so that the birth becomes a time of renewed mourning as well as of celebration.

For us, grief re-surfaced when we came to fill out a form which would entitle Sang to receive the Severe Disability Allowance. No longer could we shelter behind the pretence that he was, after all, only a schoolkid with plenty of time ahead. It felt like total betrayal of his trust in us that we should agree to words which described that this dearly loved young man was suffering from 'gross immaturity' and 'at least 80% disabled'. It was like a repeat of the speech therapist's metaphorical slap in the face.

'It's only words, Mum,' Hannah said. 'He's still the same

brother whatever the bit of paper says. Words can't hurt him. Don't let them hurt you.'

Perhaps we were beginning to reach the end of our grieving when, almost to our own surprise, we found ourselves discussing with the children over supper who we might adopt next.

19

TOWARDS THE GATES
OF MATURITY

By the time Sang was officially fifteen, a new anxiety had
snaked itself into my mind and lodged there fast. Although
he was not so profoundly retarded as to need his every
moment supervised, yet I only had to catch sight of him
with the vacant expression staring into space, or banging
a piece of wood against a chair to feel fear for his future
rearing up. The demands of Sang would be with us, now
in the present, day by day, and into the years to come for
ever and ever Amen. What eroded hope was the daily drip
drip drip, the three lurches sideways for every step forwards.
There was, for example, the three weeks teaching him to use
a can-opener so that he would be able to feed the cat, which
he liked doing, only to find that at the end of the fourth week,
his apparent success with the can-opener was entirely lost and
we began all over again at the beginning.

Alongside fear came an insidious doubt about the rightness
of his original placement with us. Clearly, said Doubt, we
had been misguided in believing that we had been divinely
led. He had always been wrongly placed in this family. Here,
where the main activities were quiet, thoughtful, academic,
intellectual, creative, was a totally inappropriate environ-
ment. Chess, music, looking at books, reading, what on earth
was there of any use or satisfaction to him in all of these?

The recurring sense of Sang as outsider, as square peg in
round family, was symptom not of his adoptedness but of his

handicap. Many natural parents have said the same, how they felt that their mentally handicapped child always felt somehow different from the others, 'doesn't fit in to anything we do', 'seems to be part of another family'.

Doubt is dangerous. It makes you go blind. In our frustrations with the present, and anxiety for the future, we didn't let ourselves see those other attributes of this particular adoptive family which fulfilled exactly Sang's needs, which had actually helped him form interests, and which provided him with his security.

Meals, family, people.

Regularly eating orderly meals together in a family, meeting other people beyond the family, going out together as a family. Scouting, camping in the woods, long sociable mealtimes with the aunts and uncles, the constant come-and-go of visitors to the house, the theatre-going. How many other ten-year-olds had had the unlikely, entirely unintended, yet as it turned out to be, wonderful experience of being taken by their brand-new father to a West End production of Dario Fo's unsuitably vicious, violent, political, satirical *Accidental Death of an Anarchist* and, without understanding a word, laughed themselves silly with delight throughout? Or to a seven-hour production of *Henry IV Part II*, in Paris, in French, and been so transfixed by the colour, movement and music of the spectacle that they did not want to go out during the interval?

But life wasn't entirely a round of theatre visits. There was the everyday to get through. Keeping our foundling-changeling happy and occupied through the weekends, the long draggy afternoons after school, became increasingly difficult. While the other children, as they grew older, became more self-reliant, absorbed for periods of time in their own interests, Sang, as he struggled out of childhood, became less and less interested in anything, less able to concentrate on any of the activities which were within his scope. The drawing, the Lego building, the playing with toy cars and little plastic men, the listening to records or story-tapes, all were

244

now despised. He knew he was not a little boy. He dismissed anything that he felt to be suitable for little boys, anything that he had formerly enjoyed, with 'Aw no, that babyish!' Yet he did not know how or want to become a big boy.

Being a teenager is always tough. We had seen how Hannah and Lawrence had been attacked by erratic periods of lethargy, uncertainty, excess vigour, restlessness. During the holidays, unable to settle outdoors or in, Sang moped miserably about the kitchen. Soon after the end of one meal, he began waiting for it to be time for the next. Eagerly and noisily he started to lay the table in the hope that this might encourage the family to emerge from whatever they were doing and re-group in the kitchen so that life could pick up its momentum again. When the table set for tea at half past two didn't make tea-time happen, he became cross and sat rocking.

Just ignore him. Teenagers need to be left alone, said the voice of wisdom. But how can one ignore someone one loves when one knows they are unhappy?

During one irksome Easter holidays, David and I found that we had to go back to a daily schedule of flexi-parenting as the only means of survival and sanity.

One morning, when it was David's turn as Sang-companion and mine to stay quietly at my desk, I found the non-stop sound effects coming through the walls were so bizarrely inconsequential, so persistently distracting, that even the clatter of my electronic typewriter wouldn't shut them out. I stopped typing and listened to what was going on next door.

Sang and David in Kitchen Entertaining Each Other One Fine April Morning

Clapping hands, clap clap clap.

Laughing.

Nose-blowing.

Happy burbling chatter with sudden change of topic from, 'Lawer, Lawer (Lawrence) back from colleger when? When he?' to 'Hannah do it. She do it.'

David: 'Do what?'

Sang: 'Can I come too?'

A moment's silence and sound of plate-stacking. Perhaps David doesn't understand the meaning of the question either.

'Dad, Dad, I found my moustache! Dad Dad!'

Sudden burst of music. Radio is turned on.

Silence. Radio is turned off.

Liquid-being-spilled noise.

'What time Dad? It two o'clock, one o'clock.'

(I glance at my watch. It is just before twelve o'clock.)

'I do weeding.' Though expressed as a statement, I know it to be a question.

Sound of Sang going to window, opening same.

'I do weeding?'

David: 'What?' David is clearly perplexed. Though I spend a lot of time gardening, Sang has never shown any interest in joining me in the flower beds.

Sang: 'Weeding? Mum say I do weeding.'

David seems to understand at last. 'Oh reading!' He knows that Sang hates reading, and that this is possibly a diversion from going out with David to fetch a barrowful of chopped wood for the stove. 'No, not now. We're getting lunch ready, aren't we? We'll finish that first. You can do some reading with Mummy this afternoon.'

Sound of window being closed.

'I glad sun is shining sometimes always. Dad, Dad, dat is meant be jags consent?'

'What?'

'I say dat is meant be jags comment? Can't you hear?'

'What? Sorry, didn't quite understand. Try again, Sang.'

'Oh don't matter.'

I gave up pretending to work, threw in the sponge, and went and poured two glasses of beer for myself and David. To Sang I gave a glass of juice and a chocolate biscuit for which he was disproportionately grateful. Even an impromptu midday snack for three persons was better than no meal at all.

Can we really, I wondered, put with with the intensity of this barrage of frustrating nonsense for the rest of our lives?

'What happens,' I said to David later that day, 'when he leaves school? What on earth are we going to do then?'

'We'll go on looking after him,' he replied calmly. 'Just as we are now.'

'We'll probably go bonkers,' I said.

'Yes, some days maybe we will. And some days we won't. Just like now.'

'But his education. He can't just rattle around at home all day. And he needs to do more than go on to Adult Training College.'

'We'll leave no stone unturned until we find just the right thing.'

Easier said than done, I thought. But David's ability to trust was, at that point, stronger than mine.

The literature we read suggested that the sooner parents start planning for their handicapped children's futures, the better. The school, however, seemed to think we were precipitous and over-anxious.

A whole year-and-a-half till his leaving date? So what was the hurry?

He was entitled to remain at school until he was nineteen. But no one at his school ever did stay on, and they had no age-appropriate provision there for older pupils. So he'd probably go to the tech wouldn't he?

There was a beginner's introductory course to various skills and trades — plumbing, brick-laying, carpentry. Through the school, Sang started going there one afternoon a week. He was bemused about why he went and what went on.

'We have good tea break. You go into canteen. You can choose.'

'Yes. And what else? What do you do in the class?'

'Ah.' Thoughtful pause. 'Today teacher shout me. Say I thick.'

'What are you learning about this week? Was it very hard?'

'I ask him what do, he say he tole me last week.'

'Perhaps he didn't understand you?'

'I not go again. Hurt your hand do that. Not doing that wall again. No thank you.'

'I'm sure it'll get better as you get more used to it.'

'Just stupid what we do there tech. He talk talk talk. Then he do writing on blackboard. I dunno what he say. He not talk properly. I can't read all that lot writing.'

He flung his notebook on the table. Each student was issued with a record book in which to note the skill for the day and the names of the tools used.

Sang's entry was written very carefully and neatly in his own hand and read, 'inEets TNOsnixfox DOMB RPEe fox Dniar'. He had, he said, copied it off the blackboard. He had no idea what these mysterious words meant, or what tools he had used during the afternoon. Since I knew the words were meant to be a list of carpentry tools, I took David's tool bag out of the cupboard to see if Sang thought any of them were the same as he had seen that afternoon. Sang didn't recognize anything, except the chisel.

We suggested that next time he could ask the relevant teacher to write the words for him. The following week 'slide rule, chisel, plane' appeared in his record book though Sang had no better idea what these items were and whether or not he had used them.

Anyway, woodwork was over. It was time for plumbing. Soon he carried home from college like a holy relic a length of copper piping, cut through and soldered into a T-junction. We knew that this is what it was because 'T-junction' was written in teacher's hand in the record book. We were all suitably impressed and the object was placed reverently on the window-shelf for admiration and approval. I dusted it some days.

Sang's pride in this piece of piping was not for his own achievement in its making but for that of the teacher. Sang had not taken any part in the cutting and soldering of the T-junction.

'Teacher done it for me. He very clever.'

The T-junction remained exhibited on the shelf as testimony to Sang's incomprehensible Fridays. It seemed to us that Sang was still a long way off being ready to start vocational training. The course had expected a greater literacy and numeracy than Sang had, and the teachers, though no doubt skilled in their own areas, didn't seem to have been specially trained for working with slow learners, or at any rate, learners as slow as Sang. Yet we were still hopeful that he'd be able to cope with something more demanding than going to an Adult Training Centre each day.

'If you have a child with any special needs,' I read in a publication put out by the National Children's Bureau, 'you will often have to take the first step towards finding services and help.' I went to the Citizens' Advice Bureau. 'Your social worker should be able to help you better than us,' I was told.

What social worker? The health visitor hadn't been to call on us for three years, nor the speech therapist, and certainly no social workers. Desperate though I felt us to be, clearly we were seen as a family who could cope admirably on our own.

So we sent away to National Development Group for the Mentally Handicapped, the Linkage Community Trust, the Voluntary Council for Handicapped Children, the National Children's Bureau, the Elfrida Rathbone Society and the Rowntree Fund, for brochures, leaflets, booklets. We listened to programmes. We went to see careers advisors and special educational directors in as many counties as we could legitimately claim we might be about to move too. We added new phrases to our vocabulary: *Development of Social skills, service options, transition to work, training for independence, open employment and sheltered housing, independent living and sheltered employment, close living situations, advanced social training units.* We saw glossy photos of gracious country houses where happy dappy young people in greasy overalls were changing car wheels, in painty overalls were re-papering ceilings, in earthy overalls were growing tomatoes, in white aprons were laying tables. Looking confident and relaxed, these young men and women were learning to be useful citizens. If only, if only, our darling boy could be one of those. If only we could find the place that wouldn't be too hard, and wouldn't be too easy, but was just right. There seemed to be fewer courses than we had hoped, and the two most likely, Dilston Hall and Pengwern College, were both residential and very far away, one near Newcastle, the other in North Wales. We couldn't let Sang be sent away, surely? We talked incessantly to anyone who might, possibly, have some good ideas. And by chance we met, camping near my mother's home, a Special Education teacher-friend of Alex's who was just about to start working on a new General Life Skills course which was not residential, and was, he said, designed for people of exactly our son's ability.

He had got to know Sang during the camp. We were very excited. So was the teacher. He discussed what might be the most vital life-skill for Sang to start work on, on a tailor-made curriculum. Since getting to the centre each day was going to be the first obstacle, learning to use the local train should become the first term's goal. The idea of Sang ever being on a train by himself seemed unlikely. But this jolly man sounded so enthusiastic, so positive, that I wished Sang were old enough to start immediately. However, he suggested we wait until he himself had settled into the new post before contacting him again to talk about the finer points of Sang's entry. We waited a couple of months, then rang up. Alas, his interest in handling difficult adolescents had already gone off the boil, and he was in fact leaving education and going to start a new career playing in a jazz band.

This small setback, discovering that one amiable young man had changed direction and lost interest in the needs of retarded teenagers, in the needs of my retarded teenager, was disappointing, but we went on turning over stones.

Our mood could be made or broken by the kind of response we got to an enquiry, by the type of casual information we picked up. How we grieved when some officious expert suggested on the telephone that we were wasting her time. But how we cheered in our souls when we read (in the National Development Group for the Mentally Handicapped Pamphlet Number 3) that 'Meeting the needs of mentally handicapped school leavers and their families is one of the most urgent tasks of community service, and also one of the least costly'.

'I not do the A-level,' Sang said, half an announcement, half a fearful question. He knew that A-levels were some great dark abyss into which he had observed Hannah tumble, and into which Lawrence was about to tumble.

We reassured him that he would not do A-levels.

'And I not do job. I not know do job. What I do, if they say, you do that job?'

'No, you certainly won't have to do a job, not until you're ready to.'

'So what I gonna do, then? What I gonna do when I leave school?'

We endeavoured simultaneously to involve Sang in the decisions about the future, since it seemed better whenever possible, that choices should be made not *for* him but *by* and *with* him, yet at the same time keep any negative details of our educational search from him.

Although his sense of time was shaky, he knew that after fourteen had come fifteen, and that after fifteen would come sixteen, which was when he saw all the big boys at his school disappearing from the scene, being swallowed up by the great unknown. And where was he going to go then?

'They go now. Not see them no more.'

'D'you know what they're doing now?' We would try to begin an optimistic conversation about the great opportunities lying ahead for young men.

'Gone away. We not see them no more never.' As far as Sang was concerned, they'd disappeared and that was the end of them.

'Well you're not leaving school for ages and ages,' we told him confidently. 'More than a year. You don't have to worry about it. You just have to trust.'

251

Did he know what trust meant? Did we know?

'Do you feel nice and safe when you're at home and it's cold outside? Do you feel safe that there'll be enough Weetabix for breakfast tomorrow morning? Do you believe that Dad and I will always try to do our best to look after you the way you need? Good. Then that's called trust. And you must trust that we'll sort out the right thing for after school. Leave the future to me and Dad to worry about and you think about the present.'

'Present? What present? When big boy leave school, sir give them a present. Pencil set and pen.'

As the time got nearer to his leaving date, he was asked to come to interviews with us. At one meeting with a careers officer, Sang seemed to close his ears and eyes to everything that was being discussed. He stared steadfastly up at the ceiling even when spoken to directly about his name, age, school, or interests. At another, when we went to the Open Day of a training college, he turned his back on, or walked away from any member of the staff who tried to start talking to him, then on the drive home afterwards, he curled up on the back seat like a small baby and sucked his thumb.

'I so tired,' he said. 'I only little boy. I been good boy today.'

How do you make someone grow up who doesn't want to?

He was not normally a loner. He liked, needed and responded to being with people. But it was always with our friends, not his. He was unable to get involved, outside home, with young people of his own age. He preferred being with adults who, out of friendship to us, made that bit of extra effort to relate to him.

Sang's hobbies were watching telly and eating meals. But in order to grow up, he needed to socialize outside home, to be with his peers. And since he wasn't able to do it for himself, we had to do it for him, like a blind date or an arranged marriage.

We tried Storytime at the junior library. The stories were at his level but he was two or three heads taller than the others gathered cosily on the floor and he soon noticed this. We tried the swimming pool. Sang was a strong but ungainly swimmer. One club was for seriously competitive swimmers only. The other was the handicapped swimming evening. We went. But a crippled woman whose disability seemed to have crippled her humanity as well as her legs yelled at Sang for swimming too splashily and for not being handicapped enough.

'Go away! Get out of the pool!' the poor woman screamed. 'Or I'll call the manager. This club is only for disabled people like me.'

When I explained that Sang was a club member too, she screamed at me, saying he certainly didn't look it.

After that Sang didn't want to go again. Nor did I much want to have to take him.

There'd always been a youth club one evening a week at school with darts, rough games, quiet games, music, and standing around in a contented adolescent way, at which students from the teacher training college came to help. But when the organizing teacher retired, there hadn't been enough enthusiasm from other staff to preserve the club's life and the volunteering students were not long enough fixed in one place to set it up alone. The local PHAB (Physically Handicapped and Able-Bodied) club seemed at first a good idea, but its members were older and wheelchair-bound rather than mentally handicapped. However, on the same premises, we discovered a new, younger-age, youth club opening up. Sang was soon enrolled into the nine-to-thirteen section. As usual, he related mostly to the helpers rather than the other kids but he was happy drawing, making cardboard models, occasionally watching other kids play darts. And the secretary agreed that even though he was over age, since he was enjoying himself in that section, he should stay.

But one evening when we went to fetch him, he was already lurking out in the corridor waiting for us. He was in great distress and so was the club leader, a heavyweight of a man. In fact, the leader was very angry.

Boys of Sang's age, he said, weren't allowed in this section. Sang wasn't to come back, not after the trouble he'd been causing. The idea of Sang as a trouble-maker sounded astonishing, even encouraging. It took a long time to unravel what had really happened. Eventually we discovered that a small gang of eleven- and twelve-year-olds, quickly discovering Sang's gullibility and keenness to please, had taught him some worldly phrases without, of course, telling him their meaning. They weren't very obscene and indeed, in Sang's usage, were mostly quite misplaced. However, hearing Sang enliven the club language with inappropriate 'Give over's, 'Push off, can't you?'s, 'Piss off!'s and 'None of your business!' caused the younger kids to riot with delight. On the entirely valid point that Sang was over-age, he was asked to leave and not come back.

Warily, he agreed to be taken to the next club, for fourteens-to-seventeens. He was instantly out of his depth. No other member was taken and fetched by a parent. We taught him laboriously to make his own way there and back. One of the middle-aged helpers taught him to play table-tennis. So long as she was there, Sang went. Several boys were starting to do the Duke of Edinburgh Bronze Award and one of the club helpers was keen that Sang should join in. Recently, amid much and proper publicity, a young woman had won the D of E Gold Award, the first-ever person with Down's syndrome to do so. The table-tennis helper assured me she would handle any problems Sang might have coping with the Bronze Award.

Unfortunately for Sang, the youth worker chiefly in charge of the D of E Bronze was the club leader who'd thrown Sang out of the younger section. But he reassured us by saying that if Sang was a keen Scout, he was already halfway to the D of E Bronze.

After less than six meetings, Sang came home early, weeping.

'Darling, what's the matter?'

Something to do with map-reading. Sang's team had to

254

plan a hike route. This involved learning to map-read. Sang showed us his wad of a dozen closely printed pages of notes. We sat down quietly over coffee and I read them aloud to him.

'But I gotta learn it. He say so. He said I stupid, not try. I not going back.'

'Sure you can go back. Course you can. No one can force you to learn all this.'

The following week, I escorted Sang to club, found the leader and explained over again that Sang was defined as having learning difficulties.

'He's a slow learner,' I said.

'That's OK. That's fine. All he's got to do is remember what I told him last week, hasn't he?'

'Quite so. Though of course as you know, being able to remember is one of the key problems of children with learning difficulties. That's why they *can't* learn quickly because they can't easily retain anything.'

'But I told him what the map symbols mean last week. Very clearly. He understood perfectly. And I said to him then, "I won't keep on telling you," and he said he understood. Now all he's got to do is learn from the notes.'

I said, 'He's illiterate, you do realize?'

'He speaks clear enough for me. I always understand what he says. And I'm used to dealing with all sorts.'

'I mean,' I said, 'he can't *read*. And since he can't read, he's not too hot on reading the map symbols either.'

'Oh no problem. Leave it to me. We get along fine.'

He was a big, heavy man, friendly, like a mountain bear might be friendly.

For a week or two more Sang tried to cope. He paid his sub out of his pocket-money. He went on playing table-tennis ever more vigorously. He agreed, only slightly reluctantly, to try once more to learn to knit a tie for his D of E craft and he completed twenty rows of plain stitch. Then one terrible evening, he returned home less than fifteen minutes after having set out for the club. Tears coursed down his face like fountains, he trembled all over and wailed unstoppably.

I took off his anorak for him, hugged him, sat him on the sofa, made him a coffee and when a sort of calm had descended, he tried to tell me, between gasping sobs, what went wrong.

'Tease me! Tease me!' he sobbed. The memory brought on new weeping. 'He say, you want come over here and do karate chop? Come and get me big karate chop. Call me Ching Ching Chinaman, want to do karate fight me. I not do fighting. Then they all laughing me.'

'Who, Sang? The kids at the club? The same ones as before? Did you get into trouble again?'

'Not kids. It the man.'

I began to get worried. Had someone tried to molest him in the street on the way to the club? Surely not in our nice quiet cathedral town?

'No, not on way. At youth club, he say it. Want me to Chinese karate fight. Call me Chinaman. Then all them laughing. So I come home. I nebber go back there, nebber, nebber.'

'Do they know you came home? The people who like you there, the lady who plays table-tennis? She'll be worried if she thinks you've disappeared.'

'I can't care.'

I didn't wait till the next week to go round and sort it out. I rang up straight away. The casual helper on the phone was indeed worried that Sang had left suddenly in a state of distress.

'You better speak to the youth leader.'

As patiently as I could I explained that Sang had come home because he felt, wrongly or rightly, that one of the other kids had teased him, had called him a Ching Ching Chinaman, and challenged him to do a karate fight.

The youth leader laughed cheerfully and I was momentarily calmed. It was, as usual, a misunderstanding.

'Oh no! that wasn't one of the kids. That was me.

Thought it'd make him feel more at home, like. Ching Ching Chinaman, that's just a friendly way of talking like. Just in fun, you know. I meant it as a joke. Karate chop — I thought at least he'd understand that sort of talk. I wouldn't ever really fight.'

I felt suddenly as though ice were being poured over me. Cold cold fury at this insensitive brute of a man, and at myself for having ever entrusted our darling boy into his care, for having forced Sang out from the security of his home.

'It sounds to me more like racial abuse,' I said. 'Whether or not you intended to insult him, you have indeed succeeded. And in front of the other people. From another kid, it might have been understandable. From a professional leader, in a position of responsibility, it sounds totally unacceptable.'

'Listen, I'm ever so sorry. Really I am. I never meant him no harm.'

'It's no point saying sorry to me,' I snapped. 'You haven't called me a Chinaman in front of everybody else. It's my son who's feeling insulted.'

'Well I tell you what. We're not closing right away. You send the lad round here, quick before we close, and I'll tell him I'm sorry.'

'OK,' I said. But Sang, now curled up like a hibernating squirrel in his bed, head under the covers, light out, had no intention of getting up and popping off to anything ever again, not even to see *Jim'll Fix It* or John Wayne.

A few days later the youth leader knocked on our front door to apologize personally. Sang had the good grace to return the man's handshake and accept the apology. But he never went back to youth club.

These blunderings by the insensitive and ignorant were, luckily, a rare incident. However, our continuing attempts to involve Sang in the outside world with young people of his own age always met with failure of one kind or another. Other parents told us how they too sometimes felt that their son or daughter had not a real friend in the world. Just at the age when we watch other teenagers striking out, breaking

257

away from parental influence, we see our retarded teenagers become increasingly isolated. They are often only too aware that they're no longer children, so are unwilling to join in childish activities, yet aren't socially and emotionally mature enough to join in ones suitable for their age. The more they stay in with parents and telly, the more they find that this is where their reality lies. The profoundly handicapped teenager, because of having to live a much more closely structured and organized day, often suffers less from isolation and friendlessness.

Outside school, Sang's chief social contact was with Scouts. He'd joined the 14th as a Cub at nine and had always been made to feel welcome, yet not exceptional. There was never pressure on him to compete, to work for badges, to move up to the Ventures before he felt ready, nor to participate if he couldn't. Although some of the expeditions were too rugged, he enjoyed the regular meetings, the five-a-side football, the ten-pin bowling. The other Scouts continued to look after him with a gruff matter-of-factness. But Scouts, however wonderful, was only two hours a week.

David tried to think up a new way of helping Sang get out and meet the world.

'What about a job?'

'But he's terrified of doing a job,' I said. 'If he can't cope with real life, how can he possibly cope with working?'

'Not a proper job. A little one. Just to get him out. A Saturday job. Or in the evenings.'

We went over the jobs that Hannah and Lawrence had started on — a paper round, working in a seaside café making hamburgers, baby-sitting. But what on earth was there for an inexperienced, ungainly young person who couldn't handle money, who couldn't read, who could not always find his way around even in the streets nearest his home, and who himself still had to be person-sat?

Obviously, for Sang, it was a ridiculous idea.

Numerous people have stumbled through Sang's life, some without noticing him, some who are desperately keen to try and do useful things for him, and some who are already too busy with their own affairs to want to get tangled up with his, yet are nonetheless instrumental in shaping his life for the better.

Soon after our unproductive discussion about whether Sang could or could not do a job, there was another of those chance encounters which was to change his prospects.

20
PERSONAL GROWTH

Sang could hardly be termed 'lucky'. To lose your family, your language, your nationality, your health and your country is not a sign of good fortune. Yet his life does seem to be 'blessed'. David and I sometimes forgot that we were not rearing him single-handed but that there were the numerous unseen, unknown angels on call.

Chris was one of those who, without making a fuss about it, helped Sang exactly when he needed it. She was a drama colleague of David's.

She was made redundant when her own college closed and was starting a sports and dance centre. There were to be exercise sessions, weight-training, a hair salon, children's classes, keep-fit for older ladies.

'We'd like to provide something for the mentally handicapped too,' she said when showing David round the half-finished premises. 'Not enough is done for them.'

She didn't know that David was the father of a handicapped person. Hoping that the dance studio might offer another social outlet for Sang to join, he asked, 'What sort of something?'

'We don't know yet,' she said.

Creating a special job for Sang as general helper at the dance centre may not have been her original intention in 'providing something for the handicapped'. But it was what she decided on.

'What would you expect him to do?' we wondered.

'I don't know,' she said. 'What can he do? Well, we'll give it a try and see, shall we?'

On the first day of his trial week, Sang soaked his clothes through to the skin while washing up two coffee cups and some teaspoons. On the second day he broke one of the coffee cups. On the third day, asked to mop the shower-room, he flooded the floor with gallons of foamy water. On the fourth day, ignoring or not understanding a barricade and a sign which said WET CONCRETE, he stepped across a newly laid floor surface, leaving his footprints forever in the concrete. On the fifth day he got paid, real money.

Four pounds was four times what he was used to as pocket money each week. It was in a real brown wage-packet with his name on the front. After examining and counting — to the admiration of Donald — the four gold coins, Sang decided he would like to go back to the job the following Monday and Chris decided that she would have him.

As he was a schoolboy, we had to take him for a medical by the educational health officer to get a youth work card guaranteeing that he was fit for the job and wouldn't be made to do anything dangerous or arduous.

He was to work for an hour-and-a-half each evening after school, Monday to Friday. We walked him to the studio and he found his own way back. Soon he learned to walk both ways himself, deciding by himself what time to set out from home.

He always came and told me he was leaving with, 'Off to work now!' and hugged and kissed me as though he were likely to be gone for a considerable time. Perhaps to him it seemed a long time.

Sang ran into many troubles, usually connected with relating to one of the other employees. He had stand-up arguments with the under-manager because he didn't like him. He fell hopelessly in love with the handsome caretaker who was himself too young to realize how his casual friendship was being received. He got cross when someone other than his new employer asked him to carry out some task. Or

261

they got cross. He was misunderstood. He misunderstood someone else. He felt grumpy because of a bad day. Someone else was grumpy because of their bad day.

Almost immediately, it seemed clear that the studio did not need him there for the amount of clearing-up he did. During the weekends the other staff managed perfectly well without his services.

'Ah, but we do need him!' Chris insisted. 'In all sorts of different ways. We're all learning so much from having him here! It's important for all of us to know that everybody working here matters. Sang must become part of the team too.'

When we tried to thank her for the opportunity she was giving him, she refused to accept our pathetic gratitude and insisted that she treated Sang just the same as all the other staff.

'She nice,' said Sang. 'She always give me big hug when I get to work. Why she do that?'

'Yes, I always hug him when he arrives,' Chris told us. 'He has to know he's loved, doesn't he? Then he can get down to work.'

'Do you hug all your employees?'

'If they need it.'

This opportunity to work at the studio was more than just a job. It was a therapy, which gave every day a focus-point, a place to get out to, a reason to brush his hair, to wash his face and hands. It was a life-line to the real world, giving daily contact with other people and the chance to start learning how to get on with them. He had to learn to control his sulks and grumps, to be civil even when he didn't feel like it. He had to learn to be reliable.

'Don't think I go to work today,' he announced after a couple of weeks when the novelty had worn off. 'It raining. I get wet.'

Further enquiry revealed that it was not so much the wetness of the rain as the fact that there was a programme on telly which he wanted to go on watching. Sang had to discover

262

that, if you want to keep a job, it has to take precedence over *Tarzan* or *Jim'll Fix It*.

His wages, because he had earned them, had a greater value to him than pocket money which was just handed out. With this new wealth he learned a new confidence about wandering around town window-shopping. He was now in a position to buy the boxes of Roses and Black Magic chocolates which he saw advertised on telly. He shared his wealth generously. The chocolates were presented to the family with a flourish of grandeur. He also discovered, more painfully, that though four pounds seemed a great amount, it was not enough for the video-recorder he craved, but that it did, after a few months, put a second-hand black and white television within reach.

He had seen it in an electrical repair shop when David had been taking our record-player to be mended, and it was going cheap at twenty-five pounds because the volume knob didn't work. Since he anyway preferred to watch TV programmes with the sound turned down so that he didn't have to bother listening to incomprehensible conversations, and since the prospect of a personal telly blaring through the thin bedroom partition alarmed Hannah if she was doing homework, this defect was almost an advantage.

Once he had worked out how to make his own way across town, he preferred us to keep away from the studio, rightly regarding it as his territory, not ours. Chris rarely reported back any of the disasters. We heard these from Sang himself. But she always told us the good news. Over the next year-and-a-half, not only could he be left to get on with his clearing-up without constant supervision, but, so Chris told us, he began to notice extra things that needed doing without being asked — to tidy out an untidy cupboard, to wipe down a messy surface. He had indeed, as Chris prophesied, become 'part of the working team'.

Naturally, at home there were still times when, like any adolescent, he felt angry, or sulky, or hard-done-by, or moody. And sometimes he felt just plain sad. But the primeval screaming, those times of uncontrolled, uncontrollable, hopeless, helpless anguish were diminishing, though so gradually that we hardly noticed how or when any more than we had really ever worked out precisely what or who triggered each one off in the first place.

Soon after he had started his job, a further opportunity for social contact came up. Months earlier, when I had had a minor operation, our GP had recommended that we apply for help to a Family Support Scheme run by the local health authority. After being on the waiting list for several months, Sang's name was now linked up with a suitable volunteer family — a young couple with a baby, a rabbit and a big black dog. Just as our other children had friends, now Sang too had some friends of his own. Every other weekend the couple took him for boisterous walks with the dog, or invited him to their home for Sunday dinner.

The job had given Sang confidence and as his vision expanded he could see how the world was filled with exciting prospects. He wanted to do them all.

Visiting Hannah in her first term at Oxford, he saw the beautiful buildings in the autumn sunlight, the cosy little college room which was all Hannah's own and he demanded, 'Where my college? When I big, I come here. Where my college?'

All the way home in the car he asked when he could go to Oxford college.

'Why she go there, not me?'

'They wouldn't let you,' said Donald getting right to the point. 'You haven't got any A-levels.'

'Hannah's kind of college,' I said, 'is for people who like doing homework for hours and hours. And who like reading books. And sitting in the library reading and writing all day. You know you don't like that sort of thing, do you?'

'I do, I do!'

'But luckily there's all sorts of different kinds of places to suit all different sorts of people. And the kind of place we're going to find for you wouldn't be suitable for her.'

If the realization of his intellectual limitations had been painful for us, it was a million times more so for him.

We saw Aled Jones on the telly singing like an angel, meeting fans, signing records, wearing snazzy glittery clothes. Aled Jones is younger than Sang. 'How old he? Why I not sing on telly?' Sang demanded. 'I want sing on telly. I gonna sing on telly.'

'Aled Jones has been training for the past about ten years,' Donald explained reasonably. 'And he's got a good voice naturally, and he can read music. And,' he added more for his own solace than Sang's, 'he's an only child, so his parents spent more time on him.'

'I gonna be on East-Ender. How much money they get pay do that? I gonna do that.'

Most of the things that Sang thought he wanted to do would never be available to him.

Facing up to who he was, and thus who he was not, what he could do, and what he could not do, required real courage. What was and still is remarkable was the positive way that he came to take possession of himself, to accept himself as he is, to accept what had happened to him and how he had come to be where he is. He saw how he had rights and how, within the confines of what was possible, he had freedom. He began to see a certain satisfaction in the uniqueness of his position, and a pride in us as his parents. Just as we used to introduce him when he first came, so now he would present us with a flourish to teachers, fellow Scouts, people at the studio with, 'This my mum. This my dad,' adding, in case there should be any confusion, 'Not my natural mum. She my adopted mum.'

Schooldays were running out fast. We were *still* searching for the right solution, for *any* solution, to continue his education. We heard that a 16-Plus Unit had recently been started in our county, offering non-vocational training specially for those mentally handicapped school-leavers who might eventually be able to work in open employment even if they could never live alone. It was so new that when

265

we tried to visit, we were told we'd have to wait as they'd hardly finished putting up the walls.

From Sang's time at the dance studio we knew he was able to learn, get on with people, and might one day be able to hold on to a real job. The leaflet describing the unit made it sound almost too good to be true, providing exactly the kind of further education Sang needed. No more classroom attempts to master the three R's, but plenty of 'experience in life', expeditions to visit factories, farms, museums, trips to markets, discos with other young people, encouragement to learn to be sociable, to dress correctly, to care for oneself, to think about other people.

But, before we envisaged him already there, Sang had to be accepted on the course. Was he a suitable applicant? What were the qualifying factors? Was he too clever? Or not clever enough? Preparing him for his 24-hour interview felt just like preparing Hannah for her interview at university. And the stakes were just as high.

When we took him over to the unit, he was very shy and very nervous. But the steadfastness he had showed at his job, his long-term enthusiasm for the Scouts, his commitment to trying to become as independent as possible all must have shone through.

When we heard that he'd been accepted, he received congratulations cards from the family and we all celebrated. It was like passing an exam, better than passing an exam. It was like winning a prize, but more important than any kids painting competition. It was the Nobel prize for personal achievement.

Sang was to start at the unit in six months when he was sixteen and a half. He would probably be able to study there for the next two years, so our immediate worries about him were over. David and I felt both relief, and delight. The long struggle was well worth it. Adopting an unhappy child and enabling him to find the right direction was the most satisfying thing in the world. It was more than that, it was the easiest thing in the world. We'd done it once. We could do it again. We had talked about it often enough. We'd just never felt that we had the energy. Now we felt we were ready.

Donald was just thirteen, Hannah at university, Lawrence about to take his A-levels. We knew that, even if they eventually set up in homes of their own, we were always going to need to maintain a permanent home base for Sang. So it seemed almost silly not to try to adopt another child.

We knew there were plenty out there. The numbers living in care had not decreased. We saw their pictures and read the brief, censored accounts of their lives regularly in the newsletters we subscribed to. As well as the estimated twenty thousand in temporary foster or Children's Home care, there were also some six thousand four hundred waiting for new parents and a chance of ordinary family life.

Before Paula came to live with us, we had to be assessed again to ensure that we were a suitable adoptive family. The procedure was less clumsily insensitive than ten years earlier, though seemed nearly as protracted. But as the adoption officer, beginning yet another lengthy discussion about our sex life and whether we had incestuous feelings towards our children, pointed out, 'These children in need have already been rejected too often. We can't afford to make mistakes. We have to make quite sure you're the right people.'

During the assessment period, the adoption workers were chiefly concerned about whether David and I were a stable enough couple to cope with a demanding fourteen-year-old. Meanwhile, members of our extended family were more worried about how the arrival of a newcomer would affect Sang.

Eventually a committee decided that we were the right family and we were allowed to meet Paula. Then she visited a few times, then she stayed for weekends, and looked at the school we had found before moving in 'forever'.

Paula lived with us for three-and-a-half months before it broke down. Or rather, in the jargon of the time, 'the placement disrupted'. After a series of committee meetings, some of which we were asked to attend, some of which were private, two social workers came in a social services minibus to collect Paula and all the carrier bags, pot plants, posters, teddies and hayfever tablets that constitute a life. We did nothing to stop them. I even helped carry the luggage out and gave Paula a kiss and a goodbye present.

But we were shattered by the loss of her, shamed by our own failure to hold on. At least it was a grief we could share with each other.

Some colleagues who had earlier set out to adopt a twelve-year-old only to have it break down, told us how for them it had been like a bereavement. 'All you can do,' they said, 'is maintain some kind of long-term link so it's there if the child wants it later on. But you don't ever get over it.'

So what went wrong with all the careful procedures?

The children talked about it, as did we.

It can hardly have been due to insufficient preparation. Whereas Sang had had virtually no 'family-work' before-hand, and hadn't even been told on the morning he was due to leave the children's home what was happening in case it should upset him, in the modern style of adoption, Paula was meticulously prepared. A 'life-story' full of photo-graphs of past events and family had been collated and hours of individual teaching had been given explaining the differ-ences between institutional and family life.

Was Paula suitably matched with us for race and cultural background? Instead of being an unknown Asian from the other side of the globe, Paula was white Caucasian, of middle-class background, and from the same area in London as I had grown up.

Was it too much money? When Sang came, there was no 'settling-in' grant and we had been extremely hard up. This time round we were sent a substantial settling-in cheque to pay for new bedding, clothes, curtains, school uniform, pocket-money, plus large fortnightly boarding-out payments which would have continued until the adoption was finalized.

We had discovered that however carefully a placement is prepared, however good everybody's intentions, it's a ter-rible risk and it *can* go wrong. After Paula had gone, there was no sense of relief, only the weight of failure. For months we grieved for the loss of the child we had not been able to love, the child we had never really even got to know. The space she had occupied minute by minute, night and day for eleven-and-a-half weeks, was still there, empty. Just because an impossibly difficult lodger has left doesn't mean you don't miss them. The visible and tangible signs of her occupation were still around too — the coat hook in the passage with PAULA on it, her blue toothbrush, (Who's reminding her to clean her teeth now? I wondered), the hoard of empty Crunchie bar wrappers still under the bed because I hadn't the heart to clear out her room, the cartoon drawing she did reminding others to clean out the bath after use.

None of us would ever be quite the same again. We felt guilt and shame.

'So you're not the perfect parents, after all?' Hannah observed acidly. Later, comforting both herself and us, she said, 'Nobody who hasn't experienced this kind of break-up really understands. In the first place, my friends all thought you were nutty. Now they think you're irresponsible ogres.'

Lawrence suffered the most blatantly obvious anxiety during Paula's stay and afterwards, with violent dreams of axes thrown and slicing off the top of his head. Maybe this was in fact a long-overdue reaction to Sang's arrival, when he had shared a room, a rocking bunk bed, his gerbils, all his toys, clothes and privacy. At least he was now old enough to be able to recount and identify these candid fears of destruction and displacement.

Paula's departure wasn't the end of our involvement. Dismantling an adoptive placement takes as long as getting into one. She came and stayed for a couple of days, this time as a visitor, not a would-be member of the family. The final event which David and I had to go to was the massive, dreaded Disruption Meeting. All parties try to recover something from the wreckage to make it better next time, if not for Paula, then for other children.

Though we were assured that this would not be an inquisition we felt as though we were on trial and that, whatever the official verdict, we were guilty — of taking a risk on somebody's else's behalf, of meddling in an unwanted, unhappy adolescent's life, of adding to Paula's sense of perpetual rejection as well as to the already alarming statistics of failure, then estimated to be about fifty per cent for the placement of older children.

One of the social workers pointed out that nothing is ever entirely wasted, that something good would probably come of it even if only that Paula had gained the experience of a different way of life and learned that she didn't like it.

Surprisingly, the whole muddling experience of Paula's much-heralded arrival, followed by her abrupt departure, strengthened rather than weakened Sang's view of his position.

Eeyore-like, he wandered around the house chanting, 'Poor Paula, she gone now. No more Paula. Poor me, got no new her no more.' Yet beneath the lugubrious soliloquy, was a hint of triumph that, where poor Paula had failed to hang on, he, by clinging limpet-tight, had succeeded. Every one of Paula's misdeeds of the past turbulent weeks, was carefully memorized and repeated. By repeatedly pointing out that Paula hadn't wanted to be part of this household, he re-affirmed his own commitment to it.

Like all adoptive parents we wanted to offer more than ordinary parenting, wanted to try to give enough love to undo at least some of the damage that has already been done. But one can only undo so much. With Sang, we had always had a residual sense of failure that however hard we tried, we were never going to be able to reverse the intellectual damage that had been done to him through malnutrition and neglect, and our long-term ambitions for him would never be realized.

Ironically, it was our total and obvious failure with Paula that enabled us to see where we had succeeded with Sang. Till then, we hadn't really believed how much he loved us and how much we needed this emotional dependence on us.

270

Every morning on his way to the bathroom, Sang always checked up on us as we lay in bed. Usually he said nothing, merely opened the door, peered myopically in before shambling out again. Sometimes we used to feel mildly annoyed by this daily inspection which invariably woke us up before we wanted to be awake. It seemed unnecessary for him to have to come and look at us every day. But after Paula's departure, we realized how we had come to rely on it, how we welcomed the sound of Sang trying and finally succeeding to turn the door knob. The dawn inspection had come to be part of the fabric of our existence, ensuring that we know who we are.

We could congratulate ourselves that, though many adoptions of older children fail, in fifty percent of cases, it *does* work out.

We wondered if and when we would try again.

21
THE JOURNEY

Sang is going to try making a train trip. Twice, he's travelled home from the 16-Plus Unit with some other students. But never before has he travelled alone. Sang is now seventeen.

This time it is his own idea to visit the Children's Home. Though the staff have changed many times over since he was there, many of the young inmates he knew as a little boy are still the same. When he's gone back to see them before, it's always been by car. When he realizes we're serious about trying the trains, he becomes less keen.

'On the train, it very difficult. I be very very nervous,' he says.

We agree with him that he might be.

'And maybe I forget get off train at right place?'

We agree with him there too.

'It much easy you take me in car.' This too is true. Door to door, it's a couple of hours' drive whereas by train, one must go first to London (one-and a-half hours) then change from Waterloo East to the Waterloo mainline station for a further forty minutes travel to Ascot. He couldn't make the changeover at Waterloo by himself. Not yet, he couldn't. But perhaps if we start practising now, go with him most of the way, then maybe one day . . . ?

We decide it's worth the risks, ignore his pleas that he's too young and start the plans, which must cover every possible eventuality, for he doesn't yet have the experience or the mental agility to think his own way out of an everyday hitch like a cancelled or delayed train. For citizens like him, progress must be taken in small, carefully measured doses.

This is how we arrange it.

First, we ring British Rail to find out about the frequency and times of trains from Waterloo to Ascot. Then we ring the Children's Home to find out which of the available arrival times would suit them best for meeting Sang. All agree that it should be in the middle of the day so as to avoid rush-hour and so that, *should* he get lost, there's several hours of daylight in which to locate him. Day and time of the journey are fixed. Then we need to know the name of every station between Waterloo and Ascot at which the train will stop. We also need to know, in advance, the cost of the ticket to Ascot.

'That's with a Young Person's Railcard,' I explain to the voice at British Rail enquiries. 'Return ticket. Going Tuesday, coming back the following Saturday.'

'What colour?'

'What colour is what?'

'Your railcard.'

'I don't know. It's not mine so I haven't got it here. It's my son's. He's at college today. I'm planning the trip for him.'

'Is it red or blue? I can't let you have the price of the ticket in advance till I know the colour of your card. They'll be different.'

'What does the colour relate to? Is it connected to age or area of issue? He's seventeen, he got it last April and it cost him twelve pounds. Is that any help?'

'No, it isn't. I don't know what the different colours mean. I just know it's a different price for a blue or a red.'

This is getting into one of the non sequitur conversations I sometimes had with Sang when nothing either of us says makes any sense to the other.

'Well,' I say. 'Could you perhaps let me have both prices — when using a red railcard *and* using a blue?'

'I suppose I *could*.' He doesn't sound enthusiastic.

Reluctantly, I disclose to this stranger's voice Sang's special needs.

'My son is mentally retarded. It takes him a long time to count out money and he doesn't always get it right. It'll be better all round if he's done it before we reach the station or we'll hold everybody else up.'

'Well fancy that!' says the BR enquiries voice when he comes back on the phone. 'Ticket's the same with a blue or a red railcard! £9.90.'

I prepare for Sang a Personal Travel Document — a small filing card which had on it the name of the station he was heading for:

ASCOT

The departure time of the train he'd be taking: 1.30 p.m. ('That's another way of saying half past one, isn't it?')

The train's ultimate destination: READING ('It's called 'the Reading train' because that's the name of the last station it's going to, at the end of its journey.')

The address and phone number of the Children's Home.

The phone number of Daddy's office so he can be called as soon as Sang arrives.

The list of stations along the way, written in big, bold capitals. He won't need to learn to say them, only to recognize them so that he could tick each one off as he reached it.

At the weekend, we practise. I read them through, my finger on each word for his eyes to follow.

Get on at WATERLOO
CLAPHAM
RICHMOND
FELTHAM
STAINES
EGHAM
VIRGINIA WATER
SUNNINGDALE
Get off at ASCOT

'And when you've put a tick by Sunningdale, you'll know you're nearly there and you'll be getting off at the next stop.'

Since Sang is now entitled to receive the Severe Disablity Allowance of twenty-three pounds a week he is able to pay for the ticket himself. He decides he will also buy a big tin of fancy biscuits to take as a present to the people still living at the Home.

But when he brings down his money jar and tips the contents on to the kitchen table to be counted, there doesn't seem to be a lot there. He's been talking about saving for a video-recorder for months, but sudden urges for chocolate, cans of Coke, and music cassettes seriously interfered with the money management.

After we'd counted out £9.90 for the train ticket, Sang is dismayed to discover that he'll have only forty pence left.

'Maybe I not go after all,' he says. 'It just waste my money, then I not have anything.'

I feel an acute stab of pain for him. He is so innocent about how his money gets used up. It seems so cruel to make him spend ten pounds on a dull rail ticket. Yet it's part of the growing-up process to discover that the Severe Disability Allowance is intended not for expensive daily indulgences but to help with the real expenditure of living. I suppress a maternal instinct to tell him I'll pay for the ticket myself. If we want to help him become part of the mainstream world, he has to live by the same rules as everybody else.

The other children don't get twenty-three pounds a week pocket-money to spend on themselves. Nor should he.

I offer to pay for the box of biscuits. Knowing when it's appropriate to give a present is important too. People in his situation who must rely so much on other people's support can so easily fail to learn to be givers as well as receivers.

Having re-counted the £9.90, we put it into a plastic sandwich bag, then across the kitchen table, we practise buying a ticket. I'm the ticket clerk. He's the traveller.

'Yes?' I say.

He hesitates a fraction before telling me his name. Then,

'Oh dearie me! That not right!' he says and starts again, this time asking clearly for a second-class return to Ascot, but adding — for the ticket clerk's benefit — his address and phone number.

By departure morning, Sang has packed enough luggage in his rucksack for a stay of several weeks rather than three nights. There is scarcely room left for the biscuits. We respect this splendid show of independence by not enquiring whether he's thought to include such essentials as toothbrush, pyjamas or change of socks.

He is almost staggering under the weight of the rucksack as he leads the way across town. But as we reach the station, he suddenly loses confidence and sidles behind me holding out his plastic bag of money. I urge him into the queue ahead of me. He has to do it himself.

'We'll each buy our own tickets,' I say firmly.

When the price of his ticket, £9.90, pops up on the computer screen, he recognizes it and is delighted.

'It's the same!' he says with delight, as though it is by happy coincidence that he has this same amount already counted out in the plastic bag. 'Same as what I got.'

Having bought his ticket, I discover that he is penniless. The forty pence seems to have got spent since the day before. He can't travel without any money, so I gave him two pounds for emergencies and tell him it is only a loan.

He shows his ticket with great aplomb, remembering the advice that one must always check that it's the correct train, even if one thinks one knows.

'Do I change Ashford?' he asks the ticket-collector loudly and clearly.

'Not this one mate. This is a straight-through.'

Often, when faced by difficulties, Sang curls up asleep like a squirrel as a way of hibernating from the demands of involvement in the world. But on this journey to London, though far from relaxed, he remains alert. But he is unable to eat any of the cheese sandwiches we have with us.

We reach Ashford.

'This where we get off,' he says. 'And change another train.'

I nod in agreement.

He has no conditional tenses. *I* know that he means, 'This is where we *would* have got off if we *had* needed to change.'

Will other people always know what he means?

We rehearse once more the routine for when we get to London.

'So then, at Waterloo, we'll look for the Reading train. You're going on the Reading train. We're going to ask for the train to Reading, even though you're not going all the way to Reading.'

'Yep. Reading. But not all the way.'

Wonderful. He is learning so well.

As we arrive at Waterloo East station, I hear a quiet mantra being chanted. Readovitch. Raddovitch. Pladoving. Raddleing, it goes. Is he talking Polish all of a sudden? We make our way towards the main concourse, and he's overcome by a fit of the panics. Instead of sticking close by me and following signs as I point them out, he blunders off course and away down a side alley. All too often, in times of stress, he unlearns everything he knows.

'Here we are Victoria,' he announces hopefully. 'Victoria the station.'

'Yes, that's right. Here we are at *Waterloo*,' I say firmly. 'Waterloo.'

'Where I am going next? Readovitch. Raddovitch. Pladding. Raddleing.' It's the Polish mantra again. 'Where I am going. The place.'

In his anxiety, he has unlearned 'Reading' too.

We are passed by a mature Down's syndrome person scurrying purposefully on his way through the crowds who seems to know quite clearly who he is and where he's going.

I yearn desperately that my son too should achieve, instantly, that aura of confidence. I try to give him a mnemonic.

'Listen Sang,' I say. 'Think of the colour red. A red postbox. A red balloon. You're going on the train that goes to a place that sounds like red. 'Reading' rhymes with the colour 'red'. Red with -ing on the end. So it sounds like Red.' Even as I say it, I know that this one won't do. 'Red' doesn't look a bit like 'Read'. He's got to be able to recognize it when he sees it written up on the timetable.

On his journey card, which has been tightly folded up in his pocket, I write READING.

'Look Sang, it's looks like the word 'reading'. On the train to Reading, you can read a book. Sang is reading. See how it looks. You're going on a train which is going to a place where people are reading books.'

'Yeah,' he says doubtfully. 'Reading the book. OK I try it.'

And he tries it, rhyming it perfectly with the colour red.

Am I trying too hard? Am I too worried?

We reach the Departures board. Like me, like all the other travellers, he stares upwards at the huge sign. But has he any clue what he's meant to be looking for? Eventually, he'll have to learn how, by looking for the three known facts:

1. time of departure
2. final destination
3. station he wants to reach

Then he can locate the correct platform. But then I notice a small detail which BR enquiries didn't tell us about, and which could make all the difference between success and failure. There are *two* trains going to Reading leaving within ten minutes of each other. One is listed as the Reading train, the other is called the Frimley train. Both call at Ascot. What to do? Since I know that he can tell the time — to the nearest quarter hour — better than he can read, I plump for the train leaving at the time written on his card.

'I see Redding,' he says triumphantly.

Yes indeed, Reading is written up in three places. But he has to unlearn that and learn all about Frimley.

But it's all getting too complicated. He switches off and stares down at his feet.

'Got my railcard, anyway,' he says. 'Cost me twelve pounds.' He takes it out and shows it to me. He is very proud of it. It has his photograph on it and it's blue. 'I'll show it to the ticket man, then I'll be all right.'

'He won't need to see your railcard, only your ticket,' I say tetchily.

In fact, the ticket collector has lost interest and doesn't want to see either.

A loudspeaker warns us that the Frimley train is not the train now standing at platform thirteen nearest the ticket barrier, but the one just coming in behind it, and that moreover, only the first six carriages of this train will be departing for Frimley. Even I find it hard to follow the crackly announcement. Sang, being partially deaf, didn't even try to listen. Certainly, he could count up to six, provided he knew where to start counting. But how to explain to someone who found left and right difficult enough, that what was the front end of a train when it arrived became the back end of that train when it left? And how did one explain where one train began and another one ended when they were drawn up right behind each other? I begin to have doubts about whether he would ever be able to handle a whole journey single-handed.

As much for my benefit as his, I encourage him about his achievements so far.

'Isn't it great to be nearly grown-up and sitting on a train all by yourself?'

'Grownup?' he giggles with disbelief. 'I not grownup!'

'Aren't you?'

'Maybe I am.' He grins at this absurd idea.

'And soon you'll be able to go travelling all over the place, wherever you want.'

'Visit Lawrence at Norwich?' he suggests. Lawrence has just started his first term at university. We all miss him, specially Sang.

When he and his rucksack are placed side by side on a seat, I discover that the carriage door nearest him is of the type that opens only from the outside and that the window is jammed firmly shut. Even if he does realize when he reached Ascot, he won't be able to get out through this door. There is just time to get him to change places to near a door with a window that isn't stuck before the whistle blows.

As the train trundles out of sight, I recall another detail I left undone. Anxiety would activate an already unreliable bladder and I failed to take him to the Gents. Will he

a) wet the seat and have to endure the ensuing embarrassment and discomfort?

b) try to follow the signs to TOILET and be still in there when the train reaches Ascot? or

c) keep calm enough to hang on till he arrives at the Children's Home?

As I make my way back to Waterloo East to find the next available train home, I ruminate uselessly about how it has taken nearly a whole working day to enable one teenager to travel, by himself, for one hour on British Rail. Next Saturday, when we reverse the process, will be the same. I'm tired and worried and wonder if trying to offer him greater mobility is really worth it.

But when I reach home and hear that he's already made it, I feel triumphantly proud. And also grateful to those guardian angels who, in the guise of ordinary everyday commuters, have watched over him as he stepped out into the world.

Thank you, community carers.

Sang's own anxiety about this giant step towards independence was contained until the morning after he got safely home again.

'Sorry. Wet bed last night,' he said, bundling his sheets into the linen basket. 'When I have dream about going on train. Maybe next time I not be scare?'

Well done, darling son. That's the ticket. Optimism and fortitude.

22
THE BEGINNING

'You still got that lad you took on?' we were asked the other day. Of course we've got him. He's one of our children. We reply defensively, though probably it's a reasonable question. The motives of all adopters are complex, obscure, highly suspect. What we are also frequently asked is 'Why did you do it?' And what we go on asking asking ourselves is, Why did it all seem so difficult for so long and why, since it was so difficult, did we go on trying to make it work? And, like Graham Greene being asked why he joined the Roman Catholic church, we used to know the answers but it's all too long ago now for us to bother to remember.

The important thing is that Sang is.

When strangers ask how it 'affected' our other children, the query carries an implication that we might somehow have risked harming them by introducing an outsider. Yet it would seem that our children were not exceptional in having shown a straightforward acceptance of, and compassion for, another child's needs. Ours were sometimes bewildered by the fact that we were so often distressed. Lawrence, at eleven, once said, 'I don't know why you keep worrying about it. He's here now, and that's the only thing that matters, isn't it?'

These days, as three teenagers and one in her early twenties, they jostle along with the bickerings, weary acceptance, teasing, fighting, tenderness, petty jealousies and private in-jokes of all siblings.

Joy had a theory that it would take an adoptee the same number of years to settle into a family as his age at placement. The two year old would take two years, the three year old three. Thus, Sang might be expected to begin to settle somewhere around the age of twenty-two, twenty-three or twenty-four depending on how old we claim him to be. But the neat formula avoids the more essential issue. Adoptive parenting is not a quality substitute for being in care, so there can be no prescribed age at which the caring and the mutual relationship ceases. Adopting is not the offer of a meal ticket and bed space for a set period of time until adulthood. Although in 1980 we may not have fully realized it, receiving Sang was literally for ever, so that whatever else may happen to him or to us, he was then, is now and will be always bonded irreversibly into the entire fabric of the extended family for generations. He is not just our son but also brother, cousin, grandson, nephew, and will likely become also uncle, brother-in-law, great uncle.

Thus, as he draws towards adulthood, it is not the end of our commitment. Rather, we are all of us only just at the beginning.

A BIG BOSSY SISTER LOOKS AFTER SANG

by Hannah

'Of course I can . . . no trouble . . . he's a human being isn't he?'

I realized that I was going to be the one to have to accompany Sang back from Marseille where my father was on a five-month research fellowship and look after him for a week in my student house in Oxford.

But I had no grounds for reacting in such a blasé fashion. The last time, four years ago, that I was substitute-mother

when the parents went on holiday, Sang had shingles . . . a
nervous complaint often arising from stress, eg separation
from parents. I should also have remembered that Sang is
the brother who makes me cry most, due to his combination
of absolute dependence and tenacious ability to love
however beastly one is.

On the ten-hour journey I realized again Sang's helplessness. He was a soul completely in my care. In the
Paris Métro he seemed to have no instinct for self-
preservation. He only stuck by me because he had been told
so often that he must. If his concentration had wandered
for two instants he could have been whirled off by
the crowd. This lack of concentration doesn't make him any
less sensitive to the people around him. When an irritable
French *madame* started haranguing Sang for not standing in
the proper queue when I was queueing to get our Métro
tickets, he sensed immediately, even without understanding
her French, that it was all his fault. I was grateful
for the opportunity provided to let off steam and give her a
garlic-scented earful.

If only Sang were less aware of how one is feeling
he would be an easier travelling companion. Sang has
refugee papers rather than a proper passport. I imagined the
French would be only too pleased to get rid of him.
In fact, the fat uniformed official made things as difficult as
possible . . . Why hadn't the young gentleman had a visa to
enter the country? . . . He should have done . . . Oh,
he'd previously lived in France for a whole year without one
had he? . . . Well he should have had a visa then too . . .

As the five hundred tired passengers behind us were
being held up from getting on to the ferry, he had to let us
board. The exchange between me and the French official
was held in French, so Sang couldn't understand the words
but he knew what was going on. It was his fault again.

After the event with the French passport man, I was
irrationally terrified on arriving at the British customs. My
breathing went very peculiar, quite out of voluntary

control. And of course Sang was aware of it. The stony-faced official spent five dreadful minutes filling in forms before letting us go.

But we'd made it home in one piece, so now all I had to cope with was the attitudes of the good citizens of Oxford. Give me bigotted officialdom any day rather than liberal-minded friends.

None of my articulate student friends understand Sang, despite all my explanations. They are not very supportive. But then, why should they be? One night after he was in bed, I just sat and cried about me and Sang, but mostly about my attitude to him. I couldn't even go and see my best friend. Susie was a good companion who talked *with* Sang as a human being, rather than at, to, or over him. But even she couldn't understand my deep anguish. There is the awful knowledge that as I get more sharp with Sang he gets more eager to please, more meek and lenient. He will carry on loving me, defending me, doglike whatever I do to him. And he has so much more than doggy loyalty. Underneath his stupidity, lack of wit or streetwise malice, he's responsive, funny, caring, generous, loving. He is so vulnerable and so infuriating.

Dear Mum,

Looking after Sang is more complicated than simply keeping him amused . . . Always the re-realization of his odd mixture of dependence and limitation, together with his enormous sensitivity and capability to love.

Just now he threw his arms around me and made contented noises. I can't cope with it. During the day I stop him from holding my hand in public as it seems inappropriate. I can't really talk to my friends about him. They don't understand. Why do I have to keep articulating my churned-up emotions when he just gets on with

284

*it? I had a good old cry then went to sleep as I'm sure you
have often before . . . I must not be offended at the
way other people treat him, and try not to see Sang as my
property. I think he's reasonably happy here, despite
his bossy sister.*

lotsa love

Hannah

Sang's need for and interest in hearing 'his stories', about the little boy found either on a pavement or in the orphanage office, about the voyage to England, about the five years in the Children's Home, and about the trip by red car to visit our family gradually decreased. He was satisfied that we should know about him and that, if ever he should want to ask, he can. These days, when asked by visitors or strangers about himself, he can and will explain confidently the basic facts of his origins, the year that he came to England, and that he is now both Vietnamese and British and that he is adopted. He refers more persistent questioners over to us.

'Don't know about that. You ask my mum and dad. They know all about that.'

It is as though he is content that we, his family, should be guardians of his past.

It is a sign not of emotional simplicity but of quite considerable emotional maturity, that he has come, by the long painful process, to an acceptance, that he will probably never return to Vietnam, nor ever know anything of his natural family. It gives him no less sadness to consider this than it would to a cleverer person. Of re-visiting Vietnam, he states simply, 'They not understand me. I not understand them. They not know me. I different now.' And when he needs to think about his lost family, he says, 'I thinking about my mother now.'

It is a privilege which he gives us, that we are allowed to share in the knowledge of these quiet and orderly times of introspective sadness.

'But what next, d'you think?'

'Of course, it'll soon be time you found him somewhere to live, won't it?'

'Have you considered the long-term future?'

People ask impossible questions. What if? When if? What next? Of course we think, fret, worry, about the future. Sang had to learn to trust in us. And we too are learning to trust in our carer who loves us, orphans and all.

Sang's Prayer for All People and Especially the Overstrand Beach Mission, Summer 1988

THANK YOU GOD for sunney
to day. Dear LORD Plaese help
other pople who is in danger
like splelial cHildren. THANK GOD for food and plants
and earth Plaese GOD can you help other pople
who is CHildren in need. THANK you GOD for
Farmers who make FOOD. THANK you for the
bearch Misson the pople lent they hut. THANK you GOD
Plaese GOD I hope
we have a very good famiy suppe to night.
THANK you GOD we got a nice summer Holiday.
THANK YOU GOD
and Father

Also from Lion Publishing

SHADOW OF WAR

Gerda Erika Baker

'At that moment the foundations of the house shake with the force of an explosion. Instinctively people cover their heads with their hands. Within the split second before the light goes out, I see that Mother is not with us . . .'

Shadow of War tells the story of a teenage girl's horror in the midst of conflict; of a family torn apart; of the privations of post-war Germany. It introduces a British soldier's young bride, and follows a personality and a faith as they are gradually rebuilt.

This book is an intensely personal account of how ordinary people's lives are devastated by war. It shows that the healing of mind and spirit can make a lifetime.

ISBN 0 7459 1873 5

A selection of top titles from LION PUBLISHING

SHADOW OF WAR Gerda Erika Baker	£3.99 ☐
HERE TO STAY Phyllis Thompson	£3.99 ☐
C.S. LEWIS – THE AUTHENTIC VOICE William Griffin	£6.95 ☐
CATHERINE BRAMWELL BOOTH Mary Batchelor	£2.50 ☐
FORTY PLUS Mary Batchelor	£4.99 ☐
WILL MY RABBIT GO TO HEAVEN? Jeremie Hughes	£3.50 ☐
LISTENING TO YOUR FEELINGS Myra Chave-Jones	£3.99 ☐
ELIZABETH JOY Caroline Philps	£1.50 ☐
FACE TO FACE WITH CANCER Marion Stroud	£3.95 ☐
CHARNWOOD Grace Wyatt	£2.50 ☐
SCHOOLS NOW Charles Martin	£2.99 ☐
WHO PROFITS? Richard Adams	£4.99 ☐

All Lion paperbacks are available from your local bookshop or newsagent, or can be ordered direct from the address below. Just tick the titles you want and fill in the form.

Name (Block letters) _____

Address _____

_____

_____

Write to Lion Publishing, Cash Sales Department, PO Box 11, Falmouth, Cornwall TR10 9EN, England.

Please enclose a cheque or postal order to the value of the coverprice plus:

UK: 80p for the first book, 20p for each additional book ordered to a maximum charge of £2.00.

OVERSEAS INCLUDING EIRE: £1.50 for the first book, £1.00 for the second book and 30p for each additional book.

BFPO: 80p for the first book, 20p for each additional book.

Lion Publishing reserves the right to show on covers and charge new retail prices which may differ from those previously advertised in the text or elsewhere, and to increase postal rates in accordance with the Post Office.